· ·

Claire Mercer is a lecturer in geography at the University of Leicester, UK. Her research is underpinned by a concern to examine critically the material and social consequences of the pursuit of 'development' in sub-Saharan Africa. Over the last ten years she has undertaken research in Tanzania and, more recently, Cameroon, and has published on the changing character and work of associational life (NGOs, hometown associations); geographies of governance with a focus on civil society and partnership; the role of the Internet in rural Africa; and postcolonial theories of development.

Ben Page is a lecturer at University College London and his research interests are broadly located within the field of development geography. He is particularly interested in the way African families, communities and places accommodate change. He is also interested in the relations between nature and society and the capacity of things (water, cities, associations, trees, meetings, soil) to provide a commentary on the interdependent relationship between environments and politics. Much of his work has focused on water supply in West Africa as a way of linking different histories and places to broader development questions about communities, the state, infrastructure, services, participatory governance, deliberative democracy and the transformation of the landscape.

Martin Evans did his postgraduate studies in geography at the School of Oriental and African Studies and King's College London. Besides diasporas and development, his research examines the complex intersections of conflict, natural resources and livelihoods in sub-Saharan Africa. This includes a critique of the 'greed and grievance' debate and reappraisal of the concept of 'war economies' by resituating them in their historical contexts and amid contemporary global inequity. He is also interested in how people gain their livelihoods in conflict and post-conflict landscapes, with a particular focus on Casamance, Senegal, scene of West Africa's longest-running civil conflict. His ongoing research there focuses on the return of the long-term displaced to their villages and reconstruction of their homes, infrastructure and the rural economy.

DEVELOPMENT AND THE AFRICAN DIASPORA

Place and the Politics of Home

Claire Mercer • Ben Page • Martin Evans

Zed Books
LONDON & NEW YORK

For Beryl, Emma, Pippa and Sue

Development and the African Diaspora: Place and the Politics of Home was first published in 2008 by Zed Books Ltd, 7 Cynthia Street, London N1 9JF, UK and Room 400, 175 Fifth Avenue, New York, NY 10010, USA

www.zedbooks.co.uk

Designed and typeset by Long House Publishing Services
Cover designed by Andrew Corbett
Printed and bound in the EU by Biddles Ltd, King's Lynn

Distributed in the USA exclusively by Palgrave Macmillan, a division of St Martin's Press, LLC, 175 Fifth Avenue, New York, NY 10010

A catalogue record for this book is available from the British Library
Library of Congress Cataloging in Publication Data available

ISBN 978 1 84277 900 2 hb
ISBN 978 1 84277 901 9 pb

CONTENTS

Figures

Tables

Currencies

Where possible the relevant national currencies are used and relate
to the approximate exchange rates at the time of the African field
research in 2005 (below), unless otherwise indicated.
£1 = Tsh2,000 (Tanzanian shillings)
£1 = 1,000 CFA francs (Communauté Financière Africaine francs)

ACRONYMS

ACONA	Asanteman Council of North America
AD3	African Diaspora and Development Day
AFFORD	African Foundation for Development
ANPRP	Association of the Naturals of Pelundo Resident in Portugal
BACCUDA	Bali Central Cultural Development Association
BACOWAS	Bali Community Water Supply
BANDECA	Bali Nyong'a Development and Cultural Association
BASCUDA	Bali Social and Cultural Development Association
BCA-USA	Bali Cultural Association USA
BCDA-UK	Bali Cultural and Development Association UK
BRC	Bali Rural Council
CBO	community-based organization
CCM	Chama Cha Mapinduzi, Party of the Revolution, Tanzania
CFA	Communauté Financière Africaine, Financial Community of Africa
CNU	Cameroon National Union
CPDM	Cameroon People's Democratic Movement
DDT	District Development Trust
DED	District Executive Director
DFID	Department for International Development
DO	District Officer (Cameroon colonial period); Divisional Officer (Cameroon postcolonial period)
FCS	Foundation for Civil Society
FRELIMO	Frente de Libertação de Moçambique, Liberation

	Front of Mozambique
INGO	international non-governmental organization
LITANEMA	Lindi Urban and Rural, Tandahimba, Newala, Mtwara Urban and Rural, and Masasi
MASU	Manyu All Students Union
MECA	Manyu Elements Cultural Association
MMES	Mpango wa Maendeleo ya Elimu ya Sekondari, Secondary Education Development Plan
NDF	Newala Development Foundation
NGO	non-governmental organization
NOMA	National Organization for Manyu Advancement
OECD	Organisation for Economic Co-operation and Development
OPSA	Okoyong Past Students' Association
RDTSF	Rungwe District Technical Schools Fund
REPOA	Research on Poverty Alleviation
RUDET	Rungwe District Education Trust
RUEDEFO	Rungwe East Development Foundation
RUWEDEFO	Rungwe West Development Foundation
SDF	Social Democratic Front
SDO	Senior Divisional Officer
SEDEFO	Selya Development Foundation
SHIMABU	Shirika la Maendeleo ya Busokelo, Busokelo Development Association
SNEC	Société National des Eaux du Cameroun, National Water Supply Company of Cameroon
TANU	Tanganyika African National Union
TTACSA	Tanganyika Territory African Civil Services Association
UMCA	Universities' Mission to Central Africa
UNDP	National Union for Democracy and Progress
UPC	Union des Populations du Cameroun
URT	United Republic of Tanzania
UWT	Umoja wa Wanawake wa Tanzania, Union of Tanzanian Women

PREFACE

....

This book is concerned with the relationship between migration and development in Africa. The 'migration–development nexus' is currently attracting attention for two main reasons. First, the 'developmental benefits' of international migration are being used as a justification by labour-recruiting countries in the Global North when confronted with the accusation that they are unjustly plundering skilled labour from the Global South. The claim is that the 'brain drain' of labour leaving Africa to work in Europe, the Americas and parts of Asia is to Africa's benefit because of the money, ideas and values that return to Africa in the form of remittances (including social remittances) from these inter-continental migrants. Second, the migration–development nexus is attracting attention because of the increasing realization of the scale of international remittances and the associated puzzle over the impacts of this money. Development policy-makers wish to steer this capital into what are perceived to be positive directions. According to the World Bank's *Migration and Remittances Factbook* (Ratha and Xu, 2008) this flow amounted to US$10.8 billion into sub-Saharan Africa in 2007. This is low relative to the remittance receipts of many other world regions, but is still very significant relative to total inward capital flows to sub-Saharan Africa. The assumption is that this 'new' source of money must have development benefits in Africa – but how?

One mechanism that may be influential in transforming the wages of African labour outside the continent into development within the continent is the grouping of migrants' remittances by diaspora associations. Rather than individuals sending all their remittances directly to their own family members for specific needs, some of those Africans living and working in the Global North are using their existing social and welfare associations to generate collective remittances, which are sent to earmarked 'development projects' within the continent. These are usually in addition to family remittances rather than instead of them. Policy proposals and political excitement regarding these African diaspora associations and their collective remittances are running ahead of detailed empirical and theoretical studies into what these associations have actually done in the past, what they are doing today and why. The aims of this book are, first, to provide such an empirical study and, second, to analyse the relationship between diaspora and development using four areas in Africa as case studies. As geographers, the concept of 'place' is particularly important to us and so we have focused on the place-based diaspora associations known as hometown associations, though we prefer the term 'home associations'. These are diaspora groups whose members are united by a shared affinity to a particular homeplace. The four places we are concerned with in this book are Bali Nyong'a and Manyu in Cameroon, and Newala and Rungwe in Tanzania.

Our argument is that the development work that these home associations have done over the years is diverse and distinctive, though often limited in scale and (from the perspective of the development business) amateurish. To some extent the strengths of these associations as development agents lie in evading the routines of the development profession even as those practices are being mimicked. In terms of their structure it is inappropriate to imagine these associations as unitary transnational networks linking home with the national and international diaspora. The reality is much more fractured with multiple, often autonomous, associations relating to any one homeplace, and uneven and irregular flows of information and capital being exchanged through some of the links. Some places are much better connected to their diaspora than others.

Existing theories of the migration–development nexus are biased towards international migrants and should pay more attention to mobility within Africa. In both the past and the present the development work carried out by associations in the 'domestic diaspora' (comprised of those people who move away from their home but stay within their country of birth) is far more significant than that carried out by associations in the international diaspora. The increased density of contacts within the country and the speed with which the 'domestic diaspora' can respond to events mean that it is better placed to be involved in developing its homeplace. Furthermore the migration–development debate has a long history within Africa in terms of the links between city and country, and associated flows of resources. The current intercontinental structure and work of some diaspora associations cannot be separated from histories of rural–urban migration within Africa.

The four case areas considered in this book have produced very different home associations with different capacities for delivering development at home. These differences are explained by different histories of migration, different national political, economic and social histories (in both the late colonial and the postcolonial eras), different current local politics, different experiences of diasporic identity (particularly in relation to ethnicity, nation and gender) and finally different ideas about modernization and change. Yet, there are significant similarities between the case studies too.

The existing analysis of remittances argues that the determining factors governing the scale and patterns of international remittance flows are fundamentally financial (relative wage levels, exchange and interest rates, investment environments, economic stability in Africa, financial services capacity). However, when viewed from the perspective of associations it becomes clear that history, politics and identity are also crucial factors in determining what development work is being done by the diaspora and why.

Whilst our analysis prioritizes 'development' it is impossible to sever the current development work that these associations do from their political work. Here politics includes not only the politics of governments, constitutions and parties but also the politics of identity and belonging. Despite the depoliticizing language that surrounds the development activities of diaspora associations, our argument is that the migration–development discourse needs to pay more attention to African politics. However, we also argue that the place-based politics associated with home associations is not always reactionary, as is so often assumed. If development policy-makers engage with diaspora groups then they are inevitably engaging with local politics, but this should not be seen as a justification for excising these associations from policy debates. The paradox of the simultaneously progressive and reactionary elements of place-based politics is opened up by distinguishing between the ideas of political belonging and of moral conviviality. Moral conviviality expresses local ideas about the right and wrong ways for diverse groups of people to live together.

ACKNOWLEDGEMENTS

Our interest with politics and development in Africa began some time ago during doctoral work on the continent (Claire Mercer in Tanzania, Ben Page in Cameroon and Martin Evans in Senegal). As geographers inspired by the historical materialist tradition of David Harvey, Doreen Massey and Neil Smith, our work has always been framed by a concern with the relations between places, the politics of uneven development, the distribution of resources, and questions of justice. In particular we find the categories and concepts of political economy still often underpin any critical geographical interpretation of the changing social relations within and between African places in neo-liberal and transnational times. However, in recent years that concern with justice has also made us engage with the insights that have emerged from postcolonial theory and from those geographers, such as Giles Mohan and Jenny Robinson, who have led the way into this unsettling but exciting theoretical terrain. In particular this reading has prompted us to consider questions of fairness in relation to episte-mology, hybridity and representation and has forced us to recognize that the privilege of our own knowledge is also often our loss when it comes to understanding the African places where we work. In this context our most important acknowledgement is to the cooperation of all those Africans (in Cameroon, Tanzania and the UK) who have talked to us as we stumbled through their words and worlds. Our work over the past four years has been made possible by the enthusiasm and openness of the people of Newala and Rungwe in Tanzania and of Bali Nyong'a and Manyu in Cameroon as well as by the devoted people sustaining a range of different diaspora associations. The banal humanity of their interests and motivations should not need mentioning, but social science has too often dehumanized Africans in a shameful way. These people are not '*our* research subjects'; we hope that we are their collaborators.

This book is based on research in Britain in 2006–7, in Cameroon in 2004–5 and 2007, and in Tanzania in 2005 and 2008, and was funded by the Economic and Social Research Council of the UK. This work builds on earlier research in Cameroon in 1997, 1998 and 2001 and in Tanzania in 1996–97, 2001 and 2003. In Cameroon and Tanzania we thank the survey enumerators – recent graduates and undergraduates of the universities of Buea and Dar es Salaam – for their diligence and good company.

In Tanzania we would like to acknowledge the assistance and insights of George Jambiya, Joe Lugalla, Sam Maghimbi, Minile Mbonile, Davis Mwamfupe and Cosmas Sokoni at the University of Dar es Salaam. We also thank Deborah Bryceson, Brian Cooksey, Rebecca Ghanadan, Maia Green, Tim Kelsall, Deus Kibamba, Rebecca Marsland, Bobby and Francesca McKenna, Lucas Mwakajinga, Benjamin Mwakasege, Mark Mwandosya and Halima Nambunga. We are grateful to the Tanzania Commission for Science and Technology for granting us permission to undertake the research and for the assistance of officers from the Ministry of Regional Administration and Local Government and from the Registrar of Societies.

In Cameroon we are similarly grateful to the Ministry of Scientific Research and Innovation in Yaoundé, local officers of the Ministry of Territorial Administration and His Majesty Dr Doh Ganyonga III, Fon of Bali, for authorizing our research. At the University of Buea we are grateful to Margaret Niger-Thomas Agbaw, Cornelius Lambi, Wang Metuge, Molem Sama, Victor and Jane Banlilon Tani, Vincent Titanji, Nkwi Walters and Emmanuel Yenshu Vubo. We also thank Nico and Susan Awasum, Christopher and Josephine Ekungwe, Jude Fokwang, Ekambi Fonkwa, John Forje, Nkong Makoge, Ernest and Nally Ndifor, Nso Valintine Nso, Francis and Henrietta Nyamnjoh, Bongayen Polycarp Tani and Samuel Tani. Above all we salute the many years of devoted service of Prince Henry Mbain, who was the archivist at the Cameroon National Archives in Buea and who passed away in 2008 just as we completed this manuscript. He will be sorely missed.

In Europe and North America we have benefited greatly from the encouragement and advice of Clare Anderson, Shirley Ardener, Nic

Argenti, Karin Barber, Dmitri van den Bersselaar, Richard Black, Chukwu-emeka Chikezie, Sally Chilver, Patricia Daley, Claire Dwyer, Gibril Faal, Richard Fardon, Ian Fowler, Peter Geschiere, Louise de la Gorgendière, Graham Harrison, Sam Hickey, Ben Lampert, Clare Madge, Valentina Mazzucato, Linda McDowell, JoAnn McGregor, Garth Myers, Jenny Pickerill, Debby Potts, Abiola Ogunsola, Stanley Okafor, Parvati Raghuram, Rachel Reynolds, Helen Robson, Malcolm Ruel, Michael Rowlands, David Styan, Ann Varley and Pnina Werbner. Seminar audiences at the Open University, University of Edinburgh, University of Aberdeen, University of Oxford, London School of Economics, University of Leicester and University College London all helped us make sense of our excess of data, as did conference audiences in Chicago, Dar es Salaam, Exeter, Keele, Leiden, London, San Francisco, Montreal and Toronto. Claire Mercer is grateful to the University of Leicester for granting two periods of research leave during the project. Two anonymous referees read the first draft of the text and made productive, detailed and fair criticisms to which we have tried to respond. We are grateful for the effort they made. Our two editors at Zed (Susannah Trefgarne and Ellen McKinlay) provided the necessary combination of pressure and encouragement to ensure the manuscript was written. The maps were drawn and redrawn with immense patience by Kerry Allen. Parts of chapters 4 and 7 have already appeared in the journal *Africa* and we are grateful to the editors for allowing them to be reproduced here.

Finally we wish to dedicate this book to Beryl Evans, Pippa Ford, Sue Mercer and Emma Page, whose limitless support is so often taken for granted.

PART ONE
Why home associations matter

HOME ASSOCIATIONS
Between political belonging and moral conviviality

A home association meeting

A group of thirty people from Bali Nyong'a in Cameroon are meeting in Hackney, east London, on a Saturday night in the spring of 2007. The meeting is in the front room of a house, the home of one of the members, and the chairs have been pushed back against the wall to allow everyone to sit down; latecomers perch on armrests and congregate in the hall. This is a regular bi-monthly meeting of the Bali Cultural and Development Association – UK, referred to by members as 'the House'. Most people have come from London and the Southeast, but some have come from the West Midlands and further north in the UK; one couple has come from the Isle of Man. People drift in over a couple of hours and start chatting and catching up on news, and go to the kitchen to drop off food and drink to be enjoyed after their discussions. As they come in they sit down, catch the eye of some of the others in the room and greet them formally by rubbing their hands together then clapping slowly and loudly three times in a measured rhythm. Those already seated join in in unison, the rhythm speeding up as the claps peter out. Drinks and groundnuts are shared as the meeting gets going.

When the meeting is deemed to be quorate the President, a young law lecturer, calls the House to order and invites one of the women to open with a Christian prayer in English. After the prayer, people sit down and listen to the President's opening remarks, including a ritual invocation to members to come on time as the meeting is already behind schedule. As often happens there are visitors and potential new members so the President then invites people to introduce themselves. Each person gives their name and the quarter in Bali Nyong'a with which they identify. This prompts some teasing and comedy as different parts of Bali Nyong'a are given nicknames that capture their stereotypes – 'Njenka Intelligence', says one man, boasting about Njenka's reputation for scholarly connections. After introducing herself, a young woman who is new is cajoled into revealing her marital status by one man who asks whether the gate to her compound is open. His ribald question produces raucous laughter, which is only amplified when the woman replies that it depends who is pushing. The minutes from the last meeting are read.

Discussions begin with a debate about the group's constitution and in particular about when they are obliged to offer financial help to bereaved members. When a group member or the relative of a member dies, the House contributes a fixed amount to the bereaved family as part of its condolences. A distinction is drawn between first- and second-class deaths, with the former being actual members, their spouses, children and parents and the latter being 'brothers, sisters, aunts and uncles'. The House currently gives £75 to a member whose family suffers a second-class death, but the President proposes tightening up the definition of 'second-class' in order to limit the House's liability. His aim is to give a more significant contribution (£100) to fewer people and also to have more money left over from group levies to give to development projects back in Bali Nyong'a. Trying to define who counts as a brother or sister proves hard, with particular disagreement about whether or not it is necessary for a sibling to come from the same womb. One member claims that, since their family are title-holders in the Palace in Bali Nyong'a, the House should recognize their status by always contributing in cases of bereavement regardless of biological relationship to the member. The discussion turns to whether the money should be drawn from the House's existing funds or whether an ad hoc collection should be made at the time of each death. It is clear that most members regard this sum as only a token (particularly if a corpse needs to be repatriated to Cameroon), and as individuals they often feel obliged to give more to bereaved families as a supplement. One member points out the extra burden faced by women, who are expected to prepare food to take to bereaved families when the House attends the wake-keeping. She asks why women are expected to bring food, which takes time to prepare, whereas men bring drinks, which do not. As a working woman she proposes that women should be allowed to take drinks to bereaved families if they so wish. This comment causes some consternation, particularly from other women, one of whom argues, 'This is a cultural House. Have you ever heard of women buying drinks in Bali?' To which others respond 'Culture evolves, culture changes.' After an extended, loud and passionate debate, the House concludes that women should be allowed to bring drinks to wake-keepings if they so choose.

During this debate a more senior member of the House arrives and announces that at 10pm they will be speaking, by mobile phone, to the traditional ruler of Bali Nyong'a, known by his title of Fon, who is in his palace in Cameroon. This is not usual during meetings but has been prompted by a land dispute back in Cameroon referred to as the 'Bawock crisis' – a violent conflict between Bali Nyong'a and Bawock over government officials' demarcation of their shared boundary and rival claims of land ownership on the boundary. The dispute has degenerated into running battles between young men of Bali Nyong'a and Bawock; homes and property have been looted and destroyed, and scores of people have been rendered homeless. The 'crisis' has made national headlines in Cameroon.

Shortly after 10pm, the man with the phone announces that he has established a connection to the Fon, and the House performs the formal greeting. The man then stands in the middle of the lounge, holding the mobile aloft on speakerphone. The Fon, who is barely audible, updates the meeting on the Bawock crisis and the Bali Traditional Council's position for over half an hour in Mungaka, the Bali Nyong'a vernacular. Not everyone can hear, either because they do not understand Mungaka or because the phone volume is low, so there is some background chatter during the call. When the Fon has finished speaking, the meeting greets him again in the formal manner, and the call is disconnected. The meeting then discusses the issues raised before pressing on with its own agenda.

The last item to be discussed is the cultural gala to be held that summer, at which the House is planning to launch its new uniform, a 'traditional' outfit made to order in Cameroon. The gala will provide an opportunity for the House to showcase dance and food from Bali Nyong'a to other Cameroonians in London so that 'people in the UK will know the Bali are here'. It will also raise funds for their annual development project, which will equip the health centre in Won, one of the quarters in Bali Nyong'a. In order to select which dances will be performed the Cultural Secretary of the House has brought to the meeting a DVD of traditional Bali Nyong'a dances. People watch while they eat the food that has been brought, including familiar dishes from West Africa such as jollof rice, fried plantains, roasted fish and chicken, fufu-corn, yam and *njamma-jamma* (a vegetable dish). It is agreed that the House will meet for rehearsals led by four members who know how to do the dances and can teach those who do not. Since there are insufficient members who know how to sing in the vernacular, and since not enough of the right musical instruments can be found in the UK to form a band, it is agreed to use recorded music. After 11pm, when people have finished their food and drink, they begin to leave, some rushing to catch the last train home, others sharing lifts in their cars.

Key themes: place, sociality and development

This meeting was just one of many we have attended and was characteristic of the hospitality offered to us as strangers and researchers. This particular meeting also illustrates three of the key themes of this book. First, this is a meeting about 'place'. A place is 'a meaningful location' (Cresswell, 2004: 7), somewhere invested with layers of meaning by humans over time. What we describe as a place is usually defined in distinction from a space. The concept of space is conceived as abstract, non-normative, generalizable and measurable. It is about distances and flows. In contrast the notion of place is associated with the local, the specific, the unique and the particular. Places are the locations that matter to people because they return to them, build memories around them, write their histories and call them 'home'. What holds the Bali Nyong'a group together, as in all of our case studies, is a shared sense of belonging to a particular place, even though some of the members have never even been there. For that reason these groups are often called hometown associations because the places to which they refer are hometowns. In this book, however, the term home association is used to emphasize the fact that the homeplace is not always a town – it might be a village, a town, an area (comprising several towns and villages) or even a nation. However, the scale and boundaries of that homeplace are often as intangible as they are contested. Sometimes the delimitation of boundaries is literal, as in the Bawock case. But, as often, it is more subtle and concerns social as well as geographical boundaries (Fanso, 1986). For example some people who are not from Bali Nyong'a choose to belong to this meeting because their husbands or wives are from Bali Nyong'a and because it is a well-run group. Furthermore though almost everyone at this meeting shares a sense of belonging to Bali Nyong'a they all identify with different quarters, compounds and families, some of whom claim a status superior to others. Place, then, is not a bounded territory in any simple sense. Members say that when you are in the meeting in east London you are *in* Bali.

Second, this is a social meeting that combines pleasure and obligation. The pleasure comes from the fun of seeing friends, sharing food and gossip, and feeling at home amongst the convivial company of those who share and understand the experience of living in Britain. The obligation is to look after members in Britain by offering mutual support, particularly in times of need. This socializing is central to the longevity of associations like this one.

Third, this is a meeting that weaves together issues of diaspora, culture and development. The essence of diaspora identity is the ongoing and shared commitment to the maintenance of the place called 'home'. This might mean the improvement of a particular geographical space, but it might also mean the maintenance of the 'culture' that is an expression of that place anywhere in the world. So, the performance of Bali dances in London and the collection of money to improve health care in Cameroon are simultaneous and inseparable manifestations of the diasporic condition. From the perspective of the diaspora, the process of development binds together a concern for the welfare and improvement of *their* people and *their* territory. Hidden in the term 'their' is the inevitability of a politics of belonging, which is about policing that boundary of who is within the group and who is outside it.

Why home associations matter

Diaspora groups are attracting attention from aid donors, governments, NGOs and academics because of the increased interest in the relationship between development and migration. The argument goes as follows. Globalization has enabled an expansion of the world economy, creating better opportunities for individuals. But, since the benefits of globalization are distributed unevenly across space, they have increased inequality between nations and provided an incentive for increasing international migration. The proportion of international migrants relative to the world population remains relatively steady at 3 per cent, so the gross number of international migrants is rising with global population growth (GCIM, 2005). There are now around 200 million international migrants, almost half of whom are women (GCIM, 2005). Remittances from these migrants to their homes form the crucial link between international migration and social and economic development (World Bank, 2006).

At a global scale, recorded remittances are now significantly larger than overseas aid flows and comprise an annual flow of around US$240 billion into the Global South (Ratha and Xu, 2008). Though only US$10.8 billion of this is estimated to be sent to Africa, remittances from migrants are nevertheless an increasingly important source of money in urban and rural areas of the continent. However, much of this flow is 'private' in the sense that it moves between individuals, who are generally assumed to use it for personal consumption and immediate social needs. This means that these remittances are not being directly invested in the provision of public goods such as schools, hospitals and water supplies. In contrast, diaspora groups, with their interest in specific development projects, offer a potential means of transferring capital and skills for the provision of public goods and services to the Global South. In addition these diaspora groups appear to have a direct knowledge of and links to beneficiaries in needy areas, which might enable them to bypass the unwieldy bureaucracies of state and development agencies. Diaspora associations might provide the crucial link between international migration and African development.

There are many immediate caveats that should be added to this argument. For example the distinction drawn between public and private is clearly over-simplistic. National economies benefit from recipients' private remittances and this benefit is in the public interest because it improves macro-economic conditions, theoretically liberating capital for infrastructure investment. For example, remittances can reduce foreign exchange shortages and offset balance of payments deficits without incurring interest liabilities or necessarily increasing the level of imports of foreign goods and services. Also those families who do receive remittances often spend them on public services, such as schools and hospitals, which generally rely on user fees. In addition the kind of consumption commonly associated with remittances (house construction, household needs and food) puts money into local economies. The argument also places a burden on diaspora associations that might well be unreasonable given their small scale and limited resources. Furthermore, the emphasis placed on international remittances in this argument underplays the significance of national remittances. Finally, it should be clear from the outset that the volume of money remitted to Africa through groups is very small relative to that remitted by individuals to their families. However, despite these objections this book takes seriously the idea that diaspora groups could be an important element of the relationship between migration and development. The book aims to understand how diaspora associations work, whether they do steer some of these remittances towards public goods, and whether donors can, or should, engage these groups as a way of reducing poverty in Africa. In so doing, the aim is also to use these associations as a means to understand better the relationship between migration and development.

Three overarching questions are used to articulate our objectives.

What is the structure and character of African diaspora groups? What development work do African diaspora groups do? And, how do we understand the political work of diaspora groups? The book is organized around these questions and we answer them by following the diaspora associations from four homeplaces: Bali and Manyu in Cameroon, and Newala and Rungwe in Tanzania (see Maps 1.1 and 1.2).

What is the structure and character of home associations?

Home associations now operate between continents, and a key trigger in the current resurgence of interest in them is the apparent shift in the scale of their operation. However, important facets of their character and structure have been overlooked because studies of domestic and international migration have tended to proceed independently of one another. Two separate lines of enquiry have been pursued, each speaking in different academic registers. The first, in African Studies, has understood home associations as ethno-territorial groups that unite indigenes of a given home through a series of interconnected 'chapters' located *within* particular African nation-states (Trager, 2001). A second, which has emerged at the intersection of work on diaspora, transnationalism, migration and development, has privileged the experience of *international* migrants and their potential contribution to the development of 'home' (e.g. GCIM, 2005).

When these two sets of debates are brought together it might reasonably be assumed that contemporary international home associations express a transnational ethno-territorial relationship that can be imagined as a network shaped like an intercontinental spider's web connecting the home with its national and international chapters. Each node (the 'branches' or 'chapters' of the association) is connected to a place ('home') by a series of lines down which flow people, money and ideas. Such a first cut at visualizing the imagined geography of a transnational home association suggests a pattern of effective, open and even communication between the nodes with the homeplace at the centre of the network. But such an imagined geography is problematic; not only does it turn out to be empirically inaccurate in terms of the structure of the associations, it also produces a misleading analysis of territory, power and agency within these associations. Whilst parts of the association's 'national' past survive in the international arena, it is wrong to think of the process of their internationalization as merely the expansion of a unitary national network.

From a development perspective the most important part of home

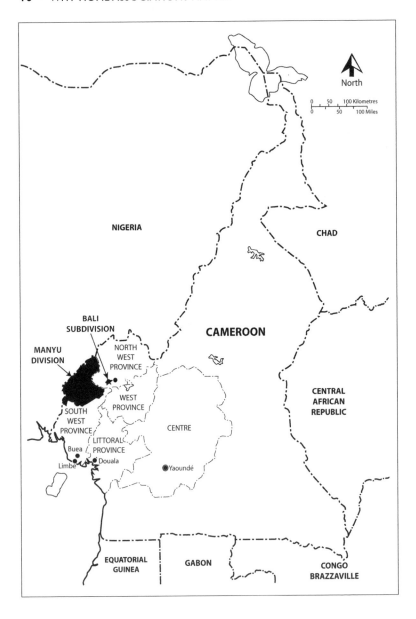

Map 1.1 Cameroon showing home areas and fieldwork sites in domestic diaspora

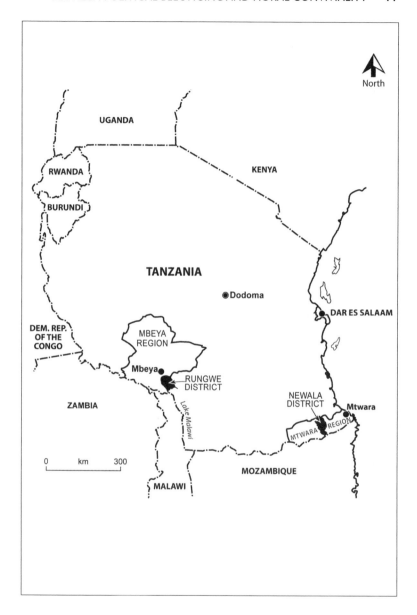

Map 1.2 Tanzania showing home areas and fieldwork sites in domestic diaspora

associations is the 'domestic diaspora'. This term refers to those individuals who have left their home area but not the nation-state in which they were born: for example, those workers who left their rural homeland in the colonial period to work on plantations or in the mines but who remained attached to a homeplace to which often they could not afford to return. According to standard definitions of diaspora this term is an oxymoron because diasporas are defined by their international movement away from a homeland. In the African context, however, the assumption that homeland and nation-state are always the same thing is erroneous. The 'domestic diaspora' is a necessary term because association members often argued that you could be outside your 'country' without leaving your nation-state, and might describe themselves as being 'abroad' whilst living and working in their national capital. The term 'domestic diaspora' better captures the ongoing shared commitment to a homeplace than the term 'internal migrants'. Furthermore, this concept addresses the bias within the migration–development nexus towards international migrants. The transnational network image says nothing about the relative size of flows of people, money or influence or the size of the membership at each point. The assumption is that the international 'chapters' of home associations make the most significant contribution to the development of the homeplace. But our own finding is that the domestic diaspora is significantly more influential in financial and managerial terms than the diaspora overseas, and as such wields more power within the association. Yet from the perspective of the village, international migrants are more closely associated than the domestic diaspora with the dreams of development and material wealth, and the allure of modernity. This gives those overseas a different kind of leverage and authority at home. The international diaspora is still relatively insignificant when compared with the domestic diaspora in terms of number of members, volume of financial flows into the home, frequency of visits home and willingness to intervene in public life at home. The capacity to travel and the proximity to home are both crucial to the 'associational entrepreneurs' who make things happen, and this largely explains why those overseas remain relatively less important. This challenges the assumption that Africa's international diaspora has the most important contribution to make to Africa's development. This bias towards international migrants suggests that people have to leave Africa in order to be able to contribute anything useful, reflecting the long-standing Eurocentric representation of Africa as a place of poverty and passivity.

In the four case studies used here, the links between 'home', domestic diaspora groups and international diaspora groups are often poorly articulated, fissile, transitory and very uneven in terms of their contribution to development at home. When things move through associations, they hop rather than flow. Certainly, the idea that one coherent association is capable of mobilizing both domestic and transnational migrants for the development of a static 'home' is generally misleading. The homeplaces themselves are not always the key territorial scale around which all associations choose to mobilize. Rather, the original 'homeplaces' sit within a wider and far more complex landscape of multiple, overlapping and sometimes contradictory 'homes', around which different associations choose to mobilize at different times. The shape of these home associations is thus unstable, as the place-based identities around which people in the diaspora form associations are not fixed in time or space. People opt in and out of home associations, which variously claim linguistic, national, clan, ethnic, regional and administrative spaces as the 'home'. Home associations are established, then become defunct as their membership drops out or switches allegiance to another group. Many individuals have overlapping memberships of multiple associations.

The idea that home associations are constituted by 'branches' or 'chapters' requires some elaboration. In most cases, branches emerge organically in both the domestic and international diaspora rather than being established in a top-down manner by a 'home branch'. Branches are marked by considerable or indeed total autonomy, for example having their own individual constitutions and registering as separate associations with local or national governments. Among Cameroonians, women's associations provide an alternative, parallel set of 'branches' that are loosely affiliated to the main home associations. Sometimes, what might look to an outsider like the 'branch' of an international network is perceived by its members to be an entirely separate organization that happens to be concerned with the same homeplace. Nevertheless, particularly outside Africa, members do sometimes describe themselves as belonging to a 'branch' or 'chapter'; alternatively, members in the home country may view or represent associations in the international diaspora as such. Furthermore, the unitary network image runs the risk of assuming an internal homogeneity *within* branches, which is not borne out in practice. Any one branch is shot through with social and political differences, for example along lines of gender, age, profession, class, status or allegiance to a political party.

Home associations are opportunistic and acquisitive in terms of communication, information and membership. A network suggests a seamless flow of information between nodes and gives no sense of the relative ease or difficulty of communication for different people. In contrast our experience has been that communication seems to be sporadic, contradictory and partial. This is compounded by the fact that many individuals who are potential members deliberately avoid the association. We had a strong sense that within Dar es Salaam and Douala the association leaderships were 'desperately seeking the diaspora' – they struggled to keep tabs on their own people. New members were always warmly welcomed and encouraged, and lapsed members were just as often lamented.

Home associations need to be understood in temporal as well as spatial terms. The image of a network tends to be static – it lacks any sense of temporality. For example, in its focus on a single homeplace in the centre it distracts from the possibility that there are other centres of operation at different times. For example, it might make much more sense to talk about London as the centre of the association for the individuals in our opening vignette. From the perspective of a meeting in Hackney, Bali Nyong'a may feel like an unimportant place – rarely visited, little communicated with, often forgotten. The existence of Bali Nyong'a is the rationale for the meeting, but as a place it is often distant. At other times, for example during the main annual dance (called *Lela*), the town of Bali might become the centre of the association. In both Tanzania and Cameroon our research suggests that for much of the time the centre of these associations is in the capital city of the African country rather than in the homeplace. This is where decisions are taken, meetings are held, money is raised. For those members who never return home but who are active members of the association, it is not useful to suggest that the homeplace is always the centre of the network. How can we re-imagine the map of home associations in a way that makes the centre of the association for some people sometimes Bali Nyong'a, sometimes Yaoundé and sometimes London? Just as separating the African and international parts of the diaspora obscures the connections between them, so too separating the past from the present obscures the continuities and ruptures between the history of associations and their present character and structure. The sudden ahistorical interest in international migrants runs the risk of breaking these historical connections, which are integral to understanding the origins of associational forms.

Existing writing tends to suggest that home associations are fundamentally ethnic in character. In some cases they are explicitly referred to as 'ethnic associations'. The 'home' to which home associations refer is often perceived to be an 'ethnic homeland', and historically the associations have often borne the name of an ethnic group. The case studies suggest that this view is problematic in at least three ways. First, it assumes that 'homeland' and ethnic territory are geographically coterminous. Second, it assumes that home associations are mono-ethnic. Third, and most significant, the idea that home associations are ethnic associations often relies on an essentialist definition of ethnicity. Nevertheless it would be perverse not to recognize that there is often a relationship between ethnicity and associational life in any place that needs to be analysed.

Each case study area contained several different ethnic groups, and their associations were often correspondingly ethnically diverse. Similarly several of the ethnic groups extended beyond the boundaries of the case study areas (for example significant numbers of people who identify themselves as ethnically Nyakyusa live in Rungwe, Kyela and Mbeya Rural districts (and beyond), yet the associations studied drew their membership from within the boundaries of a single district). There were some circumstances where different ethnic groups within the case study areas had their own separate associations, but even these often turned out to have a degree of internal heterogeneity. Home associations are always place-based but only sometimes comprise a single ethnicity. They are better characterized by an attachment to place than by an attachment to an ethnic group.

More important, however, is the way in which ethnicity is conceptualized. The term 'tribe' is generally avoided in contemporary African studies because of its associations with the primordial, the static and the uncivilized and because of the implicit distinction it draws between the character of social association in the Global South and that elsewhere in the world. Yet too often, when home associations are described as 'ethnic associations', it is this definition of ethnicity (prehistoric, fixed, geographically rooted) that is being used. In contrast, following Zelinsky (2001: 44) among many others, ethnicity is more accurately understood as a social construct – there are no objective criteria by which to measure where one ethnic group ends and another begins. Two apparently identical neighbouring groups can (and do) claim to be ethnically different – the only apparent basis for accepting this difference is that members of these two identical groups claim to be different. Because they are social constructs, ethnic groups can change over time – they have a history – and the definitions of who is included and who is excluded can also change. Indeed the history of ethnic groups is often closely related to the history of associational life, as we show in chapters 4 and 5. However, to say that ethnic groups are a social construct is not to say that they are illusions. Ethnic groups will not evaporate merely because their histories have been revealed or their changing characteristics have been demonstrated. An affiliation to one ethnic group or more is deeply embedded in an individual's conscious-ness, so the idea of a group creates its own social reality. It is the potency of this felt attachment that makes ethnicity so vulnerable to manipula-tion. An ethnic group is an 'imagined community' that is too large for personal contact between all the different individuals, but it is united by the belief that it embodies a unique set of cultural and historical features (language, religion, values, material culture, ceremony, political structure), which all members hold in common (Anderson, 1991). The boundaries of ethnic groups are defined through a relational process at the level both of the whole group and of the individual. As groups they come into being and define themselves through (often competitive) relationships with other social entities (perhaps other ethnic groups or perhaps colonial states). The identification of an individual with a particular ethnic group is a process undertaken through self-ascription by the individual concerned, but also through judgements made by other people. So, though often treated as relatively straightforward, the idea of ethnicity is actually cut through with antinomies – it is a construct but it is real, it is too large to be known yet involves immediate solidarity on the basis of shared features, and it only exists in relation to other social entities and cannot be understood as independent of them. The point is not that a fixed ethnicity can be read off from a particular home association, but that ethnicity and home associations both change over time, and the means by which they change are closely related.

Our findings contest the assumption that contemporary home associations articulate a transnational ethno-territorial relationship that can be conceptualized as a unitary network. We do not suggest that the international diaspora has no role to play in Africa's development, but we argue that the internationalization of home associations needs to be understood in relation to the history of African labour migration and associational life. Furthermore by decentring the homeplace as the focus of the network we aim to contest an inward-looking sense of the home as a physical space demarcated by boundaries and to replace this with a sense of the home being delineated by a series of social relations. This resonates with James Ferguson's (2006: 23) recent comments about globalization:

> The questions raised by considering Africa's place-in-the-world, then, are indeed 'global' ones, but not in the way that most discussions of globalization would imply. Instead, they point to the need for a new

framing of discussions of the global: centred less on transnational flows and images of unfettered connection than on the social relations that selectively constitute global society; the statuses and ranks that it comprises; and the relations, rights, and obligations that characterize it.

The pattern of linkages within African home associations is profoundly uneven. Some places are more connected than others; some people are more connected than others. The danger with thinking about home associations as networks is that this unevenness is lost. Instead, it is necessary to emphasize the way that social relations structure the association as a counterbalance to the tendency to look only at the organization when considering structure. A focus on organizations is a necessary precursor for policy-makers wishing to engage diaspora groups, but it can only ever reveal part of the story.

What development work do African diaspora groups do?

Though most contemporary home associations claim that development is one of their key purposes, there have been few critical and sustained analyses of the development work that they do (see Honey and Okafor, 1998a; Trager, 2001; Henry and Mohan, 2003; Henry, 2004; Yenshu, 2005; Mohan, 2006). Instead recent research on home associations in Africa tends to focus on the relationship between home associations and the state. The emphasis is on the role that associations have played in the emergence of a 'politics of belonging' (Geschiere and Gugler, 1998; Geschiere and Nyamnjoh, 2001) in which ethnically defined subnational spaces become the key territorial unit in which citizens have both rights and responsibilities. In these accounts home associations enable the survival of incumbent political elites during periods of economic and political uncertainty (structural adjustment and democratization). The self-declared development role of home associations is treated as a façade that masks their 'real' political function. But this is an epistemological injustice against the sincere work that certain individuals and groups do in the name of development. This is neither to endorse the naïve enthusiasm for diaspora-led development that has bewitched some of the international policy debate nor to suggest that the development work that home associations do should not be assessed critically, but it is to suggest that the claim that these associations make to be undertaking development should be taken seriously.

Currently the contribution that African home associations make to formal 'development' is fairly limited and sometimes of questionable value in terms of poverty reduction. Yet it is distinctive and articulates local desires for, and forms of, 'progress' that are innovative. These associations are important vehicles through which dreams and desires for development are expressed, debated and enacted. Members of home associations in Cameroon, Tanzania and Britain express a widespread desire for more of the goods associated with 'development'. One of the starkest empirical results from all four case studies is the demand across the social spectrum for more roads, bridges, information technology, extension workers, schools and healthcare facilities and services. Critical academics, in their enthusiasm to get with 'post-development' or 'alternative development', tend to ignore this simple point (de Vries, 2007).

Home associations are seen by many as key to the provision of developmental goods at home. Associations in the four case studies have funded: schools, health facilities, water supplies, mortuaries, community halls, libraries, internet cafes, church buildings, orphanages, museums, visits from overseas medics, restorations to palaces and other cultural buildings, legal costs in land disputes, public toilets, flagpoles, computers and cars for traditional rulers, and the restoration and equipping of government buildings. They occasionally support productive agricultural activities (for example farm-to-market roads, small oil palm plantations, and inputs for cashew farmers) but such examples are rare and generally not very successful. The projects listed are quite small, often take years to complete and are rarely objectively evaluated. In quantitative terms far more development funding comes from governments or traditional donors (international NGOs, religious institutions, mutlilateral organizations) than from home associations. But sometimes home associations are able to raise or lobby for significant amounts of money over short periods. For example, in 2003 the home association in Bali Nyong'a raised £22,000 from the domestic diaspora in just three months for a water-by-gravity project (Chapter 9). These examples are significant because they challenge the view that development has to be financed by external donors, who have their own normative view of what constitutes development and therefore of what they will fund.

Different associations, different capacities

The capacity of different home associations to deliver development is extremely variable. Whereas a focus on individual remittances tends to lead to an analysis that explains spatial differences in terms of financial factors (such as interest rates and financial stability in different remittance-receiving countries), a focus on grouped remittances and home associations points to an additional set of factors as well – in particular, history, politics and identity. For example the different histories of migration in different places have produced different types of home associations in different places. If migrants are working in poorly paid jobs on plantations their association will have far less capacity than an association whose members are professionals working in government service. Political history can also be significant. The postcolonial nation-building project in Tanzania meant that home associations were effectively illegal from the mid-1960s until the mid-1980s. This had a profound effect on their institutional memory and local credibility. Social history is also important. In two of the four case studies the early history of mission education resulted in larger numbers of individuals accessing good positions in the postcolonial civil service with concomitant benefits in terms of accessing government resources. Economic history has meant that at various times in both Cameroon and Tanzania home associations have been forced into delivering different public services because state provision has collapsed or been withdrawn due to macro-economic failures. Local politics too has an influence over the effectiveness of home associations as development agents. The second-wave democratization of the 1990s boosted the capacity of some Cameroonian home associations as they became an important mechanism through which the incumbent political party retained power. The increase in resources that flowed through home associations in this context enabled them to deliver more development goods.

Issues of identity are also key to explaining why some home associations have more development capacity than others. Identity is the process by which an individual is consciously labelled using a series of familiar social categories. Ethnicity for example is the term used to describe the facet of an individual's identity that relates to his or her membership of a particular ethnic group. Becoming a member of a home association is a form of behaviour through which an individual tells his or her and the world something about who they are and with whom they identify. In some cases that identity subsequently entails particular responsibilities that influence behaviour. For example certain ethnic identities (such as that from Bali Nyong'a) require individuals to perform in a certain way in relation to stereotypes of obedience to hierarchies or mass participation in community labour. Those case study associations that perform an identity linked with hierarchical chieftaincy can be effective in achieving broad-scale mobilization for development through that identity. Ethnicities that perform an identity tied to a flatter social structure, meanwhile, may be no less effective at mobilizing people for development projects but this may be through different means (such as neotraditional societies) and at a more localized level of identity (such as the village); broad-scale ethnic mobilization, at home or in the diaspora, may be more problematic for them.

The value of the idea of identity is its ability to reveal the relative priorities of the different social categories for a particular individual in particular contexts. Membership of an ethnic group is not necessarily the only – or even the dominant – facet of the way an individual is identified. So it is inappropriate to define ethnic group independently from other social variables such as class, nationality, religion, or gender. For example, the relative importance given to family, ethnic group and nation will influence an individual's willingness to send collective remittances to a development project via a home association.

The concept of identity has been subjected to considerable critique (Fardon, 1996; Hall, 1996; Brubaker and Cooper, 2000; Brubaker, 2002; Pieterse, 2003). First, it implies that individuals have characters that can be entirely fixed and defined by a (relatively) short list of ahistorical sociological labels. This is intuitively unconvincing. Second, the idea of an identity pays insufficient attention to the distinction between how people label themselves and how other people label them. Preserving this boundary is important because of the conflicts that arise when there is a difference between a person's own understanding of her or his self and other people's ascription of particular labels to her or him. How do individuals internalize the various external labels attached to them? How do they externalize their identity through their behaviour? How do the stories they tell the world about themselves change over time? Changes in the way these questions are answered can have a significant influence on the history of home associations. Third, in attempting to capture the multiple affiliations that are necessary to describe an individual's identity, the categories used (gender, nationality, race, ethnicity ...) become reified. Instead of treating these concepts as socially constructed they become concretized, naturalized and objectively real. For this reason it is worth introducing the concept of subjectivity as distinct from identity.

If identity describes the way that the individual consciously presents her or his self to the world, then subjectivity describes the ways that those presentations do not always work. The stories never quite work because the categories used to 'identify' people appear to be fixed and unchanging, as if they were outside history – but of course they are not, and they do change. If identity is the attempt to fix certain characteristics to an individual then subjectivity is the individual's experience of their imperfect relationship with their identity, the limits of the fit between their 'identity' and their sense of self. The expectations of the leadership of a home association may rely on attempts to assert identity; their success or failure may have more to do with the subjectivity of the association's membership. By 'diaspora identity' we mean an individual's process of becoming conscious of being a member of a particular autonomous group of people, of presenting themself as a member of the diaspora and of being understood by others as such. 'Diaspora subjectivities' on the other hand describe the unsettling experience of an individual who finds the story they tell themselves and the world about being a member of the diaspora does not always quite fit. Practising diasporic identity is about consciously articulating the diaspora group's essential characteristics, making self-conscious statements about identity, or more practical behaviour such as choices about whom to avoid and with whom to spend time. Evidence of a particular diasporic subjectivity would emerge through the expression of anxieties about belonging or other neuroses. Identity then is a concept to be treated with caution but it remains for us a crucial tool in understanding why some individuals choose to become involved with home associations and therefore why the home associations from some places are more effective agents of development than others (Chapter 8).

The distinctiveness of diaspora development

It is not the scale of the developmental work that home associations do that is important so much as its distinctiveness. Such work creates opportunities for the articulation of local desires that are innovative. In other words, it defines what counts as development differently. As the list of activities above demonstrates, home associations often undertake projects that donors would probably not consider as 'development'. This is only possible when they have their own financial resources. When home associations require external funding, they have to work within donors' current framework of development by casting their projects in recognizable and acceptable terms. Yet some home associations are still able to tailor such projects to suit their own definitions of development. In Tanzania for example, home associations undertake projects that would not normally be associated with mainstream development models. One such project was run by one of the Rungwe home associations in Dar es Salaam, SHIMABU (Shirika la Maendeleo ya Busokelo, Busokelo Development Association). In 2003 SHIMABU was awarded Tsh5 million by the Foundation for Civil Society (FCS), a multi-donor funding body, to hold a series of training workshops in Busokelo aimed at raising awareness among government officials and village leaders of the vulnerability of elderly peasants, and to offer training for the elderly themselves on how to deal with witchcraft accusations, deprivation and poor health. But it was really the witchcraft accusations that the director in Dar es Salaam considered to be the development objective. As he explained, 'this was our main topic actually. Old women are being accused and we want these things to stop.'[1] However, the focus on witchcraft accusations is less apparent from official SHIMABU and FCS project documents, which place the problem as just one of many within a more standard and familiar language of 'development problems' such as the need for poverty reduction and health education for vulnerable groups, and for good governance and leadership at the local level. Home associations have some room for manoeuvre if they know how to locate their specific concerns within donor discourses.

Home associations operate in a context where rural development has been colonized by NGOs, so they tend to mimic them in their use of developmental language, documents and rituals (project proposals, participatory meetings with 'project beneficiaries'). But at the same time, home associations have emerged organically and are historically rooted in a way that NGOs are not. It is no surprise, then, that home associations have adopted the language and form of NGOs. From the perspective of development professionals they might appear amateurish (for example in a lack of monitoring and evaluation), yet it is this amateurish quality that makes them so innovative and interesting. For example, their use of the canon of development terms casts the same words with different meanings. Take 'community participation': this term is used frequently and unproblematically by home associations, but their actual enactment of it differs from standard definitions. For home associations it is more often about the heroism of the indigenes and their commitment to place, a symbolic demonstration of what can be achieved without external help. The practice of 'community participation' is also used to produce the social relationship between those in the village and the 'elites' outside (the elites participate by giving money, those in the village participate by giving labour). Similarly 'culture', and its relationship to development, is viewed differently by members of home associations, as the following comment from the annual general meeting of the home association in Bali Nyong'a suggests:

> We are not gathered here as shareholders of a public utility company, nor as members of a democratically elected body for which our country is so rightly praised, but as members of a development and cultural association. I believe strongly that organizations such as this can only have impact if we draw on our rich, well-documented and dare I say widely appreciated culture. No money we contribute could equal that contributed by government, but our cultural capital is immense, it is immeasurable. So I

plead with delegates to speak, act and deliberate. We are here with twin objectives: to promote the development of our subdivision; and to evolve within the cultural context of Bali, one of the ethnic groups of Cameroon … We are all here for the cultural development of Bali.[2]

Here, the explicit reference to 'culture' ties it very firmly to a distinctively local approach to development, in contrast to a more common and problematic notion of culture that not only sees it as rooted in the past, but also as something to be overcome through the process of development itself. However, what this quotation also shows is that home associations are defining their work not only through responding to the world of NGOs, but also through the need to work within the framework of a national government. So, the language of culture enables the home association to take on some of the responsibilities of the state without criticizing it for failing to deliver. In general, the home associations considered here describe their work as 'complementing' government efforts.

The way in which home associations stretch definitions of development is particularly apparent in relation to their welfare activities. Another key finding of this research is that the work that home associations do to look after their members is far more important than the work specifically labelled as 'development'. Associations spend more time and money comforting members who are bereaved than they do talking about development. Yet when we suggested that development was a much lower priority for these associations than the welfare support that they offered their members, people often disagreed with us on the grounds that the welfare of the diaspora was the development of the home. In one sense this is an instrumental claim: if those in the diaspora can be helped to succeed then the homeplace will ultimately benefit. But in another sense it is a broader claim that the wealth of the place is in its people, and as such supporting each other in the diaspora is the development of the homeplace.

There is a tension emerging between the desire of international development institutions to engage African diaspora groups and the more innovative and locally specific approaches to what constitutes development that are identified here. This is because though donors have embraced diaspora-led development, they also wish to retain their own vision of what constitutes 'development'. Whilst the choice of whether or not to engage with donors is in the hands of the home associations, there is a risk that if they do, they will find that they lose the capacity to define development in their own terms. Key policy documents are taking a clear normative stance on what types of diaspora association and what types of development are acceptable. For example the Report of the Global Commission of International Migration (GCIM, 2005: 29–30) states that:

> [D]iasporas should be encouraged to promote development by saving and investing in their country of origin and participating in transnational knowledge networks... The commission commends the positive impact of diaspora and other migrant organizations that are constructively engaged in development initiatives in countries of origin, particularly through the targeted transfer of collective remittances. One way to enhance this process is for governmental and non-governmental organizations to provide matching funds for such remittances, on the condition that they are put to effective developmental use. It is of equal importance for those who are providing matching funds to ensure that diaspora organizations do not represent narrow regional, political or personal interests. Despite their potential value, diaspora organizations can be exclusionary; pursuing divisive agendas in countries of origin and even contributing towards instability and the prolongation of armed conflict. If their developmental impact is to be maximized, it is essential for such organizations to respect the principles of human rights, good governance and gender equity.

Such a policy leaves the definition of 'effective developmental use' in the hands of those who provide the matching funds. Furthermore it suggests that it is possible to find diaspora organizations that do not represent 'narrow regional, political and personal interests'. However our sense is that such interests are invariably at the heart of home associations because they are place-based. In some contexts (such as international conflict) even a 'national' homeplace might be seen as a 'narrow' interest. Rather than search for those diaspora associations that are progressive because they do not represent narrow interests it would be more useful to try and find a progressive politics of place. All these associations represent place-based interests and are therefore to some extent exclusionary, so the question is: is it possible to imagine a politics of place that is not by definition seen as parochial or where being exclusionary is not a problem?

What is the political work of home associations?

Home associations are an important institution within the contemporary politics of neopatrimonialism. They can link regional elites to the centres of political power. As such they can be springboards for the politically ambitious, and mechanisms for securing the support of rural electorates.

They can be used as part of a divide-and-rule strategy by central government to foment hostility between 'indigenes' and 'strangers' in an era of multi-party politics. Yet such a blunt reading of their political effects is unbalanced.

John Lonsdale has drawn a crucial distinction between 'political tribalism' and 'moral ethnicity' among the Gikuyu of Kenya as a means of bringing an alternative dimension to the otherwise sweeping stigmatization of ethnicity in African politics:

> my reading of history suggests that ethnicity has been the arena of common moral debate as much as a vehicle of unquestioning social ambition. Its deep political language has followed an inner logic partly independent of the changing uses to which its key concepts have been put in high politics. Its values have fired but also disciplined ambition. If that be so, the study of an ethnic imagination may not be so subversive of modern African states as is generally believed; it may be constructive. (Lonsdale, 1992: 317–18)

For Lonsdale, moral ethnicity entails Gikuyu political values being used as a potential check on politicians as the public can pass normative judgement on 'how to proceed' (Falk Moore, 1996). These values have a degree of autonomy from the way 'tribe' is brought into high politics. A similar argument can be used to mount a 'defence of place' in the politics of development (Escobar, 2001). Just as there may be a potentially constructive politics of ethnicity, so too there may be a 'progressive politics of place' (Massey, 1993, 1994, 2006).

A progressive politics of place distinguishes between 'political belonging' and 'moral conviviality'. Political belonging describes a process of exploiting affinity to place for elite political ends. Moral conviviality expresses local ideas about the right and wrong ways for diverse groups of people to live together and the process by which differences can be overcome. These two processes coexist. Loyalties to place can be used as part of a divisive and dangerous politics of belonging. This relies on the idea of rigid, impermeable socio-spatial boundaries. But there is an alternative set of values linked to places that has enabled the incorporation of a diverse range of individuals into communities whose boundaries turn out to be highly permeable. Despite the explicit attempt to draw boundaries around territories and corral those who belong there into that space, there are myriad ways in which other people are incorporated into these places on a daily basis. The values that underpin the practical means by which different people live together in places remain autonomous from the way in which the idea of belonging is being used in high politics.

In the African context this separation of place and ethnicity might initially appear counterintuitive, but it is useful both empirically and theoretically. Of the four homeplaces considered here, none are coterminous with a single or distinct ethnicity. This is underlined by the home associations themselves, none of which is ethnically homogeneous. Indeed, in the case of the Tanzanian diaspora in the UK, associations are primarily based on national rather than ethnic identities. So, using place rather than ethnicity sits more comfortably with actual practices. In addition, a focus on place offers an alternative to the straitjacket of mapping the African social landscape in terms of ethnicity, one that recognizes long histories of mobility and mixing. To imagine place as equivalent to ethnic homeland is to have allowed political belonging to erase history and moral conviviality.

Affinity to place has become more important in recent years. It is often claimed that we live in an age marked by accelerated mobility (of people, money, ideas) and of consequent changes (social, cultural, technical, economic) whose visible outcome is increasing mixture. Such changes are usually discussed together under the banner of 'globalization'. There is a sense that as space is being annihilated by time (Marx, 1973 [1857]) faster than ever, so everywhere starts to feel the same. The experience of mobility is assumed to generate anxiety and insecurity, among both those who move and those who do not. The rapid pace of change produces a desire for fixity, a desire to find a refuge from the hubbub, a place where identities are stable and homogenous rather than hybrid and changing. This desire is used to explain the way that place-based politics have returned to the fore. This shift is often described as a 'retreat' to the local. The idea that local places are outside globalization may be a fantasy but nevertheless has material effects and political consequences.

This increased loyalty to place is generally assumed to be politically reactionary. This is partly because it is thought to be based on a series of false hopes (that it is possible to escape from the experience of frenetic change; that coherent and gentle communities are coincident with particular locations). More significantly, increased loyalty to place is assumed to be reactionary because it looks inwards to small communities of interest rather than outwards to higher levels of solidarity. So classically in some of the literature on Cameroon, the increased loyalty to local places is seen to have undermined attempts to form trans-ethnic opposition parties that can articulate alternative ideologies and policies to the ruling party. In contrast, in Tanzania attempts to build political platforms based on local loyalties are considered taboo, yet rural homeplaces are becoming more important as state capacity declines (Kiondo, 1995; Kelsall, 2000). The rise of competitive localisms, a concern with boundary-making, a linking of indigeneity to representative politics, introverted historical narratives and attempts to police who belongs where are all visible signs of political belonging. Home associations are often interpreted as part of this retreat to the local and therefore as politically reactionary because they are overtly place-based.

Some African governments and elites have embraced this turn to the local in order to achieve their own ambitions and have thus amplified its reactionary consequences. The strange rise of the terms 'autochthone' (indigene) and 'allogène' (incomer) within public language in Cameroonian (but not Tanzanian) newspapers and political speeches is perhaps the most startling manifestation of this trend. However, the constitutional rise of ethnic labels on identity cards, covert government support for indigenous groups in exchange for electoral loyalty, explicit moral endorsement of indigeneity in political speeches, legislation that provides financial incentives for policing belonging (such as the Cameroonian community forestry law), and the careful manipulation of high-profile political burials all add further evidence to support the argument that there is a deliberate and knowing attempt to manipulate people's attachment to place for Machiavellian political ends in Cameroon. The result is that a loyalty to place that was already resurgent as a result of increased global mobility is sometimes exaggerated by government policy. Even in Tanzania, (generally taken to be the model for African states in erasing political tribalism) the capacity of the taboo on talking about ethnicity is being tested. This emerges in debates about the selection of parliamentary candidates. For example in 2005 in Mbeya Urban parliamentary constituency, which is 'home' to a large number of Nyakyusa 'migrants', the self-ascribed indigenous Safwa elite manoeuvred on grounds of ethnic belonging to prevent a Nyakyusa candidate from standing. This squabble was quickly censured and disciplined by the central mechanisms of the ruling party and con-demned in national papers, yet it reveals a potential tribalization of politics. In the end a Safwa candidate was selected. Furthermore, Tanzanian government ministers laud those urban elites who become engaged with development in their homeplace and involved in home associations, and this inevitably produces competitive localisms. The spectre being raised here is of a process of increasing 'political belonging'.

However, an increase in ethnic territorialization as a result of political manipulation of ideas of belonging did not always worry those with whom we spoke in either Cameroon or Tanzania. When we sketched out some of the potentially negative outcomes of pursuing place-based politics, association members were bemused by the very notion that ethnic mobilization could be problematic. This was generally also true of those in the international diaspora. In the Tanzanian case this is because there is considerable pride that ethnic conflict has largely been avoided (an outcome usually compared with Kenya or Rwanda). In the Cameroonian case there were occasions when the turn to increasingly local spheres of interest among those in the UK was regretted, but this was for practical rather than political reasons. In contrast most people, particularly in Africa, saw the rise of home associations and place-based politics through the idiom of 'healthy competition'. The activities of one elite group of migrants stimulated those of their neighbours, we were told. The incentive to get organized, form an association, and do some development work in your homeplace was that you did not want neighbouring towns to get ahead of you in the development stakes, that it would be shameful if they did. In other words, competitive localism was seen as 'a good thing' – a healthy stimulus to mobilizing communities.

One response to the finding that people were not worried about the potential for 'balkanization' of the state would be to say that they just do not understand the risks and to conclude that they (Cameroonians in particular) are 'sleepwalking towards disaster'. Given examples like the violent boundary dispute in Bawock, people must surely be either deluded or naïve if they are not conscious of the divisive political consequences of investing effort in these local competitions and excluding some individuals from communities on the grounds that they do not belong. But the people with whom we spoke are not deluded, naïve or indeed complicit – rather they are aware that ethnic territorialization is 'just politics' and that in contrast an autonomous commitment to moral conviviality is generally able to regulate the kind of competition between places. There is plenty of evidence to suggest that politically reactionary events in some of the case study areas are often justified using the language of belonging. But this is balanced by a conviction that the people know the right way to live with their neighbours. When things do go wrong (as at Bawock) it is because the balance has been tipped towards the pole of political belonging by those with particular political agendas.

The requirement to form a normative judgement about the politics of place-based associations emerges from the desire of policy-makers to intervene in the development work that diasporas do. Policy-makers want to know if home associations fall into the category of diaspora organizations that are 'exclusionary; pursuing divisive agendas in countries of origin and even contributing towards instability and the prolongation of armed conflict' (GCIM, 2005: 30). The difficulty is that home associations are inherently narrow in their interests because a loyalty to place is what motivates people to join, so it is futile to look for good or bad associations. Instead a progressive politics of place that sets up moral conviviality as a counterpoint to the dangers of political belonging shows how all associations are at risk of being exclusionary, but are not necessarily so. The merit of teasing out the rather crude dichotomy between a progressive and a reactionary politics of place is that it makes transparent what remains hidden in much of the critical analysis because of the aversion to making overt normative judgements. There is, in other words, a tendency in the discussion of the politics of belonging to move too quickly to a dismissal of place-based politics relying on an implicit suggestion that it is reactionary and to refuse to address the need and desire for a sense of attachment to place as more than just a response to globalization.

Outline of this book

The book is divided into four parts. Part One addresses the conceptual objective of rethinking the relationship between migration, development and politics when seen through the lens of diasporic home associations. Part Two deals with the structure and character of the home associations that have been studied. Part Three considers how home associations weave together development and politics in the work that they do. Part Four returns to broader questions about the relationship between migration and development, and summarizes our main findings.

After this introduction Part One continues with an explanation of the choice of Cameroon and Tanzania and the research methods used (Chapter 2). The reader is introduced to the four case study areas of Bali, Manyu, Newala and Rungwe. Chapter 3 ('Rethinking research on African diasporas and development') shows how ideas about the relationship between migration and development could be enriched by incorporating insights from the literature on diaspora and associational life. Writing on diasporas challenges conventional understandings of development in important ways: what it means, how it should be done, by whom, and where. The developmental work of diaspora associations cuts across many areas of research, yet there is a lack of dialogue between those who work on migration within Africa and those who work on international migration and transnational mobility. We argue against the epistemological separation of mobility inside and outside of Africa within the migration–development nexus because it obscures continuities and tends to underplay the significance of movement within the continent.

In Part Two ('The history and structure of home associations') the focus shifts to the four case studies. Chapters 4 (on Cameroon) and 5 (on Tanzania) outline the history of migrants' associational life in each country and show how these national and local contexts have shaped the character of the particular migrants' associations linked to each case study. The different forms that home associations take in different places is a reflection of the exigencies of political organization, social and economic history, and the associated narratives of changing identity.

Part Three ('The developmental and political work of home associations') analyses the current work that the four home associations do. Politics and development are considered together because, we argue, they are inseparable. The sequence of the chapters in this section reflects the priorities of the home associations themselves. So welfare and social support (Chapter 6), which are common to all of the associations we have encountered, is their first concern and so it is prioritized in our discussion. Home associations stretch definitions of 'development' to include the welfare and social support of those in the diaspora and those at home. This theme is continued in Chapter 7 with a discussion of home associations' role in 'modernizing' 'tradition'. The focus of the chapter is the construction of a mortuary in Bali Nyong'a by the home association. Issues around burial are a common concern among associations. The mortuary project provides a good example of the way in which diasporas do development differently and provides a lens through which we can examine the relationship between those 'at home' and those 'outside'. In Chapter 8 we turn our attention to the provision of education services. Tanzanian associations in particular have invested heavily in secondary education at home. The Tanzanian case reveals the uneven development of diaspora-led education provision by examining the differences between the Newala and Rungwe diasporas' attempts to improve secondary provision at home. Chapter 9 reflects on the limits to the capacity of home associations to provide public goods by discussing the construction of a large water supply system in Cameroon. The water project reveals the reliance of home associations on their domestic members and contacts (for example with governments) rather than on their connections with the international diaspora. But this case is also interesting because of the way in which the association dealt with the very stiff challenges it faced when the project was (initially) unsuccessful.

That the project did not fail entirely shows the strength of home associations in terms of their persistent commitment to particular places and their embeddedness in social relations, ensuring that leaders are held accountable to homeplaces.

Part Four summarizes our main findings, identifies areas where more research is needed and considers opportunities for development policy-makers to engage diaspora associations. The argument that there could be a progressive politics of place is developed further in this final chapter.

Notes

1. Interview, Rungwe diaspora in Dar es Salaam, September 2005.
2. Bali Nyong'a Development and Cultural Association AGM, Bali, Cameroon, February 2005.

2 CONTEXTS AND COMPARISONS

This chapter gives the reader information about the four homeplaces on which the book focuses. It begins with a description of the research process before turning to an explanation of the choices of Cameroon and Tanzania as the countries from which the case studies are drawn. The main body of the chapter then analyses Bali and Manyu in Cameroon, and Newala and Rungwe in Tanzania, focusing on economy, history, politics and identity.

Research design

The research for the book was multi-sited and used a range of methods. In contrast to many studies of the African diaspora, or of home associations, the research began in the four rural homeplaces and traced the associations attached to those places within Cameroon and Tanzania, and then in Britain. This gave a sense of the shape and structure of the associations in different places, and highlighted the disconnections between those locations as well as the connections. It was necessary to start in the homeplace, not only to identify diaspora connections that we could follow up, but also to understand better the relationship between those at home and those in the diaspora. Indeed, being familiar with the homeplaces made discussions in interviews in the diaspora much more fruitful.

The research was predominantly qualitative and based on interviews with association leaders and members, other community members, relevant civil servants and politicians. Research in Africa was undertaken between December 2004 and September 2005, and in Britain between October 2005 and October 2007. In Cameroon and Tanzania we interviewed people living in the four case study areas and in the principal towns and cities where diaspora associations were found. In Cameroon this meant discussions with people from Bali and Manyu in Bamenda, Buea, Limbe, Mutengene, Tiko, Douala and Yaoundé. In Tanzania interviews were undertaken with people from Newala and Rungwe in Mtwara, Mbeya and Dar es Salaam.

In addition to formal interviews as much time as possible was spent participating in the meetings and activities of the associations and wider communities. These observations were important to give a sense of how home associations work in practice and the role they play within the broader framework of community life. We were welcomed to a wide range of meetings and social events, for example a Bali Nyong'a death celebration organized by the domestic diaspora in Limbe, Cameroon; the annual general meeting of the Tanzania Women's Association in Islington, London; the installation of the new Manyu Minister as Patron of MECA in the Manyu Hall in Yaoundé, Cameroon; a Tanzanian wedding planning meeting in Slough, near London; and a Bali cultural gala and fundraising event in Dalston, London; we spent a day with one of the parliamentarians from Rungwe who was touring his constituency, inspecting progress on community-built schools and handing over money and materials collected in Dar es Salaam for further construction work. The development projects undertaken by the home associations were visited whenever possible, and project users were interviewed about the services offered there.

A social survey of 2,274 people was also undertaken in the four case study areas and among their diasporas in towns and cities in Cameroon and Tanzania. The survey was administered by local enumerators in English, Pidgin or Swahili. It aimed to gather opinions from those people who were often not actively involved in running case study associations and who might not even count themselves as members. It supplemented our qualitative research with additional information about association membership, migration and remittances, and opinions about home associations and development.

Historical material was derived from archival research in the National Archives in Dar es Salaam, Buea and Bamenda. Associations were deemed by colonial administrators to be important to politics, so relevant documentation was filed under a specific heading from an early stage, enabling effective inspection of relevant files. The Registrar of Societies in Dar es Salaam also kindly allowed access to their archive, though the scale of that resource and the relatively limited amount of information kept on each society meant that only a limited sample of their files was inspected.

Newspaper holdings at the University of Dar es Salaam and the Archives in Buea were also consulted. In addition secondary historical sources were widely used, including the excellent resource at the University of Dar es Salaam, which holds a wide range of PhD and Master's dissertations.

Why compare Cameroon and Tanzania?

It is important to emphasize the differences between places and between home associations because that variety foregrounds African agency and complexity (Abrahamsen, 2003; Mercer et al., 2003). If diaspora associations are going to be enrolled as development actors then the differences between associations will influence existing patterns of uneven development. The frustration, among those who study African society, with the crude ubiquity of particular policy prescriptions based on an assumption of homogeneity and an ignorance of context is probably matched only by the weary exasperation of policy-makers when they are told to pay attention to these differences, but given little sense of how that might be achieved.

The comparative methodology has a tendency to focus first on differences, but it can also be used to draw attention to the similarities between places (Robinson, 2006, 2007). First, for example, there is a widespread assumption that the kind of associations analysed in this book are primarily a West African phenomenon and are not found in East Africa. Home associations are indeed a more visible, elaborate and significant institution in parts of West Africa, but historically they were present in parts of East Africa and are re-emerging there because of the limits of state capacity to deliver rural development. Certainly they are different in form and character, but in broad outline there are some commonalities between East and West. The most important similarity between the four case studies is that the governments of neither Cameroon nor Tanzania can deliver rural development at the rate and scale desired by their citizens because of economic constraints. The common consequence has been a shift of responsibility onto African individuals and local communities to develop their own localities (particularly rural areas) in order to compensate for the limits of state capacity. This is not new – 1950s self-help community development followed the same logic – but it is widespread. The result is that home associations of some kind are now a common feature of social life in many different places. Such global economic structural elements have erased some of the differences between Cameroon and Tanzania and between Bali, Manyu, Rungwe and Newala.

There are further similarities and differences between Cameroon and Tanzania that make their comparison a useful exercise. Tanzania is widely perceived to have had one of the most effective nation-building policies in postcolonial Africa, whereas Cameroon has not. Tanzania has eliminated chieftaincy from formal governance whereas Cameroon has not. International migrants from Tanzania have historically tended to move east to Asia, whereas those from Cameroon have moved north to Europe or west to the Americas. The Government of Tanzania has begun to engage with its international diaspora as part of a development strategy, but the Government of Cameroon has not really done so. The two countries have similar colonial histories having both been German colonies that became League of Nations Mandate territories under British administration after the First World War. Even for African countries both have extremely high levels of ethnic diversity, yet the postcolonial management of diversity has been quite different in each. Both have rapidly growing external populations, yet their international diasporas are remarkably different in how they associate. Most important, both countries have been relatively politically stable for many decades and so provide a counterpoint to studies of refugee or conflict diasporas.

Why Bali, Manyu, Newala and Rungwe?

The four case study areas were also chosen to enable comparisons reflecting the criteria that seemed relevant to explaining the migration histories in different places and the ongoing relationship between the homeplace and its diaspora. For example in each country one case study was relatively accessible whilst one was enclaved by poor transport links; one case study had a long history of colonial education and one did not; and one case study had a history of centralized hierarchical chieftaincy and one did not. However, beyond these generalizations each place has a unique character, which needs to be summarized for the subsequent analysis to be clear.

Bali Subdivision, Cameroon

Cameroon is divided into ten provinces, which are subdivided into 58 divisions, which are in turn split into 269 subdivisions. Bali is a very small (192 square km) subdivision within Mezam Division in the Anglophone North West Province, on the southwestern edge of the area known as the Cameroon Grassfields.[1] It is densely inhabited with an estimated population of 63,800.[2] The subdivision comprises an urban centre known as Bali Town (with a population of around 20,000) surrounded by smaller villages. Bali Town, which has a mix of government services, utilities and private enterprises, is only 23 km southwest of Bamenda, the headquarters of North West Province, to which it is now connected by a tarred road. From Bali Town it is relatively easy to reach the major urban centres of Cameroon (Douala and Yaoundé) within a day by public transport or a half-day by private transport. It is a predominantly upland subdivision whose economy is dominated by agriculture (coffee, oil palm, cattle, vegetables, maize) and a long history of labour out-migration. Land shortages have contributed to this migration process. Our survey data suggest that 79 per cent of contemporary Bali residents have lived and worked elsewhere in Cameroon at some point in their lives, while 11 per cent of the total sample had lived and worked outside Cameroon, mostly in Nigeria.[3]

The Presbyterian Church (Basel Mission) was established in Bali in 1903 and so there is a long history of formal education. This placed the Bali community in an advantageous position in the postcolonial era because a significant number of people from Bali were able to get civil service employment, which provided access to central state resources and formed the basis of a self-perpetuating modern Bali elite. Many of this elite are sympathetic to the ruling government party (the Cameroon People's Democratic Movement – CPDM) but since the return of multiparty politics in the 1990s the people in the subdivision have often voted instead for the main opposition party (the Social Democratic Front) when choosing both their parliamentarian and their mayor and local council.

Bali Subdivision is dominated by the historic kingdom of Bali Nyong'a, a very hierarchical polity at whose centre is the Palace with its monarch (Fon) and associated secret societies (Voma and Nggumba).[4] The Fon and the Palace remain an important part of Bali Nyong'a society alongside the institutions of the modern state.[5] As well as being a polity, the term Bali Nyong'a is used to describe an ethnicity. Many Bali Nyong'a present themselves as a homogenous ethnic group who are distinctly different from their neighbours in the Grassfields because of their origins 300 miles to the north amongst the Chamba. The standard version of Bali Nyong'a history describes their journey south as armed raiders in the late eighteenth century and the establishment of their fondom by force at the current site around 1855. Some historians of the Bali Nyong'a choose to emphasize their Chamba roots and their martial past in order to present contemporary Bali Nyong'a as a pure, coherent, ethnic identity with a consistent, particular and unchanging character.[6] However, there is an alternative interpretation that would see Bali Nyong'a as a hybrid ethnic identity combining many different people and cultural elements (such as language, aesthetics and secret societies) from the different groups encountered on the journey from the 'Chamba cradle' to the present site. As one person in Bali put it, 'you know, Bali is like America. No one can claim indigeneity';[7] as another said, 'the real original Bali people are very few. Bali is now very cosmopolitan.'[8] In this interpretation Bali Nyong'a society and culture owe as much to neighbouring polities in the Grassfields as they do to Bali's Chamba ancestors.

The key period in the history of the Bali Nyong'a was between 1889 and 1910, when they formed a mutually helpful alliance with German colonizers (Chilver and Röschenthaler, 2002). Within twenty years Bali Nyong'a went from being a minor participant in Grassfields politics to becoming a subimperial power whose Fon was recognized by the Germans as paramount chief.[9] In 1891, two hundred Bali Nyong'a men were trained and supplied with rifles by the Germans to form a *Balitruppe* who were able to exert control over neighbouring groups. The legacy of this period is ongoing animosity with their neighbours: not only did the Bali Nyong'a use their new power to assert control over more land, but they were also responsible for supplying forced labour to German plantations on the coast, where the mortality rates for workers were extremely high. The result is that in 2007 the outgoing president of the Bali home association in Cameroon observed that 'the recent Bawock crisis revealed the actual depth of feeling against us... and much as the violence of the propaganda came as something of a surprise, it also confirmed what we have always suspected: that when the chips are down, we in Bali have no one but ourselves to count on'.[10]

Not everyone in the subdivision identifies themselves as ethnically Bali Nyong'a however. In addition to the people of Bawock who identify as Bamileke (Chilver, 1964) there is a group in Bossa village who identify as Meta and a number of villages of semi-nomadic cattle herders who identify as Mbororo (Fulani). In sum, of the four case study areas Bali is the closest to being ethnically homogenous but not only are there minority groups within Bali, but also the Bali Nyong'a ethnicity itself is internally highly heterogeneous.

Within Bali there are a number of home associations. The largest is BANDECA – the Bali Nyong'a Development and Cultural Association. This had several precursors, which operated under different names dating back to the 1940s. BANDECA only operates within Cameroon. In parallel to BANDECA is Nk'umu Fed Fed, a women-only home association that is autonomous from BANDECA but often collaborates with it. Outside Cameroon there is BCA-USA (the Bali Cultural Association USA) and BCDA-UK (the Bali Cultural and Development Association UK). In addition in Cameroon the groups in Bawock and Bossa have their own home associations while the Mbororo have an association that represents the interests of all their groups across the Grassfields (Hickey, 2004, 2007a).

Manyu Division, Cameroon

Manyu occupies the northern part of the Anglophone South West Province of Cameroon. It forms the upper part of the low-lying and densely forested Cross River basin. Manyu is a large (9,565 square kilometres), relatively sparsely inhabited division with a total population of over 200,000. It contains four, predominantly rural subdivisions: Mamfe Central, Upper Banyang, Eyumojock and Akwaya. Mamfe, which is by far the largest town in the division (estimated population 20,000), was established by German colonial administrators after an insurrection in 1904–5 (Ruel, 1969; Niger-Thomas, 2000; Michels, 2004). As a divisional headquarters the town of Mamfe has a wide range of government offices and services, though electricity and water have recently been leased to private sector operators. For reasons of accessibility, fieldwork in Manyu was conducted in Mamfe Central and the neighbouring Central Ejagham area of Eyumojock, though no geographical restriction was made when contacting migrants from Manyu during fieldwork elsewhere in Cameroon or in the UK.

Manyu has fertile soils and a climate favourable to the production of a diverse range of products (particularly cocoa, palm oil, coconuts, maize, vegetables, tropical and citrus fruits) with relatively high profit margins. The bulk of production still comes from smallholders. The other principal economic activity in Manyu is cross-border trade with Nigeria, which provides a crucial source of revenue in the area, particularly for women (Niger-Thomas, 2000). However, economic opportunities in Manyu have been stifled in recent decades because the area has very poor transport links. Routes to the south (which lead to the markets of Kumba and the coastal towns), east (to the urban centres of North West and West provinces and ultimately Douala and Yaoundé) and west (to Nigeria) are notoriously poor. To reach the major urban centres of Douala and Yaoundé is a time-consuming and difficult journey, which would generally take more than a day if travelling by public transport during the dry season and longer during the rains. However, Manyu was not always enclaved. During the British colonial period Mamfe was the junction of the two main roads in the territory: the north–south route connecting Buea to Bamenda and the east–west route connecting Enugu (Nigeria) to Southern Cameroons (the name of the Mandate territory). As a result Manyu attracted inward migration in the colonial period from both Nigeria and the Grassfields. At the same time there was also outward migration from Manyu to the plantations on the coast and to urban centres in Nigeria.

Manyu is currently very loyal to the CPDM, the governing party of Cameroon, and there has been a minister from Manyu in every government since independence. The general sentiment however is that the rewards for this loyalty have been relatively meagre. Some people suggest that this is a consequence of the junior posts held by the ministers, who have therefore been unable to steer resources towards their home area. Others suggest that it is because the elite puts more effort into its own political survival than into the development of the division. Manyu has not always been politically pliant. In the early 1990s there was a brief period when an opposition party – the National Union for Democracy and Progress (UNDP)[11] – wielded significant influence. Indeed the current CPDM parliamentarian for Mamfe Central and Upper Banyang constituency (who holds the post of First Vice President of the Cameroon National Assembly) was originally elected under the UNDP banner.

The boundaries of Manyu are the creation of colonial and post-colonial governments. In 1961 independent Cameroon inherited Mamfe Division from British colonial rule, changing its name to Cross River Division in 1969 (Ruel, 1969) and then to Manyu Division in 1975. In 1992 the boundary changed again when Lebialem Division was carved out of Manyu. Manyu encompasses a number of different ethnic groups with overlapping territories. Before it was created as a unit of administration, the different societies of the area were never governed as a single unit; nor did they imagine themselves as such. Certain groups predominate in the Manyu diaspora and politics, particularly the Banyang and Ejagham, but there is signficant linguistic and cultural variation even within these. Occasional indications of tensions between the two groups were encountered during fieldwork, although these must be set alongside this internal heterogeneity and their long history of cohabitation, cultural exchange and intermarriage.

In common with most other groups in South West Province, the Banyang and Ejagham are characterized by their relatively flat social structure, variously described as acephalous, decentralized, diffuse, segmentary or stateless (Ruel, 1969; Nyamnjoh and Rowlands, 1998;

Konings and Nyamnjoh, 2003; Röschenthaler, 2004). The village is the most important unit of political geography in Manyu. Ties may exist at higher levels, usually through clans – groups of villages perceived to have common descent – but historically these have had limited political authority. Chieftaincy is often a wholly colonial construct but nevertheless it is perceived to be very important, as the effort that goes into numerous long-running disputes over village chieftaincy titles shows. The main institution that provides a higher level of territorial allegiance and integration is Ekpe (also known as Ngbe, Nkwo, Nyamkpe) – a male initiation society made up of numerous autonomous lodges that operate at village level. A large village will have a number of Ekpe lodges. The society's functions are recreational, political and economic – it is used to endorse laws, enable trade and protect the property rights of its members. Ekpe's reach is far wider than Manyu, stretching down as far as Calabar, in the area of Nigeria where it is believed to have originated. Ekpe does not provide any logic for an identity that maps neatly onto the space of Manyu, but it does provide a unifying institution for most Manyu men. Ekpe provides a meaningful historical identity that transcends the mosaic of village loyalties.

The main home association for Manyu is MECA – the Manyu Elements Cultural Association – which operates at the scale of the whole division. This has separately constituted autonomous branches across Cameroon, the US and Europe. In addition there is Efokhoyu, a network of Manyu women's groups such as the Manyu women's association MOHWA, among others. There are also associations that refer to the different subdivisions, and many village-scale home associations.

Newala District, Tanzania

Newala District (4,015 square kilometres) is located on the Makonde Plateau, which rises to an average altitude of 800 metres from the surrounding plains of Mtwara region along Tanzania's border with Mozambique. According to the 2002 census, Newala has a population of 183,344. Just 11 per cent of the population is urbanized, living principally in Newala Town (URT, 2003). The town is the administrative, commercial and religious centre of the district. Together with Lindi region, Mtwara is considered to be among the poorest parts of Tanzania (Seppälä, 1998a). It is estimated that 43 per cent of the population live below the national poverty line.[12] Since Tanzania moved to a system of multi-party democratic politics in the early 1990s, all parliamentarians for the district have come from the ruling party, Chama Cha Mapinduzi (CCM).

Much of southeast Tanzania is often described as 'peripheral' (Seppälä and Koda, 1998; Wembah-Rashid, 1998) because of its geographical isolation from the rest of the country, which is compounded in Newala by the physical elevation of the plateau. The main urban centre in the southeast is Mtwara Town, 130 km away to the west along a poor sand road, while Masasi Town is 60 km to the east. The main southern inland route bypasses Newala entirely. Although the bridge over the Rufiji River was opened in 2003, it still takes at least two days to reach Newala by bus from Dar es Salaam in the dry season, and for six months of the year Newala is effectively cut off from the rest of the country due to the rains (Mesaki and Mwankusye, 1998).

The economy is based on smallholder farming, producing a limited range of crops for the market and for subsistence (the latter crops include sorghum, millet, cassava), but there is also a substantial rural informal sector including extractive activities, craft, trade and services (Seppälä, 1996). Agriculture is rain-fed and uses hand-hoe technology and bush fallow methods, with few inputs (Tadreg, 2007). Farm plots tend to be scattered and are often located some distance from farmers' residences (Mihanjo and Luanda, 1998). The principal cash crop is cashew, which was introduced during the colonial period as a soil conservation measure and encouraged as a cash crop particularly after 1945. Cashew production was severely disrupted by forced resettlements under villagization, which were extensive (Hyden, 1980; Seppälä, 1998b). Nevertheless the region remains a cashew producer, exporting raw nuts for processing in India or Singapore. Between 1990 and 2000, cashew production increased fourfold but since 2000 it has struggled (Tadreg, 2007).

Islam spread in pre-colonial inland southern Tanzania through Arab trade with the more centralized polities neighbouring the Makonde Plateau from the end of the seventeenth century (Liebenow, 1971). During the early twentieth century the influence of Islam became more widespread across the south as a result of contact with Swahili society, and the upheavals associated with German colonization and with the Maji Maji uprising in particular (Alpers, 1972; Becker, 2006). Islam's move on to the plateau was characterized by widespread conversion, while the influence of churches has always been erratic and limited to 'islands of Christianity' (Seppälä, 1998a: 29). The Universities' Mission to Central Africa (UMCA) founded a mission at Newala in 1878, but withdrew to the plains in the 1890s leaving only a single teacher at each of the two plateau missions. The Newala mission station was re-established in the 1920s, and a Catholic Benedictine mission was founded in the 1930s in another part of the plateau. Neither the UMCA nor the Benedictines established secondary schools on the Makonde Plateau, instead focusing their efforts on lowland missions (Clayton, 1993). The consequent lack of secondary education in Newala District continued until as recently as 1989 when the main home association, the Newala Development Foundation (NDF), upgraded St Peter's Middle School to Newala Day Secondary School.

Most people living on the plateau identify themselves as ethnically Makonde but significant minorities identify as Makua or Yao. The Makonde[13] are not coterminous with Newala District, which is just one of three Makonde-dominated districts (the other two being Mtwara Rural and Tandahimba). The Makonde are divided into four dialect groups, two of which are spoken in different parts of Newala (Nangumbi, 1998). The history of the Makonde Plateau is not just one of 'penetration' and interference by Arabs, missionaries, Germans, British, the Tanzanian postcolonial state and agents of the global cashew nut trade, although they have all left indelible markers of their presence. The settlement of the plateau is a story of around four centuries of movement (Liebenow, 1971). The interior of southeast Tanzania was reportedly largely uninhabited in 1616, but by 1800 the migration of Makonde, Makua and Yao across the Ruvuma Valley was well under way (Iliffe, 1979). Though without water, the plateau was a natural place of defence. The dense vegetation coupled with the Makonde preference for scattered settlements offered a degree of refuge from the slave trade (Ranger, 1979; Clayton, 1993). In the 1860s and 1870s the Makonde were one of many mobile groups, and the plateau absorbed many of these migrants and refugees. Newala's first two prominent leaders were in fact Yao (Liebenow, 1971). The basic Makonde social units were small matrilineal kin groups (*litawa*), of which there were several hundred. Related *litawa* formed political–territorial units (*chirambo* (s.), *virambo* (pl.)). There were approximately one hundred small scattered *virambo* by the end of the nineteenth century, each led by an *mkulungwa*, a pioneer colonist or a matrilineal descendant (Liebenow, 1971). A centralized Makonde polity never arose. The various Europeans who engaged with the Makonde assumed, as they did elsewhere in Africa, that ethnicity was the central organizing feature of African politics and sought to produce an ethnic territory, when in fact political authority in southeast Tanzania depended on 'knitting together fragments of ethnicities' (Ranger, 1979: 63). Indirect Rule heralded a more systematic transformation of society on the plateau. For administrative purposes and to make tax collection more efficient, everyone had to belong to a single *chirambo* and recognize a *mkulungwa*, including non-Makonde groups. The British attempted to fix *virambo* boundaries and membership, and to amalgamate smaller *virambo* into larger units, which were easier to administer. This meant that non-Makonde groups such as the Machinga, Maraba and Mawia became 'lumped together as "branches of the Makonde" with the stroke of a district official's pen' (Liebenow, 1971: 103). The British even appointed an *mkulungwa mkuu*, a post similar to that of paramount chief. Indirect Rule was abandoned in 1942 but seven years later the British resurrected their attempts to govern the Makonde as an ethno-territorial unit with the Umakonde Umoja project which tried to bring the Makonde in Newala and Mtwara districts together into one administrative unit. It was aborted in 1954, officially because the British considered the differences between the relatively 'progressive' and 'wealthy' Newala Makonde and the more 'apathetic' coastal Makonde too great. An attempt in 1951 by the Makonde of Lindi District to establish the Wamakonde Union was quashed. By the late 1950s, emergent Makonde unity was at odds with the prevailing nationalist strategy.

During the 1920s and 1930s the introduction of forced labour penalties for tax evasion obliged many plateau residents to engage in labour migration or cash-cropping. Makonde went to the southern coastal sisal plantations and later to the infamous Nachingwea Groundnut Scheme in neighbouring Lindi District. With the 1950s sisal boom, labour migrants moved further up the coast to Dar es Salaam, Bagamoyo and Tanga (Kingdon, 2002). Seppälä (1998a) argues that ideas of Makonde unity were forged as much through labour migration as through British attempts to establish Indirect Rule. Today the out-migration of both educated and uneducated groups is characteristic of Newala District (Mihanjo and Luanda, 1998). The combined effect of Indirect Rule and labour migration has been to generate a degree of Makonde unity in the twentieth century, but this struggles to overcome the highly decentralized character of Makonde society.

The main home association in Newala is the NDF – the Newala Development Foundation, which was registered as a District Development Trust in 1988. It has only two 'branches': one in Newala and one in Dar es Salaam. It has no international branches or affiliates. It appears to be the only home association that refers to Newala district.

Rungwe District, Tanzania

Rungwe District (2,211 square kilometres) comprises Tukuyu town and a large rural hinterland in Mbeya Region, in the Southern Highlands of Tanzania near the border with Malawi. It is an upland district, with the Mporoto Mountains in the north, and the Livingstone Mountains in the east rising to 2,265m. The southernmost part of the district slopes down towards low-lying plains alongside Lake Nyasa, which comprise Kyela District (carved out of Rungwe in 1972). Rungwe has a population of 307,270, around 15,000 of whom live in Tukuyu (URT, 2003). The district is well connected to the national and regional transport network and is bisected by the tarmac road that links Dar es Salaam (a twelve-hour bus ride away) to Malawi. The same road links Rungwe to the regional centre of Mbeya, 72 km to the north. However, internal transport connections within the district are more basic. Rungwe is divided into two constituencies, both of which have returned parliamentarians from the ruling CCM party in all three multi-party elections (1995, 2000, 2005), some of whom have served as cabinet ministers at different times.

The district's extraordinary range of altitudes produces a correspondingly diverse range of crops. For much of the district, agriculture has provided a reliable income, the major cash crops being tea (currently the most profitable), potatoes, vegetables, coffee and cocoa. An estimated 32 per cent of the district population live below the national poverty line against a national average of 36 per cent (URT, 2005).[14]

After the First World War the population of Rungwe became increasingly engaged in labour migration. Initially migration seems to have been unpopular, and the 1923 District Report claimed that people from Rungwe had 'a great aversion to leaving the district'. Most of the migrant labourers recruited in Tukuyu in the 1920s actually came from Nyasaland (Malawi) or Northern Rhodesia (Zambia) and were sent either to the coastal plantations north of Dar es Salaam or to the Lupa goldfields northwest of Mbeya (Willis, 2001). Yet by 1938 the Lupa goldfields were employing 42,000–52,000 men annually, one third of whom were from Rungwe (Ellison, 1999). Droughts and food shortages in Rungwe in the early 1930s were influential in driving this change. So extensive was the migration from Rungwe to Mbeya that in 1941 it justified a detailed inquiry by the District Officer, who described it as an 'invasion'. Later, men from Rungwe began to migrate further afield to the mines of Northern Rhodesia and South Africa. In 1942, approximately 600 men from Rungwe entered Northern Rhodesia; by 1947, 2,000 men from Rungwe were employed there (Iliffe, 1979). The numbers from Rungwe were large enough to warrant the establishment of a recruitment office in Tukuyu for the South African mining industry (Willis, 2001).

The majority of the population in Rungwe identify themselves as ethnically Nyakyusa, though there are minority groups of Ndali and Safwa who live principally near the western and northern borders of the district. There are also many Nyakyusa people in the neighbouring district of Kyela. The pre-colonial Nyakyusa were not a centralized hierarchical society with a paramount chief. Political authority in Rungwe was small-scale and exercised by a constellation of separate *abanyafyale*,[15] (who later modelled themselves as 'chiefs' under Indirect Rule) and *amafumu*, elders who were redesignated as 'headmen' in 1935. The Nyakyusa are well-documented in the anthropological and historical literature (Wilson, 1959; Charsley, 1969; Koponen, 1995; Ellison, 1999) and are known for their unusual social organization based on the 'age village' rather than kinship group, and for their creation as a 'tribe' under Indirect Rule. Wright (1971) characterizes pre-colonial Rungwe as a fractious political landscape in which *abanyafyale* competed with one another for spheres of influence. However, while accounts of Nyakyusa history highlight the diverse nature of the pre-colonial population, they pay less attention to the continued relevance of a single group identity that developed once these different groups were absorbed by the category 'Nyakyusa' in the first half of the twentieth century. By the end of the 1930s many of these small groups had been amalgamated into a single Nyakyusa 'tribe'. Colonial rule provided two key centripetal forces in the creation of this tribe. The first of these was the Europeans' insistence that political authority in Africa rested on hierarchical tribal territories, at the pinnacle of which was the chief. The second was the imperative that colonial rule placed on Africans to migrate to find waged labour. Despite the abolition of chiefs in Tanzania in 1962 and four decades of repressing ethnic identities in favour of national unity, the idea of being Nyakyusa survives.

Historically Rungwe was, like Bali, a national leader in the field of education, again a consequence of the early establishment of (Moravian) mission schools in the 1890s in the wake of German colonization. At independence in 1961 the educational advantage that the missions afforded meant that (along with the Chagga and the Haya, from the north and west of the country) Nyakyusa people from Rungwe were well positioned to access government jobs. Now, however, there is a general sentiment of having fallen behind, particularly in education. In 2004 the district had 195 primary schools and 29 secondary schools; that year, only 25 per cent of students who passed the Standard Seven National Examination were able to enter secondary school (Rungwe District Council, 2005).

There is a wide range of home associations that refer to different parts of Rungwe District, but all are limited to a diaspora *within* Tanzania. The Rungwe District Education Trust (RUDET) operates at a district-wide scale. There are other associations that operate through the two local parliamentarians at a constituency scale (Rungwe East Development Foundation [RUEDEFO] and Rungwe West Development Foundation

[RUWEDEFO]). The needs of smaller areas are the focus of smaller funds such as the Selya Development Foundation (SEDEFO), which is concerned with four wards, and Shirika la Maendeleo ya Busokelo (Busokelo Development Association, SHIMABU), which concentrates on Mwakaleli.

Conclusions

This chapter has introduced the four homeplaces in terms of their agricultural economy, their accessibility and their political, migration and educational histories. It has paid particular attention to the creation and representation of ethnicity. In all four places there is a story in which identities, particularly ethnic identities, are shown to have changed over time. The difference between home associations in Bali and Rungwe on the one hand and Manyu and Newala on the other is particularly shaped by transport and educational history. Both Bali and Rungwe are within a day's travel of the main centres of population and both had an educated elite at the time of independence, which enabled them to access good positions within postcolonial bureaucracies. In both cases this has fostered a relatively well-placed diaspora, which is more actively engaged with development through home associations and is discussed in more detail in Chapter 8.

In all four places farming is dominated by smallholders, though Rungwe and Manyu also show significant development of larger, commercial agricultural enterprises. But there are also dramatic economic differences between the profitability and reliability of agriculture in each place, which shape the relationship between those outside and those at home. In Newala the combination of poor transport connections and a fragile environment produce an overdependence on cashew, a crop with an erratic price on world markets. In Bali, the shortage of land effectively precludes a robust agricultural economy. In Manyu the considerable agricultural potential is frustrated by poor transport links, though some enterprises are flourishing and so there is more interest in the sector from those outside. Lastly, in Rungwe, the combination of good transport links, diverse environments, and some land availability has resulted in a profitable agricultural economy. While these differences do not show up dramatically in our survey data (Table 2.1) they were perceived to be important by those in the associations. These differences have a significant impact on the interest and willingness of those outside to invest in development at home. Where the agricultural economy is strong, family members are less dependent on those in the diaspora, though there

Table 2.1 Monthly household income in the homeplaces and among the domestic diaspora (survey data)

	Bali residents	Manyu residents	Rungwe residents	Newala residents
<£10	39%	17%	47%	35%
£10–£49.99	47%	46%	41%	43%
£50–£199.99	10%	27%	8%	15%
£200+	2%	4%	0%	3%
No data	2%	6%	4%	4%
Number	303	311	323	324
	Bali domestic diaspora	Manyu domestic diaspora	Rungwe domestic diaspora	Newala domestic diaspora
<£10	8%	8%	24%	25%
£10–£49.99	43%	46%	43%	50%
£50–£199.99	39%	32%	21%	15%
£200+	5%	6%	3%	3%
No data	5%	7%	9%	7%
Number	241	253	254	264

Note: 2,273 people were asked (in either English, Pidgin English or Swahili) to estimate total household income from all sources except remittances, using given categories in local currencies.

is more potential for those at home to support those in the city during times of crisis.

Finally the political structures of pre-colonial and late colonial society also impact on contemporary associational life. The highly centralized society in Bali provides a history of authoritarian leadership, which enables the current association to take on an effective, if coercive character based on a Bali Nyong'a identity that takes pride in showing obedience to neotraditional structures. The associations in Rungwe reflect a society in which 'tribal identity' and 'traditional rulers', though imposed through Indirect Rule, achieved a degree of unity and authority, notwithstanding the abolition of chieftaincy in the 1960s. In Manyu, ethnic diversity and a less systematic imposition of Indirect Rule mean that overarching unity is only achieved successfully through membership societies such as Ekpe, and associational life is correspondingly fragmented. Village-scale associations are more coherent than the division-wide association. In Newala the profoundly decentralized organization of Makonde life, combined with the ambivalent and partial imposition of Indirect Rule, have resulted in a situation where home associations that rely on a feeling of unity connected to a Makonde identity face an uphill task. Development strategy that relies on diaspora groups will need to acknowledge the dramatic unevenness of associational life in different places.

Notes

1. Throughout the book the term Bali is used to refer to the subdivision, the term Bali Town to refer to the main urban centre in the subdivision, and the term Bali Nyong'a to refer to both the ethnic group and the historic and present kingdom.
2. Divisional Medical Office records, 1 February 2005.
3. 307 randomly selected residents in Bali Nyong'a were asked, 'Have you previously lived or worked elsewhere in Cameroon? If so, where?' The survey was administered in English or Pidgin by Cameroonian research assistants. A subsequent question asked about international work experience.
4. The key early published sources on Bali Nyong'a's history and anthropology are Hunt (1925); Jeffreys (1957) and Chilver and Kaberry (1961).
5. Bali Nyong'a has had just four monarchs since around 1865: Galega I (1865–1901), Fonyonga II (1901–40), Galega II (1940–85) and Ganyonga III (1985 to the present). The longevity of their reigns has enabled them to exert an authority within their polities that was probably unparalleled within the Grassfields.
6. The Bali Nyong'a are not alone in the Grassfields in their selective interpretation of history (see Yenshu and Ngwa, 2001; Yenshu, 2003).
7. Interview, Bali diaspora in Bamenda, March 2005.
8. Interview, Bali diaspora in Bamenda, March 2005.
9. The history of the Bali Nyong'a fondom is rich, complex and highly contested. See Hunt (1925); Jeffreys (1957, 1962); Chilver (1964, 1967, 1970); Bejeng (1985); Nyamdi (1988); Titanji et al. (1988); Fohtung (1992); Fardon (1996, 2006b); Fokwang (2003).
10. Outgoing speech by the President of BANDECA, Bali, April 2007.
11. The UNDP was a party led from North Cameroon by Bello Bouba Maigari – a former prime minister under Cameroon's first president, Ahmadou Ahidjo. It had some significant electoral success across South West Province based on a nostalgia for the northern leaders of the past and on the fact that it was an opposition party but was not the SDF, perceived by many in South West to be monopolized by Grassfielders. For more see Takougang (2003).
12. The Tanzanian poverty line was set at Tsh7,253 per 28 days at December 2000 prices (URT, 2005).
13. The Makonde of Mozambique claim a similar origin to the Makonde in Tanzania. Although both groups have similar social and political organization, they are linguistically distinct (Kingdon, 2002).
14. See note 12.
15. The *abanyafyale* (s. *umalafyale*) are referred to in different accounts as chiefs or as princes.

RETHINKING RESEARCH ON AFRICAN DIASPORAS AND DEVELOPMENT

Thinking about the African diaspora opens up new ways of understanding African development and change. The development work that diaspora associations do challenges standard ideas about what development is, where it can be done, and by whom. Yet to date there has been relatively little critical debate about the relationship between development and diaspora beyond the question of remittances. In this chapter we aim to show how work on diasporas and associational life can enrich understandings of the migration–development nexus. This discussion begins with a critique of the ways in which African diasporas have been conceptualized, researched and represented. It then turns to the research on Africa's diasporas, arguing that Africa's internal and international diasporas should not be treated as separate entities. This is followed by a discussion of African diasporic associational life that weaves together research on domestic and international diasporas. A distinction is drawn between those associations that are organized around a homeplace and those that are not. We argue that, in general terms, associations whose members share an affinity to a common homeplace tend to be more interested in developmental work in Africa. In discussing associational life in the domestic and international diasporas together, the aim is to demonstrate how an understanding of contemporary transnational home associations, the social relations through which they are created and maintained, and the work that they do, is enhanced through an appreciation of their historical and contemporary work in Africa.

Beyond the migration–development nexus

Diasporas have recently attracted the attention of scholars and policy-makers concerned with the 'migration–development nexus' (Davies,

2007; Merz et al., 2007; Faist, 2008). Yet the distinction between migrants and diasporas, and the nature of their relationships with development, have been unclear. Policy-related research on diaspora and development has run ahead of academic research and, in focusing on the needs of policy-makers who wish to harness the developmental potential of diasporas, it has tended to be preoccupied with the social and economic remittances of individual migrants (Ammassari and Black, 2001; Levitt, 2001; Nyberg-Sorensen et al., 2002; Sander and Maimbo, 2003; Pantoja, 2005; Farrant et al., 2006; Ionescu, 2006). The slippage between 'migrants' and 'diasporas' is also evident in initiatives such as the UN's High Level Dialogue on International Migration (GCIM, 2005; OECD, 2006) and national policies being formulated within aid ministries of the Global North (DFID, 2007; Murray, 2007). Despite occasional perceptive internal critiques of these ideas (Ghosh, 2006; de Haas, 2005), much research has concentrated on how diasporas can be incorporated into existing models of migration and development rather than on new conceptualizations of what diasporas bring to development.

Research has shown that diasporas undertake a range of large- and small-scale ventures at home, including house-building, support for education and training, fundraising and charitable donations, trading with and investing in businesses at home, paying taxes, and transferring technology and knowledge (Vertovec and Cohen, 1999; Al-Ali et al., 2001; Newland with Patrick, 2004; Vertovec, 2004, 2006). The development impact of return migration and 'brain gain' has also attracted interest (Ammassari, 2004; Germenji and Gedeshi, 2008). China, India and Mexico are often portrayed as archetypal 'success stories' in that their diasporas have made astute use of knowledge and technology transfers in the case of China and India, and remittances in Mexico (Bolt, 1996; Orozco, 2002; Orozco with Lapointe, 2004; Davies, 2007; de Haas, 2007a).

Beyond individual economic and social remittances, the development work that diasporas undertake collectively, such as their support for infrastructural projects, has also attracted interest (Vertovec, 2004). Here the shift is from a concern with migrants as individuals, to diasporas as groups of migrants. Research on Latin American diaspora groups, and their home associations in North America, indicates that their contributions to improving public goods can be substantial, with investments in health and education facilities, sanitation, infrastructure and information projects (such as libraries and internet cafes) at home (Smith, 1998; Portes and Landolt, 2000; World Bank, 2001; Orozco and Welle, 2005; Orozco, 2006; Orozco and Rouse, 2007; Portes et al., 2007).

Orozco estimates that Mexican home associations in the USA donate a minimum of US\$30 million a year, equalling local government budgets for public works in some small rural towns. Their development projects expand public services and provide employment for those involved in construction work. The Mexican government has been particularly proactive towards home associations, offering matching funding programmes through different levels of government (national, regional and local) for investments in public goods.

Diasporas make important contributions to development in material terms. Yet discussion of the significance of diaspora identities and of the nature of diasporas' relationship to development has been limited to date (compare Mohan, 2006, 2008). The easy elision of 'diaspora' and 'migrant' masks the theoretical differences between them. Migrants are often conceived as 'problems' in a way that diasporas are not – 'diaspora' is a less pejorative term that pre-empts the rehearsal of certain prejudices (particularly in relation to concerns about assimilation), and opens up debates about mobility to new ideas. Migration as a concept also treats the movement of people as the agglomeration of the rational acts of individuals governed by the logics of incentives and opportunities. 'Diaspora', however, with its association with the strange dialectic of simultaneous flight from and longing for home, foregrounds questions of emotion and desire. The standard definitions of 'diaspora' all include an explicit notion of 'home' and an implicit sense of its maintenance and reproduction (Safran, 1991; Clifford, 1994; Cohen, 1997).

Diasporas, then, cannot simply be 'added' to the migration– development nexus. Indeed, bringing diaspora and development into dialogue poses challenges to both diaspora studies and development studies. In particular, the development work of diaspora groups reveals a shared attachment to a home*place* that is much more material than a wistful longing or a myth of return. Yet the diaspora literature, which has worked hard to establish an analytical framework that understands diasporic identities as non-local, hybrid and fluid, is reluctant to entertain the notion that a home*place* still matters. In order to emphasize the cosmopolitan, deterritorialized qualities of diasporas it has been necessary to assert their *placelessness* – the idea that identity is divorced from location. Where the homeplace does appear in accounts of the diaspora, its effects may be powerful but are relegated to the register of the imagination. Instead, writing on diasporic space tends either to draw attention to the fragmented global space in which a diaspora somehow maintains its unity despite effectively being nowhere (Hall, 1990; Clifford, 1994; Gilroy, 1994; Brah, 1996; Cohen, 1997; Anthias, 1998;

Braziel and Mannur, 2003; Brubaker, 2005) or it draws attention to the local space in which individuals within the diaspora actually live (Tölölyan, 1996; Werbner, 1998, 2002). In neither case is the *place* of origin held to be that significant: indeed treating it as significant is sometimes taken to be inherently reactionary (Manger and Assal, 2006: 16). From a theoretical perspective the great achievement of diasporas is that they are at home anywhere, they have multiple unbounded homes, defined not by nation-states or geography but by social relations. However, in their determination to assert this liberation from place, those who write about diaspora have sometimes overlooked the ways in which a place of origin continues to be important for some groups who describe themselves as diasporas (compare Werbner, 2000). The determination not to reify or essentialize bounded places as 'home' answers more to Western academic agendas than to the words and actions of those in the diaspora. This is not an attempt to recuperate or defend a sense of primordial 'rootedness', but simply to recognize the very immediate ways in which some diasporas reterritorialize home.

In the context of diasporas, developmental work, the celebration of their capacity to break the link between territory and identity is only part of the story. Diasporas do break the link between identity and place because they make new homes in new places, but through their development work they also constantly remake the home they came from. Place and identity are continually co-produced by the diaspora. This is a concern that is as yet underdeveloped within diaspora studies (Carter, 2005). Bringing diaspora and development together provides an opportunity to link political economy with questions of culture and identity, and to avoid treating them as separate areas of analysis (Mohan and Zack-Williams, 2002). Highlighting home associations' paradoxical role in decentring 'home', while at the same time convening a shared commitment to it, offers a way forward for such an analysis. The proposal that diasporic space is cosmopolitan and transnational is an exciting one, which should not be lost. However, the evidence of commitment to a place of origin or homeplace (in words and deeds) suggests that such versions of diasporic space are only ever partial; they are necessary but not sufficient frameworks for understanding the spaces of the diaspora experience.

In the same way that development work challenges theorizations of diasporas, so diasporas challenge core assumptions about space and agency that are deeply embedded in development studies' epistemology. Perhaps for this reason critical development studies has only recently begun to engage with debates about diaspora (Zack-Williams, 1995; Adi,

2002; Mohan and Zack-Williams, 2002; Mazzucato et al., 2004). For example, debates on global civil society and transnational development networks, of which diasporas are surely a key constituent, have to date proceeded with little reference to diaspora groups (compare McIlwaine, 2007; Faist, 2008). Instead the focus has been on networks that link familiar and professionalized international NGOs and donors to grassroots actors (such as local NGOs and CBOs) in the Global South (Keck and Sikkink, 1998; Bebbington, 2000). Development studies – and development policy – struggles to move beyond the assumption that the agency for improvement of transnational development networks lies with institutions in the Global North (Henry et al., 2004; McFarlane, 2006). Though diasporas are geographically located in the West, they are culturally located elsewhere – they are not seen to be Western enough to be development agents. The welfare, support and development activities of diasporas in the Global North challenge the standard spatialization of development as a process located in the 'Developing World' (Jones, 2000). Since the success of diaspora engagements with home depends partly on the economic well-being of those in the diaspora, an effective diaspora development policy involves investing in the diaspora outside the 'Developing World'. The Spanish government is among those proposing to fund the activities of diaspora groups within Spain from its overseas aid budget (Sieveking et al., 2007). Whether this is normatively justifiable is of less interest here than the challenge it poses to the way the spaces of development are imagined.

One of the few extended critical treatments of the nature of development undertaken by diasporas recognizes precisely these tensions. Giles Mohan (2002) sets out a threefold classification that distinguishes between development *in*, development *through* and development *by* the diaspora. These three types of diasporic development, though different, are clearly interdependent. Development *in* the diaspora refers to benefits that accrue to the host locality as a result of the presence of international migrants. Such benefits are independent of the fact that these workers are members of a diaspora and relate simply to their function as labourers who propel economic growth within the host country. Development *through* the diaspora refers to additional benefits experienced in the host country as a consequence of the ongoing transnational connections that are a particular feature of diaspora groups. These benefits may serve the interests of individuals within the diaspora in particular, but are also of value to the host country more generally. Finally, development *by* the diaspora refers to benefits that diasporic communities bring to their countries of origin. Diasporas, then, contribute to socio-economic well-being and economic growth in the host country as well as back at home (see also Al-Ali et al., 2001), thereby redefining the nature and scope of development.

This intellectual trajectory is taken further through a discussion of what Mohan (2006), following Hart (2001), identifies as the difference between 'D' and 'd' development. The former refers to planned development interventions undertaken by states, while the latter indicates the uneven unfolding of capitalism. Historically, 'D' development contained the inequalities that emerged from 'd' development by providing public goods through the state for those who saw only limited benefits from capitalist accumulation. However, over the past 30 years the rise of neoliberalism has deliberately undermined 'D' development in order to instigate a further round of 'd' development. In response, diaspora development has had to expand to fill the void left by the incapacitated state (Levitt, 2001). However, Mohan also wishes to get beyond what Gibson-Graham (2004: 410) refers to as 'capitalocentric' readings of development. The economies of diaspora are not necessarily capitalist economies. They do not always follow capitalist logic, but instead are tied to a politics of obligation based on kin and community. For Mohan, non-state diaspora development and the reproduction of the state have become interdependent, and the boundary between 'D' and 'd' development has been blurred by diasporas' engagement with the development of an 'ancestral town' (2006: 869).

Diaspora engagement with development at home is thus more complex than is often acknowledged in discussions that focus on the economic and political 'impacts' of migrants. Diasporas are distinguished by their *collective* engagement with home, which draws on the shared sense of obligation that diaspora members feel to each other and to their homeplace. This underpins a unique approach to development that is expressed through a range of social, cultural and quotidian political activities, as well as by the more familiar activities associated with economic development and high politics. However, recognizing that diasporic development weaves together development in both home and host country requires a re-examination of the idea of the 'homeplace' in standard definitions of diaspora. And specifically in research on Africa's diasporas, there is a similar need to re-focus attention on the places that are 'home' in Africa.

Reframing African diasporas

The term 'the African diaspora' has been applied across vast temporal and spatial scales to refer to many dispersals of people from the African continent. It first emerged in the 1950s and 1960s to describe the history of the dispersal of communities of African ancestry around the world, and the social, cultural and political connections between them (Manning, 2003; Boyce-Davies, 2007). The term also had political purchase, particularly for pan-Africanists, for whom the concept was closely associated with the social and political struggles for decolonization in Africa and the Caribbean, and for civil rights in the USA (Sherwood, 1995; Adi, 2002).

In this book we reframe Africa's diasporas to include domestic as well as international forms of mobility. In so doing we respond to some of the systematic absences and biases in the Anglophone literature on African diasporas. Historical and Cultural Studies perspectives, which have become dominant in studies of the African diaspora, have tended to privilege the experiences of Africans in the North Atlantic while paying less attention to the links between contemporary practices in the diaspora and a differentiated African continent (Akyeampong, 2000; Byfield, 2000; Manning, 2003). In particular, historical writing on diaspora has unwittingly homogenized the continent of Africa in its attempts to develop 'a theoretical framework and a conception of world history that treats the African diaspora as a unit of analysis' (Patterson and Kelley, 2000: 13; see also Shepperson, 1976; Kilson and Rotberg, 1976; Cohen, 1997; Gomez, 2005). 'Africa' itself has become an undifferentiated place even while 'the African diaspora' has been conceptualized as dynamic and multi-layered. The treatment of diaspora by Cultural Studies has also turned the spotlight away from Africa, focusing its glare almost exclusively on the North Atlantic. The publication of Paul Gilroy's landmark book *The Black Atlantic* (1993) drew attention to black modernities in the diaspora, but it also established a research agenda biased towards the North Atlantic in general, and the transatlantic slave diaspora in particular (Byfield, 2000; Zeleza, 2005; Manger and Assal, 2006). Ter Haar (2004) argues for example that the experience of the transatlantic slave diaspora should not be seen as archetypal since Africans in Europe did not enter that continent through slavery and therefore have a very different sense of diaspora identity and exile. The widespread presence of Africans around the Indian Ocean, particularly its western littoral, has also been sidelined by the focus on the transatlantic slave diaspora (Alpers, 2000; see also de Silva Jayasuriya and Pankhurst, 2003; Zeleza, 2005; Campbell, 2006; de Regt, 2006, 2007; de Silva Jayasuriya, 2007).

In order to avoid some of these problems we follow Paul Tiyambe Zeleza (2005), who has called for a framework for the study of Africa's diasporas that recognizes multiple diasporas at different geographical and temporal scales, and their different connections with Africa. Zeleza's approach is unusual in diaspora studies because he is willing to deal specifically with migrations that take place *within* Africa as well as those outside of it. Thus his categorization of 'modern historical diasporas' includes the intra-African, Indian Ocean, Mediterranean and Atlantic diasporas, while his 'contemporary African diasporas' include the diasporas of colonization, decolonization, and the era of structural adjustment. He is thus critical of recent attempts to characterize 'new African diasporas' (e.g. Koser, 2003a) as distinctly postcolonial phenomena. The 'intra-African' diasporas are identified based on the primary reason for dispersal, including:

> the trading diasporas (the Hausa and Dioula in western Africa); the slave diasporas (West Africans in North Africa and East Africans on the Indian Ocean islands); the conquest diasporas (the Nguni in southern Africa); the refugee diasporas (for example, from the Yoruba wars of the early nineteenth century); and the pastoral diasporas (the Fulani and Somali in the Sahelian zones of western and eastern Africa). (Zeleza, 2005: 45)

Zeleza's 'intra-African' diasporas are echoed in Colin Palmer's observation that, in the pre-colonial period, 'people who left their ethnic homeland were, strictly speaking, residing "abroad"', leading him to wonder whether 'it is more historically accurate to speak of Yoruba, Akan, or Malinke diasporas for much of the period up to the late nineteenth century or even later' (Palmer, 1998). Richard Fardon has taken this a step further by pointing out that it was quite possible to be 'cosmopolitan' without ever leaving colonial Nigeria (Fardon, 2006a). Given the socially constructed nature of ethnicity the idea of an 'ethnic homeland' is one that needs to be treated with caution and put in careful historical context. However, by drawing attention to the historical record of mobility and diaspora formation within the African continent, these writers alert us to the fact that Africa's diasporas have not always been defined by their relationship to the boundaries of postcolonial nation-states (see also Akyeampong, 2000; Byfield, 2000). The task, then, is to explore which migrations under what historical conditions have led to the formation of diasporas within Africa as well as outside of it, and the connections between them.

Analysis, then, needs to break down the gulf between research on Africa's domestic diasporas and research on Africa's international diasporas. To date this has meant that accounts of associational life in the international diaspora often treat migrations within Africa as historical relics, important only insofar as they prefigure the formation of diasporas outside the continent (compare Manchuelle, 1997; Frost, 2002; Kerlin, 2000; Uduku, 2002; Abdul-Korah, 2007). However today diaspora associations continue to be an important part of associational life within Africa as well as outside of it; indeed the two are often connected in diverse ways. The formation of contemporary domestic diasporas needs then to be understood as part of the process of the formation of international diasporas, rather than as temporally and spatially separated from it. Such a shift makes visible the connections between domestic and international diasporas, their similarities and differences, and how they change over time (de Haas and Bakewell, 2007). Those studies that recognize this produce a more convincing and holistic account of diasporic global networks (Mazzucato, 2005; de Haas, 2007b; Kabki, 2007; Smith, 2007).

African diasporas and associational life

A focus on African associational life provides scope to reflect critically on what it means to treat diasporas as part of civil society. It provides an opportunity to go beyond the apparently more 'problematic' or 'exotic' groups: those Africans whose visibility in the West emerges from their transgression of legal, geographical or cultural boundaries. Refugee communities are one example here (Koser, 2003b; Pérouse de Montclos, 2003; d'Alisera, 2004), but research has also focused on 'criminal diasporas' engaged in illegal transnational economic activities such as 'Nigerian' advance fee ('419') scams (Glickman, 2005); and the involvement of Ghanaians in drug trafficking networks linking Asia and Latin America to Europe and North America (Akyeampong, 2005). This research dovetails with wider public concerns in Europe over 'problem' African communities, such as 'Somali gangs' in London (e.g. Laville, 2007), African churches and child abuse (Sanders, 2003; Ranger, 2007), and the numbers of 'illegal immigrants' arriving from Africa (Pinkerton et al., 2004; Black et al., 2006; de Haas, 2007b). There is also concern over diasporas' political roles, particularly in civil conflict. These include the mobilization of national opposition, subnationalist or rebel movements, whether through print or internet propaganda or through funding of political or military activity (e.g. Brabazon, 2003; Collier, 2000; Collier and Hoeffler, 2001; compare Nathan, 2005). However, it is also recognized that diaspora groups can mediate in peace processes, as in Uganda (Rigby, 2006); help to rebuild post-conflict home states, as in Somalia/Somaliland (Farah et al., 2007; Kleist, 2008) and Eritrea (Clapham, 1998); or lobby for issues like human rights, such as among the Zimbabwean diaspora in the UK

(Chikanda and Dodson, 2007). These groups are interesting and important, but they are certainly not the only African diasporas.

Far less attention has been paid to more quotidian forms of associational life in the African diaspora, which are extremely varied. Within Africa and beyond, migrants come together in all sorts of formal and informal associations, which unite members of a faith, political group, nation-state, age group, gender, profession, business group or homeplace; those in need of welfare or refuge; members of burial societies, rotating savings groups, old boys' and girls' school networks, sports clubs, and arts and cultural groups (Ndofor-Tah, 2000). All these groups compete for the time, resources and loyalty of individuals, even though they often overlap in terms both of their membership and their activities. However, a key difference between African diaspora associations is the extent to which they are concerned with development on the African continent. This is linked to whether the association membership has a basis in a shared attachment to a homeplace.

Though the focus of this book is on home associations it is important to remember that such groups are only one element within a wide array of everyday associations in the African diaspora. This section of the chapter looks at diaspora associations based on faith, trade, occupation, and politics before turning at the end to home associations. Although we separate these associations for heuristic purposes, many associations perform multiple roles. What unites all the groups considered below (and makes them different from home associations), however, is that their developmental focus is generally on improving the quality of life for those away from home, rather than those remaining at home.

Diaspora faith groups have attracted particular attention. Studies show that, among other things, faith groups meet certain needs of migrants including spiritual, social, cultural and sometimes material needs. However, there is little evidence that diaspora faith groups are making the kinds of contributions to development in Africa found among other groups such as home associations. This is not to say that religious organizations do not engage with development at all – many operate in Africa as NGOs with development portfolios, often funded by a mix of local contributions and funds from international donors. But less formalized faith groups are usually concerned with welfare and support away from home. To return to Mohan's (2002) three-fold typology above, their activities resemble development *in* and *through* the diaspora, but generally not *by* the diaspora.

Documentation of the recent growth of organized faith groups in the international diaspora is still in the early stages with Christian, particularly

Pentecostal, groups attracting most attention. Far less is known about African Muslim communities with the exception of the Murids (*Muriddya*), a Sufi brotherhood that originated in nineteenth-century Senegal (to which we return below). Ter Haar (2004) suggests that this is because African Muslims are more likely to worship at mosques that cater for many diaspora groups than to form their own congregations. In contrast, Christians have been establishing independent African churches in the diaspora for some time. Independent African churches first appeared among Nigerian communities in Britain in the mid-1960s (Killingray, 1994; Harris, 2006), but their rapid growth across Europe has been more recent. As Pentecostalism has grown in popularity across Africa (Gifford, 2001), so migrants have established Pentecostal churches abroad. Ter Haar (1998) records such churches in the mid-1990s in Belgium (frequented by Zaireans, Brazzaville Congolese and Angolans), Germany (frequented by Nigerians, Ghanaians and Zaireans) and France (frequented by many Francophone Africans and more recently by Nigerians and Ghanaians). Less is known about African independent churches in North America, although a recent estimate counted at least 50 Ghanaian churches in Toronto alone (Kwakye-Nuako, 2006).

Recent research in the UK and Ireland has revealed the popularity and dynamism of African independent churches (Ajibewa and Akinrinade, 2003; Styan, 2003; Maxwell, 2007). These include independent churches founded in the diaspora, churches with a link to a 'parent' church in Africa or the diaspora, churches that are part of a global religious organization, and previously existing churches that now cater for African diaspora groups (Kwakye-Nuako, 2006; Ugba, 2006). Churches emerge, disappear, extend, move and develop branches (ter Haar, 1998). New churches are constantly created, sometimes on national grounds. In general terms there is a difference between the mainstream and Pente-costal churches in terms of their imagined geographies, which for the mainstream churches are expressed through linkages with parent churches in, and a socio-cultural orientation towards, Africa, while Pentecostal churches in contrast are oriented to an international 'Pentecostal ideological space' (van Dijk, 1997; Englund, 2004; ter Haar, 1998). Pentecostal congregations are, then, less likely to be oriented towards an African 'homeland'.

Most churches provide a welfare and support role for their congregations. For example, Hepner (2003) argues that Eritreans in Chicago are more likely to attend churches than a home association meeting because they offer better opportunities to share social and cultural activities. In

North America and Europe, many new immigrants drift away from the mainstream churches (Presbyterian, Catholic, etc.) to which they belonged in Africa, preferring to join African-led churches, some of which served by clergy sent from home and which incorporate practices of worship from home such as language, music and dance. Kwakye-Nuako (2006) reads the exodus from mainstream churches in North America as a desire to incorporate culture into worship; others working on Europe have argued that it is a response to a feeling of alienation from mainstream churches in the host society (ter Haar, 1998). For example, Ugba (2006: 169) notes that in Ireland, African Pentecostal churches attract new members 'because their activities are uniquely relevant to the experience of African immigrants'. They provide moral support to those dealing with unfamiliar bureaucracies and facing marginalization and loneliness. Although he cautions against a functionalist view of the experience of racism and the need for cultural expression (see also Herbert et al., 2008), he argues that these churches are crucial supportive sites where members are able to produce a sense of community and belonging.

Another form of faith association that has attracted attention is the *dahira* (Islamic solidarity association), which has flourished among the Murids of urban Senegal and beyond (Beck, 2001; Riccio, 2003). Originally conceived as a religious body (a prayer circle or Koranic school), the *dahira* moved from the rural to the urban setting with migrants as a way of delivering mutual support, retaining varying degrees of ties with villages of origin (Diop, 1981; Manchuelle, 1997). The *dahira* has since adopted other social, economic, developmental and political roles in urban Senegal and abroad. Analysing Murid life in New York City, Babou (2002) finds a division of labour between *dahiras*. Individual 'branch' *dahiras* carry out social support functions among their members including social networking, integration into urban life, support with housing, jobs or the authorities, events such as marriages and baptisms, and repatriation of the dead to Senegal for burial. An 'umbrella' *dahira* brings together the whole Murid community in New York, mediating between them and the City authorities, financing local projects, and collecting money for the functioning of the brotherhood in Senegal. International *dahiras* connect the diaspora more directly with the Murid holy city of Touba in Senegal. They raise money for projects to maintain and develop Touba, including urban sanitation and health care, mirroring the activities of those groups of Murids in Dakar who, since renewing the site for the great mosque in the 1950s, continue to organize remittances for public goods in Touba (Gueye, 2002). Copans (2000), however, challenges the effectiveness of *dahira* investment in the city, claiming that this investment reflects a longer-standing lack of development by the Murids of their heartland, the 'Groundnut Basin' of west-central Senegal (Cruise O'Brien et al., 2002).

The Murids form an interesting case here because they could be considered as a 'trade diaspora' as much as a religious one (see, for example, Diouf, 2000; Buggenhagen, 2001). Since the Second World War they have expanded into Dakar and other Senegalese cities and from there into Europe, the US and elsewhere. The concomitant development of Murid commerce has created networks that now link Dakar, Paris, New York, Jeddah, Hong Kong and many other cities globally. The Murids show that distinct categorizations of different diaspora groups can rarely be sustained empirically. For example Riccio (2001, 2003) demonstrates that the dynamic trading networks of Senegalese (mostly Murid) migrants in southern Italy are partly built on the brotherhood's vertical and horizontal ties. *Dahiras* initially developed in Senegal as a result of internal labour migration, and with later transnational migration they provided the basis for traders' networks, performing welfare functions such as helping migrants to find accommodation and work. The traders have also established non-religious organizations to represent their interests within Italy, known as Senegalese Associations of Italy, united by a Coordinamento (CASI). However, the religious aspect of the Murid brotherhoods continues to shape life for those in the diaspora, providing moral and spiritual support, including visits by *marabouts*. Their complex ties and activities based on faith, commerce, ethnic and place-based affinities differentiate the Murids from other migrant trading networks such as those developed by Congolese *sapeurs* (MacGaffey and Bazenguissa-Ganga, 2000), Senegalese traders in Barcelona (Kothari, 2008), and the Soninke across Africa and beyond (Simone, 2001).

Finally, African diaspora associations have included those formed for distinct political purposes. According to Adi (2002) the first such association in Britain (The Sons of Africa) was formed in the eighteenth century by Olaudah Equiano and Ottobah Cugoano to campaign against slavery and racism. In the twentieth century, a range of African associations coalesced around struggles against racism (Sherwood, 2007), for representation and recognition as citizens, and for political independence in Africa. Organizations often brought together people of different nationalities, such as the West African Students' Union (WASU), founded in London in 1925 and comprised of people from Nigeria, Sierra Leone, Gold Coast and Gambia; the League of Coloured Peoples, which emerged in the 1930s and 1940s and had members from the middle-class Caribbean and African communities; and the African Progress Union (Killingray, 1994; Adi, 2002). WASU was particularly active, weaving its initial remit to act as a representative for African history, culture and law with a later concern with independence and West African statehood. Other associations emerged in response to more localized issues of concern, such as the Colonial Peoples' Defence Association, established in Liverpool in the late 1940s to assist African seamen targeted by government for repatriation (Killingray, 1994; Olukoju, 2007). A key concern in the first half of the twentieth century was politics in Africa rather than in Britain, although clearly the two were linked. Pan-African, regional and country-specific associations had political agendas oriented towards home, such as the British Somali Society (mid-1930s) and the Somali Youth League (1940s). Egbe Omo Oduduwa, a Yoruba cultural association established by Chief Awolowo and other students in London in 1946, became a political party in Nigeria in 1948 (Killingray, 1994).

Where any of the above diaspora associations have engaged with development at all, they have mostly been concerned with development *in* and *through* the diaspora. In the final section of this chapter, we turn to development *by* the diaspora, and those African associations specifically concerned with developing the homeplace, however defined by a diasporic group. An associational focus on a place is crucial in facilitating a developmental engagement with home.

African home associations

Home associations have captured the imagination of those interested in the relationship between diaspora and development because their international 'chapters' have become increasingly visible in the European and American cities where academics and policy-makers live and work. Our aim here, however, is to historicize them more carefully in the context of their development and growth in Africa from the first half of the twentieth century. Indeed one of the arguments of this book is that contemporary African home associations cannot be adequately under-stood as development actors without an understanding of the conditions in which they emerged within Africa, and the work that they do there. The preoccupation with Africa's international diaspora has meant that there has been a surprising lack of reference to previous work on home associations within Africa, despite the fact that African Studies has long recognized home associations as a response to the social, economic and political dislocations of migration. This research has shown that home associations maintain and enhance solidarities from home in the new, usually urban environment for the purposes of conviviality and mutual support. Home associations are not uniquely African (Moya, 2005) but here we focus on African associations only.

African home associations have emerged and changed with historical circumstances, and their shifting geographies and activities reflect this. Some of the earliest recorded forms of African home associations are to be found as far back as the mid-sixteenth century among African slaves transported to Cuba (Ishemo, 2002). In Africa itself they are a twentieth-century phenomenon. Research has shown, for example, that home associations were established in early-twentieth-century Dakar in the form of *chambres* among Soninke migrants,[1] each *chambre* bringing together migrants from the same village (Manchuelle, 1997). The *chambre* provided cheap communal housing and food for the migrants including support for unemployed members, who did household chores while working migrants made regular contributions for rent and food. The *chambre* also provided 'an emergency fund for illness and repatriation to the Soninke homeland, a mailbox, and a place to meet, to exchange news from the village, and to hold festivities' (Manchuelle, 1997: 124). Order was maintained by a system of fines, and the *chambres* of a given village recognized the oldest man present from the chiefly family as their leader. This form of organization was modelled on village youth associations, and even extended into the international diaspora. Communal housing and village mutual aid funds, similar in organization to the Dakar *chambres*, were recorded among migrant Soninke traders in the French and Belgian Congos in the early twentieth century and among Soninke seamen in France after the First World War, forming early transnational home associations. In 1930s Marseilles, for instance, the Soninke, arriving as sailors and stowaways, were the largest African group. They congregated in particular cafes and hotels and formed village mutual aid associations. Each had its treasury, which covered lodging, food and costs due to sickness or death among its members, and paid for the repatriation of undesirables. In certain cases the village funds pooled their resources into a common treasury. Despite the hiatus in activity during the Second World War, these collective efforts helped to establish the Senegalese Sailors' Hostel in Marseilles in 1948. Early transnational home associations were formed among other Senegalese migrants too. In the 1950s and 1960s, increasing rural–urban migration from Haalpulaar villages in the Senegal River valley led to the establishment of solidarity funds (*caisses*) among the migrant *chambres* in Dakar and, later, in France (*foyers des migrants*; Schmitz, 1994). Clearly, in the current era, it is therefore the *expansion* of transnational home associations that is new, rather than their internationalization *per se*.

It seems, however, that such early expansion into the international diaspora was unusual. During the interwar period, it was migration within Africa that encouraged the growth of home associations. Often this was migration to plantations and mines as well as to towns and cities. Migrant organizations existed in Nigeria as early as the 1920s (Abbott, 2006), but it was from 1930 onwards that home associations burgeoned in Anglophone and Francophone Africa (Offidele, 1947; Little, 1965; Cohen 1969; Foucher, 2002; van den Bersselaar, 2005; Yenshu, 2005). Peer interaction influenced the spread, structure and activities of home associations, as neighbouring villages copied and competed against each other in trying to establish and run effective associations. For example Little (1965) attributes the origin of home associations in Nigeria in the 1930s to Igbo moving to towns in the west and north of the country. During this time, home associations became subject to increasing academic, political and cultural attention (Offidele, 1947). For colonial officials, they were a reservoir of individuals who could act as advocates for their vision of development (Chadwick, 1950). In turn, their role as a channel for engagement by African populations with colonial administrations increased (Ruel, 1969; van den Bersselaar, 2005). For African novelists of the 1950s, home associations were a key social group through which ideas about modernity and African independence were articulated, for example in Chinua Achebe's (1960) *No longer at ease*.

Assumptions about social transformation and particularly the post-independence focus on nation-building meant that home associations were expected to be superseded by modern associations based on class interests or ideology rather than ethnicity and attachment to place. This may explain why they all but vanished from the literature in the 1970s and 1980s (compare Little, 1972). Where they do appear it is in the margins of broader discussions of politics. Boone (2003), for example, writing about Côte d'Ivoire in the mid-1970s, describes the expectations placed on ruling party members, high-level bureaucrats and parliamentarians living in Abidjan to become figureheads in their home localities, which included becoming leaders of home associations.

Home associations re-emerge as a focus of research in the 1990s in the context of discussions about legitimacy, democratization and citizenship (Pratten and Baldo, 1995; Hickey, 2007a). However, they are strangely absent from the explosion of work that documented donor efforts to shore up the continent's democratic transitions through 'building capacity' in Africa's civil societies (Mercer, 2002). Instead, they emerge in discussions of politics, indigeneity and territory. Political and economic liberalization created the conditions that encouraged home association growth as development became a race to access resources. In this way home associations have been treated as emblematic of the persistence of ethnicity in Africa and its impact on politics since the 1990s (Barkan et al., 1991; Osaghae, 1994; Olukoshi, 1997). The changes ushered in by adjustment and liberalization propelled those who could to seek opportunities elsewhere by moving to towns, cities or neighbouring countries, or by leaving Africa altogether. Although it is generally recognized that home associations have moved with African migrants to their new destinations, the focus on transnational associations in current research obscures a widespread collective amnesia about their emergence in Africa. Any sense of historical continuity (and rupture) has often been lost (compare Henry and Mohan, 2003; Abbott, 2006).

Contemporary place-based associations in the international diaspora are extremely varied. They can be organized according to national identities, such as among Ghanaians in Canada and the UK (Owusu, 2006; Mohan, 2006; de la Gorgendière, 2007), Nigerians in North America (Abbott, 2006), or Senegalese in Italy (Riccio, 2001); by ethnic identities, such as among Yoruba in Toronto (Adeyanju, 2000), Igbo in Liverpool and Chicago (Reynolds, 2002; Uduku, 2002), or Asante in New York (Attah-Poku, 1996); or through identification with a home town, region or kin network, such as migrants in Portugal from the Guinea-Bissau village of Pelundo (Kerlin, 2000). There are some examples of 'ethnic supra-unions' such as the Asanteman Council of North America (ACONA) (Amoako, 2006) and the Igbo World Congress (Uduku, 2002). In practice, however, such distinctions can be difficult to disentangle, particularly given associational change over time and people's multiple memberships (e.g. of national and ethnic associations). Furthermore the members of any given home association often share relations based on kin, ethnicity, homeplace and nation, as exemplified by the 400 members of an Igbo association in Chicago who come from 125 families sharing the same homeplace, a 130-square-kilometre region of Nigeria's Igboland (Reynolds, 2002). Members of associations that ostensibly bring together those of a given profession can also turn out to share an affinity to a place (Frost, 2002; Lampert, 2007), or home 'places' are effectively replaced by an *alma mater* in alumni associations (Nyamnjoh and Rowlands, 1998). The fluidity of place-based associations through time is demonstrated by the associational life of the Ghanaian diaspora in Toronto. In the 1970s the community was relatively small, and the Ghana Union was established for all migrants. Its popularity waned within a decade as more Ghanaians migrated to the city and ethnic associations such as the Ashanti Multicultural Association, established in 1982, became more popular. By the mid-1990s there were 28 active Ghanaian associations in Toronto, including 16 hometown associations, 7 ethnic associations and a National Congress of Ghanaian Canadians (Owusu, 2000). Both hometown and ethnic associations were popular sites of social and cultural practice and vehicles for hometown development, while the national association represented a united Ghanaian voice in Canadian civil society (Owusu, 2000). However, research on the Ghanaian diaspora in the UK also shows that migrants may choose to distance themselves from the balkanization of associational life by establishing broader national associations or by not joining one at all (Henry and Mohan, 2003; Mohan, 2006). The proliferation of associations tied to ever smaller places is not just related to increased migration, though increased migration is a necessary prerequisite for this process.

There is disagreement on the 'typical' membership of home associations. Based on their work among Ghanaians in Toronto and Asante in New York, Owusu (2000) and Attah-Poku (1996) argue that short-term immigrants, often characterized by lower incomes and lower educational attainment, are the most likely members. Manuh (2003) adds that among Ghanaians in Toronto, new immigrants are more likely to be active in home associations while longer-term residents dominate the larger ethnic and cultural associations. Such an 'assimilationist' position is common in North American studies, where the appeal of ethnic associations is said to diminish for professionals 'whose occupational institutions come to lie outside the ethnic framework' (Owusu, 2000: 1156; see also Caglar, 2006). However, others point to the middle-class leadership and membership of many home associations. Riccio (2003), for example, reports that it is well-educated and established Senegalese migrants who lead associations in Italy. In the USA, Reynolds's (2002) research on professional Igbos in Chicago shows that home associations are just as popular among middle-class Africans while in the UK, Mohan (2006) reports that the majority of Ghanaian home associations are dominated by male professionals and entrepreneurs. Also in the UK, McGregor's (2007) research shows how low-paid care workers from Zimbabwe are constrained from joining associations through lack of time and resources.

What unites these different associations is that, in contrast to the faith-based, political and trade associations discussed in the previous section, they are primarily defined by a shared attachment to a homeplace. Yet there has been little comparative discussion of the role of place in diasporic associational life. Analyses variously invoke nation, ethnic group or homeplace as the explanation for the character of the diaspora association, rather than something that itself requires explanation. This is problematic for two reasons. First, it means that the ways in which home associations co-produce place and identity are overlooked. In this book we argue that although they are place-based, home associations do not simply 'reflect' a sense of belonging tied to naturalized and bounded places. Second, it obscures the uneven geography of Africa's international diaspora. The general lack of comparative work on African diasporas has meant that differences in mobility – who moves how far, and who does not – have gone largely unremarked. Yet if we pause and ask a basic question about which diasporas have attracted most attention in Anglophone scholarship, it quickly becomes clear that research has focused on just a few groups including the Ghanaian, Murid and Nigerian (particularly Igbo and Yoruba) diasporas. Clearly this is to do with relative population, but it is also to do with relative mobility and its relationship to the history and geography of development. For example, much research on the 'Ghanaian diaspora' has actually concerned the Akan-Asante people whose history marks them out as mobile and well-educated relative to other groups in Ghana and even Africa. The slippage between ethnic group and nation serves to obscure not only the basis of members' shared sense of attachment and obligation to a place, but also the uneven historical-geographical relations that have shaped these diasporas relative to others (see Ndione, forthcoming, for a good example of how this unevenness plays out between homeplaces at a very local scale). Put simply, the extent to which any given village, town, ethnic group or nation in Africa has sons and daughters 'abroad' is highly uneven and, as we show in parts Two and Three of this book, is bound up with their history and geography. Discussions of the developmental role of Africa's diasporas need to pay attention to the fact that not every homeplace can count on the support of a well-placed international, or even domestic, diaspora.

The work that home associations do

Although African home associations have courted attention for their capacities as developmental actors, research into home associations both in Africa and in the diaspora reveals that they are principally concerned with the welfare of members away from home. They engage in familiar community activities surrounding birth, marriage and death; and provide space and time to share language, banter, music, dance and food associated with home (Honey and Okafor, 1998a; Trager, 2001). They offer support and advice in terms of education, housing and employment, all of which can be challenging in different and sometimes acute ways for national and international migrants. The role of home associations in offering legal advice and support, often in the context of racialized labour markets, is therefore particularly important (Mohan and Zack-Williams 2002). Owusu (2000) argues, for example, that many Ghanaians in Toronto seek membership of home associations partly in response to the hostility they encounter in their everyday lives.

The development of home, in contrast, is something that only some associations have dipped in and out of over time (Offidele, 1947; Little, 1965). The earliest recorded evidence for developmental work points to Nigerian home associations that began to undertake development activities within a few decades of their establishment in the early twentieth century. Urban migrants sought to construct hospitals, schools and roads equal to those they encountered in the city where they lived (Barkan et al., 1991; Honey and Okafor, 1998a; Grillo and Riccio, 2004). However, it makes little sense to separate home associations' welfare activities from their more 'project-based' development work. Home associations weave together their welfare and developmental work, recasting development as an ongoing process of care and improvement of both people and place in the diaspora and at home. Indeed, the two are inextricably linked since the improvement of the people is also the development of the place.

For most contemporary home associations, then, development in the form of social welfare remains their primary concern. Repatriation of the bodies of migrants who die 'abroad' and support to the bereaved are paramount (Mazzucato et al., 2006; van der Geest, 2006; Page, 2007). Assistance is also typically provided at other key life stages such as birth, baptism, marriage and illness, or at times of crisis such as bailing members out of prison (Schmitz, 1994). But home associations are also active in other, related ways. They identify, fund and construct public infrastructural projects such as roads, water and electricity supplies; support public institutions such as schools, hospitals, libraries, market places, town halls and post offices; and contribute to the beautification of the homeplace. They invest in the maintenance of 'tradition', such as through donations to palaces, cultural artefacts and cultural festivals. And they serve as a mouthpiece for the homeplace, lobbying government officials for resources and representing their home in local, national or international debates (Barkan et al., 1991; Hickey, 2007b).

Home associations have been considered the archetypal postcolonial development actors because they are self-organized, entrepreneurial and popular. They are also 'organic' in that their insider knowledge about the community at home means their interventions are more likely to be appropriate, sustainable and accountable than are externally driven projects (Honey and Okafor, 1998a; Vertovec, 2004; Chikezie, 2005). As Trager (2001) argues, little development would take place in the home-place without them.

Activities are funded through a combination of membership dues, special levies, collections and fundraising events to which home association members and elite networks contribute. Occasionally grants are obtained from NGOs, donors or government. There is scant information on the actual amounts raised by home associations for discrete projects, but resources can be considerable: Barkan et al. (1991) estimate that the Otan-Ayegbaju Progressive Union in Oyo State, western Nigeria, raised approximately 90 per cent of its cash contributions from its urban branches, and in the late 1980s was able to raise as much as N50,000 a year (US$11,000). This figure increased for specific projects. For example, during the early stages of construction of a 25-bed hospital at home the Union raised N250,000 (US$55,000) annually. There are limits to what can be achieved by home associations: the hospital had to be completed with the assistance of the World Health Organization, Oyo State Ministry of Health, and the teaching hospital of the University of Benin. Nevertheless, home associations can mobilize substantial resources. This is often assumed to be the main strength of the international diaspora although, again, specific figures for projects are few. Exceptions include Attah-Poku's (1996) research on the Asanteman Association of New York, which raised US$7,000 for Kumasi hospital between 1989 and 1992 from around 1,000 members. ACONA contributed US$10,000 to the restoration of Kumasi Museum and sent a delegation to congratulate Otumfuo Opoku Ware II on his silver jubilee (Amoako, 2006). In Europe, Kerlin's (2000) study of the Association of the Naturals of Pelundo Resident in Portugal (ANPRP) provides some detail on fundraising among Guinea-Bissau's diaspora. ANPRP's budget is mostly taken up with the concerns of its 223 members in Portugal but in 1997 it spent US$2,300 on the purchase and shipment of a generator for the village mosque, representing almost one third of its annual income. However, such contributions need to be put in the context of the other heavy, and often more pressing, demands on diasporas' resources. Research that looked at Ghanaians' remittances from the Netherlands, for example, suggested that contributions to community development projects at home are a much lower priority for migrants than investments and expenditures in businesses, housing, education, general subsistence, and funerals there (Mazzucato, 2008).

The few detailed accounts of home association development activities contrast them with projects that are conceived, funded and managed externally. A key difference here is that home associations are motivated by a mixture of civic pride and a sense of obligation to home (Trager, 2001; Mohan, 2006). Home associations are considered to provide participatory and sustainable alternatives for addressing local development problems (Trager, 2001). Honey and Okafor argue that: 'hometown associations constitute important institutional resources that are part of the indigenous knowledge system... [they] bear eloquent testimony to the creativity, adaptability and responsiveness of indigenous knowledge systems' (1998b: 2).

Such accounts recognize that home associations tend to be dominated by male elites (local and diasporic) and can also be exclusionary on grounds of ethnicity, class or generation (Mahler, 1998; Goldring, 1998). But it has also been argued that elite participation is central to home associations' success, since elites are often the ones with the ideas, resources and networks on which successful projects must draw. There are mechanisms for wider community participation such as AGMs and open community meetings where programmes are debated and agreed. 'Women's wings' are often attached to home associations but work independently. It is possible for community members to express disapproval of projects by withholding contributions, which are a kind of 'voluntary taxation' (Trager, 2001), although there is social pressure to be seen to contribute. As Barkan et al. (1991: 462) point out, home associations 'make "public policy" even though they remain private bodies'.

A more common theme in research on home associations has been their role in mediating the relationship between urban and rural spaces (Englund, 2002; Geschiere and Gugler, 1998). Early home associations were commonly formed and led by *évolués*: educated, modern, moneyed young men who, in their new status, challenged the social norms and gerontocracy of the village. Foucher (2002), for example, recounts the essentially modern activities brought by *évolués* to their home villages in the Casamance region of Senegal in the post-war period, such as vacation classes for children, football and social events, which crystallized into home associations, while Schmitz (1994) shows how the *chambres* of young single men from the Senegal River Valley reproduced village political structures in Dakar in the 1960s. They often comprised members of the same age group, regardless of social status, but positions of responsibility were reserved for sons of the local aristocracy. The migrant *caisses* in Dakar maintained social relations between the city and the village through a system of penalties ranging from fines to ostracism of relatives remaining in the village: recalcitrance in town could therefore have implications for those back home. Schmitz (1994) also notes that in the early 1970s their investments in rival mosques and cemetery walls enabled them to bypass accusations from those remaining in the homeplace that they had assimilated with whites and abandoned the village. As migrants became better established in town from the mid-1970s onwards, *caisses* were able to fund a wider range of public goods at home including post offices for receiving remittances, health centres, warehouses for receiving food aid, boreholes for water supply and primary schools.

Home associations have also become entangled in gender politics. Lambert (1999), looking at Casamance (Senegal), records how during the 1940s and 1950s a regional men's association maintained a vigil at Dakar port, checking to see if women arriving on the ferry from Casamance had their parents' permission to migrate. Similarly, among the Banyang of South West Cameroon, Ruel (1969) records attempts to stop female migration to plantations and urban areas on the coast. Female migrants were characterized as 'prostitutes'; one clan union, an early form of home association in the area, had 'the extermination of prostitutes' among its stated aims (Ruel, 1969: 265). Punishments included fines and ostracism when they returned to the village, unless they agreed to marriage, and women were sometimes even forcibly repatriated. In both these cases, women were seen as absconding from their duties in social and economic reproduction – as abandoning their roles as wives, daughters and farmers – and escaping patriarchal control. However, both authors record how attempts to control women had largely foundered by the late 1950s as migration (male and female) became increasingly embedded in the societies in question; in Casamance at least, however, attempts by village associations to regulate female migration continued until at least the mid-1970s (de Jong, 1999; Lambert, 1999).

The stated aims of home associations often include pledges relating to 'development' and 'culture', or to 'develop culture', which refer to their work in maintaining cultural buildings and artefacts, the production of literature in vernacular languages, and support for cultural festivals. These stated aims also refer to efforts to pass on cultural knowledges to children. In the diaspora, home association meetings and events are key sites where children can learn the language, rituals and dances of home (Lentz, 1994). Trager's (2001; 129) work among Ijesa home associations in Nigeria reveals the ways in which the development of tradition is re-imagined as a route to development and modernity. She shows how 'new traditions' such as community days and national days, as well as older traditions such as coronations, are modified by elites in order to provide public gatherings that unite the community through the 'display [of] symbols of unity, success and development of the hometown'. Such gatherings might include fundraising events for specific development projects, but importantly they also serve to draw the diaspora home for purposes of mutual support. Their identity work is indivisible from their developmental work. However, elite appropriations of the home 'culture' can be problematic. Lentz's (2006a, 2006b) research among the Dagara of northwestern Ghana reveals how members of the elite-based Nandom Youth and Development Association, a home association for the Nandom area, draw on Dagara ethnic identity, which serves both as a political platform and as a marker of a more problematic rural 'custom' that the urban elites must change. She argues that '[t]he professionals become cultural brokers who are deeply immersed in the dominant notions of development and progress that they try to instil into their rural tribesmates' (Lentz, 1994: 165).

The political work of home associations has been a further area of sustained scholarly interest. They have been identified as closely allied to the rise of the 'politics of belonging', 'in which the village and the region assume new importance as a crucial source of power at the national level' (Geschiere and Gugler, 1998: 309; also Nkwi, 1997; Nkwi and Socpa, 1997; Eyoh, 1998; Geschiere and Nyamnjoh, 1998; Nyamnjoh and Rowlands, 1998; Nyamnjoh, 1999; Jua, 2005; Kuba and Lentz 2006; Ndjio, 2006). This group of scholars became alarmed at the rise of autochthony discourse – statements about who really belongs where – and its political effects in Africa, which they argued were ushered in as a result of fraught political and economic conditions following the shift to multipartyism. Geschiere and Gugler argue that some countries have witnessed the 'villagization of national politics' (1998: 309), in which ethnicity and autochthony have become the key markers of social difference. In the new political dispensation, the question of autochthony casts home associations as convenors of the interests of ethno-territorial units, manipulated by governments for their own political ends (Woods, 1994; Hagberg, 2004; compare Hickey, 2002). Others have gone further and argued that 'elite' or 'ethnic' associations have emerged as key conduits through which governments attempt to harvest rural votes (Bayart, 1993; Geschiere and Gugler, 1998; Nyamnjoh and Rowlands, 1998). This leaves agency in the hands of the elites. However, home associations are also a response to the same political change at a more local level. Commenting on Nigeria in the 1990s, Trager (2001) suggested that home associations should be understood in the context of political repression and insecurity that compelled people to seek safety in their homeplace.

There is scope to understand better the relationship between home associations and the politics of belonging. Less attention has been paid to home associations tied to the village than to the larger ethnic associations and elite associations that represent regional interests (Nkwi, 1997; Nkwi, 2006). There is also potential to ask what the politics of belonging means in the international diaspora. In North America, for example, it is often considered that Africans have 'stronger' ties to home compared with other immigrants, which militate against assimilation (e.g. Arthur, 2006). Equally, journalists have sometimes claimed that Africans remain insulated from mainstream European society. The British *Economist* magazine, for example, has asserted that 'strong ties of origin reinforce black Africans' insularity' (2004: 25). In this context, the politics of what it means to belong are part of the discussion of the politics of integration.

An attachment to place is frequently invoked as significant to home associations (Barkan et al., 1991; Trager, 1998; Gugler, 2002), yet rarely is this attachment examined in any detail. Place is thus sometimes unwittingly treated in primordial terms (Agbese, 1998; Honey and Okafor, 1998a). Others see it as dynamic and socially constructed (Lentz, 1994; Trager, 2001; van den Bersselaar, 2005; Kuba and Lentz 2006; Mohan, 2006) but not sufficiently interesting to warrant greater attention. Place is most commonly inferred in relation to discussions of territory. While some authors have stressed the deterritorializing effect of multi-sited home associations, others have pointed to their reterritorializing work such as the settling of disputes at home and lobbying for administrative boundary changes (Trager, 1998, 2001; Lentz, 2006b). There is, then, scope for a sustained analysis that considers not only these apparently contradictory effects of contemporary home associations together, but that also takes their internationalization into account.

Conclusions

The preoccupation of the migration–development nexus with the economic and social impacts of migrant groups, and particularly with remittances, has so far rendered it unable to respond imaginatively to those diasporas that push the boundaries of development. Yet diasporas provide scope for thinking about development in new ways. Reciprocally, the development work that diasporas do challenges theorizations of diaspora to get to grips with the very material ways in which diaspora groups, such as home associations, co-produce place and identity. In the determination to assert the transnational cosmopolitan qualities of diasporas, the place of origin has understandably been downplayed. However, empirical realities require a conceptual re-engagement with the homeplace. This notion of homeplace captures the spatial expression of memory, emotion and obligation, and provides a conceptual vehicle that enables the articulation of space, political belonging and moral conviviality.

The migration–development nexus has also been unable to overcome the temporal and spatial separation of Africa from discussions of the contemporary transnational African diaspora. This has impoverished understandings of diaspora formations such as home associations, which need to be understood in the context of their historical development in Africa if we are to gain insights into what they do well, and why. The study of African diaspora associations needs to pay attention to the histories of associations inside and outside Africa. We now, in Part Two, turn to an examination of the histories of home associations in Cameroon and Tanzania.

Note

1.   The Soninke are a Mande sub-group in the area straddling the shared borders of present-day Senegal, Mauritania and Mali (Manchuelle, 1997).

PART TWO
The history and structure of home associations

4 HOME ASSOCIATIONS AND THE NATION IN CAMEROON

The next two chapters develop the claim that the form and function of contemporary home associations are shaped by the history and geography of particular places. The focus is on understanding how different associations are organized and why. These structures reflect, first, a mixing of the particular templates on which home associations were modelled and, second, an African response to the national political-economic context in which they operate. So, in both Cameroon and Tanzania, these associations were initially created by Africans (often urban and often migrants) in the interstices of the colonial state, drawing on a range of experiences and ideas. Different social relations, environments, personalities and historical narratives in the four case studies have produced an associational landscape that is dramatically uneven.

The form and functions of home associations drew on a range of models, which their leaders would mimic and mutate. These templates include both the cultural repertoire of 'traditional' associations (particularly the dance groups known as *ngoma* and membership societies such as Ekpe and Voma) and the 'modern' associations (clubs, unions, cooperatives, professional groups) active in the cities, mines and plantations. Both have a dynamic quality: they are not fixed or timeless but evolve. Indeed in recent years associations have started to mimic NGOs and the language of participatory development. The result is that current structures reflect both the particularities of each homeplace (for example the home associations in Bali are more unitary than those in Manyu because social organization in Bali is more hierarchical and because Manyu is much larger and more diverse) and the particularities of where people meet in the diaspora (for example those in plantation or mine areas place more emphasis on welfare because their members are often less financially secure than those in capital cities, some of whom are more concerned with lobbying and politics). Local histories have a significant impact on the shaping of the structure of associational life in African states.

The differences between places within Cameroon or Tanzania are, to some extent, reduced by the imposition of national policies and legal frameworks. This is why the following two chapters separate the two case study countries. The insertion of the nation-state into the African social landscape is one of the most profound changes of the colonial and post-colonial periods, and associations therefore have national characteristics. Home associations in both territories were tolerated by the colonial state, even tacitly encouraged, because they were 'tribal' and served useful welfare and disciplinary functions. In the postcolonial era, however, national attitudes to ethnicity and freedom of association were very different in the two countries. In Cameroon an explicit policy of regional balance has fuelled a process of ethnic competition in which home associations are active, if sometimes unwitting, participants. The tacit endorsement of subnational identities in the era of multi-party politics persists even as nationalist rhetoric denies it.

This chapter introduces the home associations in Bali and Manyu on which this research was based, before putting their histories into the context of Cameroon. Although Bali and Manyu would often be separated in analyses of Cameroon because one is a centralized, hier-archical society in the North West and the other is a decentralized, segmentary society in the South West, the comparative approach used here reveals some striking similarities between the templates for the contemporary home associations. In particular, in both places home associations draw on a long history of ranked membership associations and use those associations as templates for their own organization. The Manyu secret society Ekpe and the Bali Nyong'a secret society Voma, for example, have much in common. Both are male membership associations with a series of ranks where initiation is made by payment, discipline is maintained through fines, and esoteric knowledge of paraphernalia, terminology and secret signs are used to articulate the hierarchy. Both are closely associated with performance (dance, masquerade and music) with a semi-secret quality through which their authority over non-initiates is demonstrated. Both secret societies exercise the important function of protecting members' rights (for example over property) and provide a venue for socializing. Both have thrived in recent years as competition for titles and authority at home has increased (Fisiy and Goheen, 1998). The claim that Ekpe and Voma are similar (at a superficial level) would be anathema both to those anthropologists whose careful exegesis of such associations is concerned to draw out their distinctive nuances and also to their Cameroonian members for whom such associations are an outward sign of the fundamental differences between communities. Yet it seems reasonable to claim that the long history of ranked membership societies in these separate places provides a shared model on which to base home associations with branches, rules, obligations and multiple functions.

The structure of home associations in Bali and Manyu

BANDECA

The Bali Nyong'a Development and Cultural Association (BANDECA) is a constitutionally established cultural and development association. It comprises both people living in the Bali Nyong'a fondom and people with an affinity to Bali Nyong'a living elsewhere in Cameroon (the 'domestic diaspora'). Its explicit aim is to 'leverage cultural identity' (BANDECA, 2007) in order to foster development at home. Though it does not explicitly set out to provide welfare services for members living away from home, it does seek to 'develop unity' and 'cater for the socio-cultural and economic interests of its members and to promote their development'. A Bali women's association called Nk'umu Fed Fed parallels BANDECA, working with the main organization but retaining its autonomy and carrying out its own projects. In addition there are at least three international Bali Nyong'a associations: the Bali Cultural and Development Association UK (BCDA-UK), the Bali Cultural Association USA (http://www.bca-usa.org/), and Friends of Bali (Germany). None of these is formally part of BANDECA; they are separate organizations that sometimes work with BANDECA. So this is not a transnational association but a group of associations that have some shared goals.

BANDECA's constitution outlines a hierarchical and integrated national structure. The National Executive Committee (NEC) of twelve elected officers, led by the President-General, forms the core of the leadership. The NEC is drawn from the National Council, which is a larger body including elected representatives from each geographical area where the organization has members. Officially the National Council is the key decision-making body though it rarely contradicts the NEC. Specific committees with particular interests (culture, development, water supply) draw their members from the National Council. BANDECA is run by successful individual 'sons and daughters of Bali'. They include some powerful national figures as well as individuals with a wide range of professional and commercial experience and contacts. The President-General from 1999 to 2007 was a Minister-Plenipotentiary who presided over Cameroon's convention centre, the *Palais de Congrès* in Yaoundé. Within the regions there are divisional councils that bring together the basic meeting groups or branches, known as *nda kums*. Some divisional councils are much more active than others. The *nda kums* predate the formation of BANDECA, which has appropriated these groups to form its mass membership. Other related associations such as Nk'umu Fed Fed are treated as auxiliary members of BANDECA. All members are entitled to vote in the anuual general meeting, which is usually held in Bali Town around Easter. BANDECA was launched in Cameroon in 1999, but there is a long history of similar associations in Bali Nyong'a dating back to 1941; these associations have expanded and contracted under a series of names and constitutions.

The Fon of Bali is the patron of BANDECA; the association works closely with the Palace institutions and is always careful to observe the correct protocol and deference. Yet it is also distinct from the Palace, a position supported by many association members who suggested that the Palace lacked financial accountability. This suspicion must not be overstated though. For almost all Bali Nyong'a migrants the Palace remains an important symbol and a key element of 'home'. Furthermore the Fon of Bali, a well-known figure in Yaoundé, can be an asset for the home association when lobbying for funds from government. BANDECA also relies on the Fon's authority to deliver community work and to endorse changes in 'cultural practices'. The Fon is kept closely informed of plans and it is unimaginable that he would not be involved in BANDECA activities. The BANDECA leadership have had to steer a careful path that avoids personal and political enmities between its members and the Palace.

The claim is sometimes made that everyone from Bali Nyong'a is a member of BANDECA, but the reality is not so straightforward. Membership is closely related to a Bali Nyong'a institution called *nda kums*, which were originally village or quarter-level meeting groups within Bali. When Bali Nyong'a migrants went to the coast during the colonial period they organized themselves into new *nda kums* on the plantations in order to socialize and support each other.[1] There are now 53 Bali Nyong'a *nda kums* in Cameroon. In some larger towns there are multiple *nda kums*, some with very different social characteristics and financial obligations. Membership is voluntary and people generally choose to join the group with which they have most in common socially. BANDECA used the network of *nda kums* to create a membership, organizing all the *nda kums* in the same city into 'divisional councils' of BANDECA, each with their own presidents who are often also the Fon's appointed 'head' of the Bali Nyong'a diaspora in the given city or town. There is also a divisional council in Bali, which refers to itself as the 'home' branch of BANDECA. Not only are *nda kums* expected to register as group members (for a fee of 10,000 CFA francs),[2] but they also collect an 'annual development levy' (1,000 CFA francs for men and 500 CFA francs for women) from individual members, which goes to BANDECA. So while BANDECA claims that its membership includes all those who are active in *nda kums* across Cameroon, it cannot be assumed that these individuals have actively opted in to BANDECA; it is more likely that they have joined their *nda kum*. Second, though BANDECA claims to be an 'umbrella organization' for all Bali Nyong'a associations, not all groups are that enthusiastic about being brought under its cover. The most obvious example here is the women's group (Nk'umu Fed Fed) which, though it cooperates with BANDECA, is also keen to preserve its independence. Third, many in the domestic diaspora choose not to join either a *nda kum* or BANDECA. Sometimes this is because membership carries financial obligations that they would rather avoid, sometimes because they disapprove of these 'traditional' structures, and sometimes because they use their spare time in other groups (such as church groups). As one young Bali Nyong'a woman in Douala put it:

> I do care about development in the village; if there is a project and I can see what they are doing then I contribute ... I just don't have time or the inclination for the *nda kums*. Sacrifice and jujus, I don't have time for them. Other people go because they are worried about a family member dying, but if one hundred people come to a death celebration, only twenty of them really care, the others just want to eat and drink.[3]

So, though the BANDECA leadership aspires to include everyone who is a part of Bali Nyong'a in the association, in reality mobilizing the membership remains a challenge.

Home associations in Cameroon are often described as 'elite' associations in the literature (Nkwi, 1997; Nyamnjoh and Rowlands, 1998) but there is no consistent definition of who counts as an elite. Rather a combination of family history, professional achievements, economic assets and social engagement produces a highly subjective and contextual label. Not all elites are migrants and not all migrants are elites. Many elites will have a home in Bali Nyong'a but may only stay there occasionally. Not all elites are wealthy, especially those resident in Bali Nyong'a and treated as elite because of their position within the Palace or because of professional achievements. Many who are highly respected may be retired civil servants on relatively low incomes. On the part of many Bali Nyong'a residents who are unambiguously not elite there is a perception that BANDECA is an association for migrants and elites. They are not hostile to BANDECA's activities or ungrateful for its efforts, but they do not perceive it to be their concern.

In the UK there is just one Bali home association, the BCDA-UK. It is the oldest of all the international associations included in this research, having been established in London in 1966, and some current members have been participating since the 1970s. It meets bi-monthly and people travel from across the UK to attend meetings, which are usually held in London. Most members come from London and the Southeast, but members also travel to meetings from Birmingham, Wolverhampton, Newcastle-under-Lyme and the Isle of Man. At the time of research there were 38 registered members, mostly first-generation migrants who arrived in Britain in the 1980s, although some members were born in Britain and some have arrived in more recent years. Nevertheless, all members are socially and economically established in Britain. Members pay an annual membership fee (£100), which is used first for the Trouble Bank (from which group contributions to members in times of death and sickness are made) and second to cover the cost of refreshments at meetings. Additional contributions are sought at times of birth, marriage and death, and for particular projects in the diaspora or at home. The American association, BCA-USA, is much larger and maintains more direct links with BANDECA.

MECA

The Manyu Elements Cultural Association (MECA) is the home association on which this study focused in Manyu but is only one of a wide range of home associations operating in the division. MECA is the home association for the whole of Manyu Division – a vast area comprising one main town (Mamfe) and many small towns and villages. There is no MECA branch within Manyu itself; the association exists only among the Manyu diaspora. MECA has a devolved structure: it is not a single coordinated association with a single constitution and a single set of aims. Rather, it is a series of independent home associations, each of which takes the name MECA (for example MECA-Douala, MECA-Yaoundé, MECA-UK, MECA-USA) but registers separately, draws up its own constitution (though using a similar format and wording within Cameroon) and conducts its own affairs. In other words different MECAs are autonomous. This means it is easy for groups that meet in the US and

Europe to take the MECA name without being committed to the projects and politics of the association in Cameroon. Attempts to turn MECA into a single federation of these various groups have so far been unsuccessful, although MECA-Yaoundé maintains a degree of primacy among MECAs in Cameroon. Its official spoken language is Pidgin or English.

There have been home associations referring to Mamfe since the early 1940s, but MECA itself evolved out of the Manyu Investment Group in Yaoundé in around 1963. By 1980 there were around 600 people in MECA-Yaoundé. There has always been a minister from Manyu in government and he (to date the minister has always been a man) has automatically been the patron of MECA-Yaoundé. A large hall has now been constructed by MECA-Yaoundé in the suburb of Essos for Manyu functions. Manyu diasporas in other cities and countries emulate the Yaoundé model. A MECA can be established where there are at least 50 members. There are four subdivisions in Manyu and the presidency of MECA-Yaoundé rotates between them, with the three vice-presidents representing the other subdivisions. The president, vice-presidents, treasurer and financial secretary are elected while other posts are appointments from the four subdivisions. An unelected 'council of elders', made up of 'very big people' in Yaoundé and back home, was established in the early 1980s to act as advisors.

Today MECAs also exist in Douala and most urban centres in Anglophone Cameroon including Bamenda, Buea, Kumba and Limbe but, unlike BANDECA, as already mentioned there is no MECA in the homeplace itself. MECAs are also found in Nigeria, the US and some European countries (the UK, the Netherlands, Germany and Switzerland). In the UK, MECA groups have formed locally where there are enough members; so, for example, there are two MECA-UK groups in London, a MECA-Leicester and a MECA-Birmingham. There are at least 13 'chapters' of MECA-USA organized along state lines (Georgia, New York, Texas, Florida and California are prominent). The 2004 MECA-USA convention in Atlanta had around 2,500 participants. There is also a significant splinter group in the USA called the National Organization for Manyu Advancement (NOMA), which left MECA after a dispute. As noted above, each MECA remains largely autonomous in its activities, usually supporting home development projects on a bilateral basis, although MECA-Yaoundé sometimes acts as a liaison point for overseas MECAs funding projects in Manyu.

Membership of each MECA is 'open to all Manyu citizens' (MECA-Yaoundé 1996: 2) resident in the city concerned. Membership is not direct as individuals but through 'family groups', organized usually around affinity to a particular village or sometimes clan within Manyu. Family groups pay dues to MECA as a group, the amount depending on the size of the group. So for example there are 24 family groups in Yaoundé, which form the basis of MECA-Yaoundé, and 41 in MECA-Douala. The average family group is around 40 members, suggesting that there are around 960 financial members in total in MECA-Yaoundé. If a husband and a wife are from different villages they will probably be members of the husband's village's family group, though his wife may choose also to attend her own family group (though she is unlikely to pay dues there). Women often take prominent roles in family group meetings as treasurers and secretaries and take an active part in deliberations. The MECA-Yaoundé executive committee estimates that 30–35 per cent of Manyu people in the city are members, of whom more than 70 per cent are civil servants, with the rest working in the private sector. Some professions, such as the armed forces, tend not to join because they have their own support structures. Other Manyu groups loosely affiliated to MECA include the Manyu All Students Union and, in Yaoundé, the Manyu Solidarity Foundation, which rewards successful Manyu students in an annual ceremony. MECA also engages with Efokhoyu, a network of many women's groups in Manyu (the name means 'umbrella' in Kenyang).[4]

In common with most home associations elsewhere, mutual support was the initial motive for the Manyu diaspora in forming such groups, but MECA's current aims (Box 4.1) also include cultural preservation and development at home. Although it is an association for the whole Manyu Division, MECA's development projects (such as support for the hospital) have concentrated on the divisional headquarters, Mamfe town. To some extent this is a conscious policy: to strengthen services centrally where anyone in the division can in theory use them, and to sidestep the risk of MECA leaders favouring their home villages.[5] Still, most groups are more concerned with welfare in the diaspora than with development at home, although not all MECA members would recognize such a stark distinction between the two (Chapter 6).

In principle MECA is apolitical but the practice is different. During national elections the president of MECA-Yaoundé may make a declaration that all Manyu people are going home to support the ruling party, the CPDM, and he may well go to Manyu to campaign with the government minister who is the MECA patron. However, many civil servants would be expected to go home on campaigns anyway and would be given money for that purpose, so it is hard to distinguish individual support for the government from MECA support for the government

---

Box 4.1 The aims of MECA-Yaoundé (1996 Constitution)

1. To revive, develop and maintain the culture of the Manyu people, thereby creating a sense of attachment to, and awareness of the cultural legacies of the Manyu people among the members of MECA – Yaoundé.
2. To participate in cultural and development projects initiated in Manyu division.
3. To foster the spirit of loyalty, cooperation, unity, collective responsibility and patriotism among Manyu elements of all walks of life in Yaoundé.
4. To interact with Manyu student associations or organizations.
5. To collaborate with other Manyu and non-Manyu cultural and development associations having similar objectives and interests, within and outside Yaoundé.

---

during election time. Despite a backlash against such partisanship from some MECA members, the president of MECA-Yaoundé always works closely with the Manyu minister and all MECAs raise money for the minister's 'homecoming' celebration after he is first appointed. Indeed the sums raised for the homecoming easily exceed those raised by MECA for development projects. However, much of the discourse of Manyu elites was that it was necessary to work with and show support for the current Manyu minister as a means of getting him to bring development goods to the division through the government. The homecoming is a particularly important part of this charade: it is a form of flattery that the minister may take into account in lobbying for future development support, and shows the government that the minister is popular at home and can thus help carry the constituency for the ruling party.

It is impossible to describe home associations in Manyu without also discussing village-scale development associations. These are home associations that refer not to the whole division (as MECA does) but to specific places within it. There are at least 24 village development associations in Mamfe Central Subdivision alone, commonly run by the village chief and traditional council at home in conjunction with senior elites in the domestic diaspora. Villages copy each other in this respect: it has become 'fashionable' to have a village development association.[6] In many ways these village associations are closer to the standard model of a home association than is MECA because the scale is more meaningful as a 'home' than Manyu, which is large and essentially a colonial creation. The village associations tend to have a more unitary structure with a single constitution and a series of 'branches' in different centres of population, which meet as 'family groups'. Because the villages are mostly small, however, it is not easy to form branches outside the largest cities because of the lack of potential members. Village development associations find it particularly hard to gather enough people to meet overseas, and village diasporas will often federate in order to get a working number of members. Still, there is a US branch of the Ewelle Social and Development Association based in Atlanta, and village-scale meeting groups have also been identified in the UK.[7] The individuals who pay membership dues to join a branch in the city are clearly association members, but there is more ambiguity about whether those in the village itself are members – sometimes they are treated as *de facto* members despite not paying levies. Though the homeplace is smaller and more homogenous than Manyu as a whole, these village associations can still be fractious, with large villages having competing associations whose disputes often reflect battles over chieftaincy titles.[8]

Common village-scale development projects include construction of town halls, classrooms, health centres and farm access roads, and the rehabilitation of pipeborne water systems. Their projects pivot around the village's 'cultural week', which is often timed to coincide with the Easter holidays.[9] Domestic diaspora elites use the long weekend to come home and discuss potential projects with the traditional council and village community. Once priorities are determined, cash contributions are agreed for members, levied either as a flat rate or on a sliding scale according to income. Elites may also use their positions or connections to lobby central government for support or seek donations (cash or in kind) from external sources, usually Western embassies in Yaoundé. Villagers pay a considerably smaller cash levy, sometimes nothing, but provide labour for construction. The effectiveness of the village development associations thus relates closely to the size and dynamism of the village diaspora. A single strong elite is sometimes the key to success: for example the Deputy Rector at the University of Yaoundé I is frequently lauded for his efforts in developing his Akwaya village, Bache. Such individuals are important in mobilizing action and acting as brokers with the state (Hagberg, 2004).

Pressure is therefore put on urban elites to return with their 'wealth' – money, skills and connections with the wider world – and share this with those at home in accordance with socially rooted notions of obligation (Nyamnjoh and Rowlands, 1998; Hickey, 2004; Mohan, 2006). Elites failing to do this may be admonished or sanctioned for selfishness. Within Manyu, this is usually effected through the village's neotraditional structures, including the Ekpe secret society. One member of the diaspora likened his village development association membership booklet to a 'passport' for entering his homeplace: it recorded his payment of death dues in Yaoundé and levies for various development projects. Non-payment would expose the defaulter to sanctions, usually fines, from the traditional council if he wanted to take a body home or receive one there.[10] But such situations seem relatively rare: Manyu elites were generally loyal to their village association and sometimes passionate about its development efforts. Only in very exceptional cases will association leaders ask government authorities to compel community members in the village to participate.

The broader vision and knowledge brought by elites are generally welcomed at home and any disagreements over priorities, it was claimed, were resolved through constructive dialogue, usually in the public meetings of cultural week. However, diaspora elites do not always use their considerable influence in village development appropriately. One Western donor representative complained that such individuals may impose projects on their village with little engagement with their pur-ported constituency.[11] Such projects may be inappropriate or unrealistic, driven more by a desire to make an impression than by real need. One urban elite criticized the evident 'town hall inflation' in Manyu, with every village wanting to show that it has 'big sons' through an 'egocentric project'.[12] Such problems may also arise between domestic and overseas elites: the same man complained that his association's 'US branch sent us bogus plans for the town hall that we can never realize. They are dreamers ...'

Another problem is that, because of their small size, village associa-tions lack resources and have erratic funding streams; this sometimes leads to divisions over priorities. Half-built, sometimes overgrown town halls and churches are a familiar sight in Manyu villages and sometimes divert resources from other projects.[13] One UK-based Manyu elite criticized the size and cost of a new village church, arguing that water supply was a more pressing need.[14] Financial constraints also mean that efforts to create productive enterprises rather than public goods are rare, and village youths were often critical of association projects, which they saw as no substitute for the creation of much-needed jobs.[15]

The structures and characters of the home associations in Manyu and Bali – MECA and BANDECA – are therefore very different. Whereas the former is decentralized, with separately constituted multiple autonomous organizations operating under the name of MECA both nationally and internationally, the latter is more of a national unitary organization with a single constitution operating across different branches. The international Bali diaspora operates through separate organizations that do not even take the name of BANDECA and sometimes choose to intervene in development through different institutions (such as local government). Whilst BANDECA has an active home branch, with members from Bali itself on the national executive, MECA has no home branch. Unlike BANDECA, MECA has to compete with the numerous smaller-scale village-scale home associations. Within Manyu these associations provide most of the diffuse rural development projects across the division, while MECA focuses most of its projects on Mamfe, the main town in the division. Finally whereas BANDECA draws its patron from the Palace (the Fon), MECA relies on the government (the Manyu minister) for its symbolic authority.

At the same time these two groups also share some structural similarities. First, they draw membership from pre-existing networks of groups in the cities of Cameroon. Second, they both rely on 'tradition' or 'culture' (the Palace in Bali, Ekpe in Manyu) as the basis of their unity. Both are also defined in part by ideas of 'elite obligation'. Most crucially, however, both organizations are Janus-faced, looking not only back towards the home but also out towards the Government of Cameroon. This relationship is addressed in the following section on the history of associational life in Cameroon.

The case study associations within the history of home associations in Cameroon

From 1916 to 1961 the part of Cameroon where this research was conducted was governed first as a League of Nations mandated territory and then, after 1945, as a United Nations mandated territory (Delancey and Mokeba, 1988). In effect, however, it was treated as an extension of the British colony of Nigeria. The colonial administration in Cameroon appears to have had little interest in the way Africans associated in the 1920s. However, the reverse was not true, and throughout the colonial period there is evidence of associations seeking legal endorsement from the colonial state. The following is a typical request for legal recognition made to the District Officer (DO) in Victoria (present-day Limbe) in 1929 by the Le Likumba Society and signed 'P. de Kombe'. We know nothing more about this group but can infer that it is connected to the Likumba Plantation (one of the coastal plantations dating from the

German colonial period) and (on the basis of the name) that the author of the letter was Bakweri (the ethnic group in that area):

> Sir, we have the honour most respectfully to put the following complaint before you, which we hope will meet you in good consideration. (1) For your information, we beg to state you that we made a certain club in our town, which we hope ourselves to be love each anothers. It is not made by following the Government's laws. (2) In our rulebook, there are some laws fixed by us, we beg the DO to look after them, if any against the Government, select it and may be scratched. (3) We beg the DO not to refuse this our present of 5/- [5 shillings] send to him, is a thing all the members in the society present to him to look that, all agreed in one opinion to make this club.[16]

The attached club rulebook clearly baffled the DO whose note on the letter described the club's laws as 'weird', but the association was neither proscribed nor registered. The DO simply returned the five shillings and insisted that the club did not have the legal right to extract monetary fines from members, and that its only legal sanction against defaulters was expulsion. Soon afterwards (in November 1935) a group of taxpayers from Manyu (then called Mamfe Division) met in one of the plantations on the coast at Tiko and formed a similar association called the Nkenkwa Hope Rising Club.[17] However, associational life on the plantations seems to have placed more emphasis on immediate material concerns, particularly the education and upkeep of children, through credit unions and *njangi* (rotating savings and credit associations [Ardener and Burman, 1996]) than on home.

By the end of the 1930s the colonial state started to take a more active interest in African associations. This shift was driven by the politicization of associations in Lagos, as a result of which in July 1936 a general circular from the Criminal Investigations Department required District Officers to undertake a survey of African associations across Nigeria. This survey revealed an unnumbered (and by implication a large) quantity of contributions clubs and funeral savings clubs (referred to at this time as *isusu*) in the coastal plantations.[18]

Probably the first recorded home association in the archives in Cameroon is the Ibo Tribal Union. The Victoria branch of the Union was founded in 1935 with the declared aim of 'the advancement of goodwill and mutual understanding between its members', who by 1941 numbered over 100.[19] The Ibos were migrants (or 'strangers', to use the term in the archives) who had come from Nigeria to the mandated territory of Cameroon either to trade or work in the plantations. The letter lists the Union's work in bearing the funeral costs of members, feeding those who fell sick and repatriating stranded Ibos. Within a couple of years the Union had also started lobbying on more contentious issues, requesting a seat on the Victoria Federated Native Authority and a role as the official body collecting tax among Ibos in Victoria District.[20] The DO refused both requests. The record also shows that the Union brought together smaller Ibo family groups that met on the different plantations and sent delegates to the main Union, which was in the process of constructing a meeting hall in Victoria.[21] By 1953 there were eleven separate branches of the Union in the coastal areas of Cameroon.[22]

Individual colonial officials were initially broadly sympathetic to these migrants' associations. For example, in 1939 the DO commented on an Ibo association that 'the objects of the society are entirely praiseworthy and I approve of its formation and operation'.[23] A decade later the DO in Buea wrote that the Ibo Union 'has behaved with commendable moderation and good sense during a trying period, and its influence has been salutary and widespread'.[24] Local African officials were also grateful for the Union's role in maintaining discipline among Ibos in Victoria.[25] But within a few years these associations were causing the administration some anxiety precisely because they enabled particular groups to achieve a degree of unity and autonomy. As a later DO in Victoria wrote to the Ibo Union, 'I ask you to remember that you are strangers in the Cameroons; that you have been permitted to live, trade and farm here by the local inhabitants, and that it is your duty therefore to conform to local customary laws, and not to set yourselves up as independent people.'[26]

Soon after the founding of the Ibo Tribal Union, Cameroonian migrants adopted the same model. The Bakweri Improvement Union was established in 1939 (Ebune, 2004) and by the early 1950s at least 15 other similar Cameroonian home associations were known to officials, usually referred to as 'tribal unions'.[27] These often had significant 'international' memberships:[28] several give a head office address in Lagos and list branches in the coastal plantations of Cameroon, most often Tiko or Victoria. Indeed, these associations began away from home: 'Almost all the tribal unions now existing in Nigeria were found, not in the very towns of the tribes represented, but outside their own villages, and sometimes their own tribal territories' (Offidele, 1947). Whilst they depended on keeping the connection with those villages the impetus for organization was among migrants.

The earliest home association in Bali dates from this period and is characteristic of it. The Bali Improvement Union initially had an educational focus. It launched a scholarship scheme, funding a number of students to go from Bali Nyong'a to the US and Europe for higher education. Some sources suggest that the Union was founded in 1943 inside Bali Nyong'a by Fon Galega II (Ndangam, 1988: 43–66), others that it was formed outside by Bali Nyong'a migrants, especially those in the police force.[29] One template for the Union likely came from similar associations established by Nigerians working in the Cameroonian plantations. The Bali Improvement Union subsequently evolved into the Bali Youth and Elders Association,[30] which faltered in the 1950s because of problems over financial accountability.[31]

The forties saw the establishment of the Mamfe Improvement Union (a precursor of MECA), in 1943. From its 'headquarters' in Lagos it sent money home to Mamfe to sponsor a candidate to stand for election in the Eastern Houses of Assembly. However, no candidate was put forward and those in the diaspora unsuccessfully sought the help of the administration to retrieve the money from those at home.[32] By 1947 the police were observing the Union, which they believed to be involved in organized smuggling.[33] After 1947 a group of other tribal unions connected to Mamfe (Manyu) emerged: the Ejagham Union (1947),[34] the Banyang Improvement Union (1950), the Union of Mamfe Natives (1950),[35] the Bangwa Improvement Union (1950), the Ossing Development Union (1951) and the Mamfe Overside Improvement Union (1953).[36] These groups are more akin to today's village-scale home associations. There was already a structural tension in the area between the district-wide association and the more local associations (Ruel, 1964).

In 1947 Lord Hailey's visit to Nigeria prompted another covert survey of associations and political organizations in Cameroon during which the tribal unions were described as 'self-help societies, and if engaged in political activities at all, it is only in connection with their own home-towns'.[37] This survey also identified nascent nationalist political groups, often emerging under the guise of 'welfare' and 'cultural' associations – the Cameroon Welfare Union (1942) is particularly significant (Ebune, 1992, 2004). Their history, along with those of other political parties, is relatively well known and covered in most textbooks on Cameroonian history (LeVine, 1964, 1971; Mbuagbaw et al., 1987; Fanso, 1989, 1999; Ngoh, 2001).

The question of registration continued to vex African members of the tribal unions. In the 1940s they attempted to register under the Trades Union Ordinance and the Land Ordinance (1933) and to support their requests some associations claimed to have legally registered in French Cameroun[38] or to have a Certificate of Incorporation issued by the Nigerian Government.[39] A policy was established maintaining that since the unions were private clubs they were not government's concern: 'A

Resident or any Govt. officer is not required to approve a private union's rules and aims or to provide a "legal guide", which is a way to trap Government's support of the Union.[40] The British colonial government in Cameroon in the 1940s was always a minimalist administration operating with a skeleton staff, so this attitude to registration was driven as much by practicality as principle.[41]

From the early 1950s the migrants' associations start to drop the terms 'tribal' and 'improvement' from their names and to include the term 'welfare' or 'development'.[42] It was around this time that Cameroonian associations started to collect money among their members in the coastal plantations to fund the construction of town halls, roads and maternity units in their home areas.[43] In 1951 for example the Mamfe Youths Association (Victoria) applied to raise money throughout the plantations from 'all Mamfe Indigenes and patriotic sons from Mamfe Division and other interested personalities all over the country'[44] for a new independent town hall at home in Mamfe. Such collections were propelled by the introduction of rural self-help schemes supported by Colonial Development and Welfare funds and ideas. Colonial officials expressed some anxiety about whether these collections were entirely voluntary but still expressed sympathy for their developmental aims.[45] The associations also became active in lobbying government and sending petitions to colonial officials requesting government services in their home areas.[46]

In the 1950s the tribal unions also took a more ambiguous political role. As a British official put it in 1958, they were 'semi-social and semi-political'.[47] On the one hand they often vigorously and explicitly claimed that their agenda was non-political, a response to the relatively tight policing of modern associations in Nigeria that were perceived to espouse nationalist ambitions. Insofar as these Unions were fundamentally about recreation and mutual support among members they could reasonably claim to be apolitical. On the other hand, however, because they brought people together to discuss their home areas they inevitably began to articulate political complaints about both the non-delivery of services and the non-representation of Africans in decision-making processes.[48]

By 1951 the overarching Mamfe Improvement Union was described as having 'been moribund for many years'[49] within the division, though it still operated from Lagos and took an interest in affairs at home and appeared to be trying to organize its revival.[50] In 1952 it was active in lobbying the administration for better services in Mamfe town (in particular water supply, town planning and hospital services).[51] The Union argued that community development (the self-help participatory strategy being used elsewhere in Cameroon) was not 'workable' in urban

Mamfe because it was a 'cosmopolitan town'.[52] Trying to achieve unity in Manyu's development was clearly already problematic by this time. During the visit of the mission of the Trusteeship Council of the United Nations Organization to Cameroon in 1952, the Mamfe Improvement Union was able to achieve a degree of influence and present itself as the representative body for Africans within the division. In a memorandum to the visiting delegate it defined its organization and its aims:

> The Mamfe Improvement Union is an organization of the entire Mamfe District comprising indigenes from all parts of the division. The Union aims at saving the present and succeeding generations from the scourge of disunity and its effects. It is out to foster the spirit of tolerance, cooperation and mutual understanding among the respective ethnic groups in order to ensure future mutual understanding and inter-tribal harmony. It seeks to fight in conjunction with other political, social and economic organizations in order to guarantee political emancipation, social welfare and economic security for the Mamfe Division in particular and the Cameroons in general.[53]

When the Union representatives met the UN delegates they took the opportunity to articulate their opposition to any future incorporation of Mamfe in an independent Nigeria. Over the following decade this anti-Nigerian sentiment appears to have governed the agenda of the Mamfe Improvement Union.

From independence in 1961 to unification in 1972, Cameroon had a federal constitution and there were two state governments: Anglophone West Cameroon and Francophone East Cameroon (Kofele-Kale, 1980; Njeuma, 1995; Chiabi, 1997; Awasom, 1998, 2000). For the first five years of independence modern associational life in West Cameroon was marked by continuity. Like the former colonial administration, the new government saw some value in home associations as a means of policing specific communities.[54] Furthermore 'community development', in which local contributions of money and labour were combined with technical support from government and international NGOs, remained the key mechanism for rural development, so home associations could also be enrolled there.

However, in 1967 the legal framework changed dramatically. Federal Law No 67-LF-19 required all associations to be formally declared to the local Senior Divisional Officer (SDO).[55] Association leaders had to complete a form, stating their association's name and purpose and the names of the office-holders. In line with the nation-building project of the time, it was declared that 'associations of exclusively tribal or clan character... or whose purpose is to undermine the integrity of the Federal State or the form of Government shall be null and void'.[56] Covert surveillance of associations was required to police this law. The violent internal conflict with the Union des Populations du Cameroun (UPC) rebels was still a significant feature of political life in Cameroon in 1967, and such authoritarian practices were easy to justify in the name of public security (Hickey, 2004).

In Bamenda the 1967 law had been pre-empted by the Prefectural Order No 1 of 17 May 1966, which required associations to register and give the location and date of their meetings.[57] Between October 1966 and December 1968, 179 different associations filed registration documents in Bamenda. The majority of applications are for *njangi* and many are for individual death celebrations. Place-based names are given for 85 of the associations, many of them home associations formed by indigenes of a particular place who were living in the Bamenda area. After 1968, permits for Cameroonian groups began to be refused on the grounds that they were tribal, whilst officials pandered to anti-Ibo sentiment by banning their association entirely (Kleis, 1980).[58] In another round of name changes, associations now described themselves as 'family unions' or 'progressive unions' to signal a move away from tribal identities.

Individuals in the administration were caught between sympathy for the mutual aid aspects of home associations and suspicion about their political motives. In September 1969, for example, the Divisional Officer (DO) in Victoria called 22 groups to a meeting which was also under Special Branch surveillance. The DO said that the associations were good 'because contributions are made there for self help in time of need' but that they were illegal because they were tribal and because some of them criticized the government. He advised them to change their names so that they did not sound tribalistic and to open membership to anyone: 'Discrimination and tribalism should not exist in Cameroon, he observed.'[59] The police were unimpressed, observing that 'changing the names of such associations from the original to the other names means changing only the calabash ... leaving the contents undiluted'.[60] In effect the 1967 law had the effect of driving home associations underground.

The ban on ethnically based groups in the interests of post-independence nation-building (Hickey, 2004) does not seem to have prevented migrants from Manyu from associating together. For example the Manyu All Students Union (MASU) began meeting from 1965, and there was a Mamfe Women's Club and a Mamfe Elements Union meeting in Bamenda in 1966.[61] MASU meetings were observed by the secret police and photos of members were kept on file. It was described as 'incitive if not subversive'[62] because discussions suggested that Manyu was not favoured politically. MASU was kept under surveillance.[63] Despite the ban, home associations continued to work along community development lines by collecting money for home development projects. For example in March 1971 the Ewelle Improvement Union (a village-scale home association in Manyu) 'agreed that the villagers who are not all working should contribute the sum of 600 francs each while all the Ewelle indigenes working both inside and outside Manyu Division are to contribute the sum of 2,000 CFA francs each for the construction of the school'.[64] Manyu associations were unapologetic about using coercion to extract money from the domestic diaspora and would ban individuals from returning home unless they could show a receipt for their donation. In Ossing for example it was decided that 'anybody who refuses to contribute will be prosecuted for being against development'.[65]

Soon after the abolition of the federation and the introduction of the unitary constitution in 1972, Cameroon became a one-party state under the leadership of President Ahmadou Ahidjo and the Cameroon National Union (CNU) (Amazee, 1994). Home associations responded by again changing their names and incorporating the CNU into their title. For example (on the advice of the Manyu SDO) the Ossing Youth Progressive Association became the Talagaye, Ossing, Ndekuai and Ntenako Development CNU Committee for the Badi Water Project.[66] Under a new formula established in the 1970s home associations justified their existence by claiming to be conduits of information between communities and government. Associations continued with the same basic functions but showed they could adapt to changing political times. Throughout the 1970s and into the 1980s, however, it was the framework of state-sanctioned 'cultural associations' that provided the principal means for hometown associations to continue meeting without infringing the law. 'Culture' became the acceptable way of talking about ethnic identity.

The Cameroonian government walked a fine line between, on the one hand, proscribing tribal associations as part of the nation-building project and, on the other, explicitly expecting migrants to take on the responsibility of developing their homeplace by forming associations that brought them together. Sometimes it was hard to sustain this contradiction. For example in 1971 the SDO in Limbe publicly banned the annual meeting of the Manyu Elements Association in Tiko that would have brought together representatives from Buea, Victoria, Tiko, Muyuka and Meme. He described the meeting as tribal and contrary to the spirit of national unity.[67] In response one member wrote to the police objecting to the ban and arguing that the government was encouraging citizens to help their home villages and that the meeting was planning to raise funds for a maternity unit in Bachuo Akagbe and the water supply in Bachuo Ntai. He claimed the meeting was not tribal because it was based on a small village and said:

> The CNU, our national political party, and the Cameroon Government have been campaigning for militants and citizens to organize themselves in social groups for the development of their towns and villages. In this respect the sons and daughters of Bachuo resident in Fako and Meme Divisions considered it duty bound to assist the Bachuo Village Council with financial aid because they cannot put in their own labour physically in any project.[68]

Whilst nationalist rhetoric condemned tribalism, then, the practice of rural development relied on mobilizing ethnic affiliations and loyalties.

The main Bali home association was also typical of this period. Despite the change in the law it was relaunched sometime in the late 1960s under the name the Bali Social and Cultural Development Association (BASCUDA).[69] This had three branches around Cameroon: one in Fako (covering both the plantation area and Buea, the one-time capital of the federal state of West Cameroon), one in Yaoundé (the national capital) and one in Mezam (the nearby city of Bamenda and surroundings). Each branch operated under a different name and acted largely independently. Later there was also a home branch in Bali Nyong'a itself, called the Bali Central Cultural Development Association (BACCUDA).[70] During the 1970s each branch of BASCUDA undertook to finance separate development initiatives, most of which were concerned with improvements to the Palace such as construction of a grandstand, repairs to the Palace fence, levelling of the ground used for the annual Lela dance and purchase of a car for the use of the Fon. It was through this organization that members of the Bali Nyong'a diaspora in the USA first contributed to their homeplace too. All these groups sent money to the home branch (BACCUDA), which then dispersed the funds. Explanations for the collapse of BACCUDA and BASCUDA in the 1980s are hazy, but there appear to have been leadership tussles following a loss of trust between those individuals outside (the 'external elites') and those running the organization at home.[71] In particular there were suspicions about whether the money collected by those outside was being spent, when it reached Bali, in the way that was intended. There followed a period during which the Bali home association was dormant.

In the first half of the 1980s the new President of Cameroon, Paul Biya, toured the country speaking repeatedly about the need to move away from tribal identities: 'We must show greater determination to replace the narrow-minded solidarity based on ethnic and religious affinities with solidarity based on ideas. By so doing, we will gradually move from a juxtaposition of our tribal groups to their effective integration within what will then become a real nation.'[72] Discussions with those who were at school during this period often make the point that students were completely unaware of their friends' ethnic identities. Yet BANDECA and MECA continued to work throughout this period, apparently with the blessing of the state. So while it was increasingly unacceptable to talk about ethnicity it was also publicly expected that those living 'outside' should continue to take a special role in the development of their homeplace and the state endorsed financial collections for this purpose.

The 1990s and the early years of the twenty-first century have seen an efflorescence of home associations, now almost uniformly called 'cultural and development associations'. The current Fon of Bali, with the encouragement of the most important government official in Bali (the Divisional Officer), re-established the home association in Bali in the mid 1990s under the name BANDECA – a single organization, which would work on co-ordinated rather than independent projects.[73] According-ing to the new constitution BANDECA aimed to assist the government's development efforts. For the first few years BANDECA was largely inactive. However, by removing the association's office from the Palace and by transferring the key leadership roles away from local elites and towards those living outside Bali Nyong'a, trust with the wider domestic diaspora was re-established. Elections for the key national and divisional roles within BANDECA were held in 1999, after which the organization began to collect levies for development.

Since 1999 BANDECA has raised tens of thousands of pounds (mostly from migrants within Cameroon) and has undertaken a number of projects. It has renovated a building in Bali Town for its own headquarters and has also renovated the Divisional Officer's office and helped to equip the offices of the new gendarmerie brigade in Bali. This illustrates the close public relationship between BANDECA and the Government of Cameroon. BANDECA has provided bail for five Bali Nyong'a residents arrested after a violent land dispute with people from a neighbouring subdivision. It has overseen a library, with books provided by the Bali Nyong'a diaspora in the USA,[74] and it has organized a cancer-screening exercise. However its two largest projects were the equipping of the town mortuary and the reconstruction of the water supply (chapters 7 and 9).

In recent years various MECAs have supported improvements at Mamfe General Hospital. In a long-running, expensive and as yet unfinished project, MECA-USA has constructed a building to house a mortuary in the hospital grounds but has failed to provide the necessary equipment, and the building remains unused at time of writing. The opening of a private mortuary in Mamfe has probably further under-mined this project. The benefits of a few other MECA projects are spread around the division, notably medicines distributed to subdivisional and village health centres. There have been projects to establish internet and reprographic facilities in Mamfe, as well as a library, which were funded not by MECA but by NOMA from the US. There is also a long history of diaspora groups giving scholarships in Manyu, continued today by the Manyu Solidarity Foundation.[75]

The revival of home associations in Cameroon in the last two decades is a consequence of several factors. First, the 1967 law was repealed and a new more liberal law of association was introduced in 1990 – a precursor to the subsequent episode of relative political openness.[76] To register an association, the leaders now give the SDO their constitution, rules and regulations, the names of the executive, the minutes and place of first meeting, and pay 5,000 CFA francs. The association is then issued with an authorization to operate. Second, the state has largely moved away from the nation-building project and its associated goal of the elimination of tribal loyalties. The official (if generally implicit) removal of the taboo around public declarations of ethnic loyalty was compounded by an emerging politics of ethnic competition, in which different areas fought to compete for the limited resources of the central government (Jua, 1997; Nkwi and Socpa, 1997; Gabriel, 1999; Nyamnjoh, 1999; Geschiere and Nyamnjoh, 2000; Konings, 2001; Fonchingong, 2004; Oben and Akoko, 2004). Such a policy had always been present under the guise of 'regional balance' but reached a new level in the 1990s when multi-party politics threatened the existing political establishment and home associa-tions were seen as a means to undermine putative opposition alliances. Ultimately this re-ethnicization process found expression in the new 1997 constitution with its requirement that Cameroonian ID cards should carry an individual's ethnic affiliation (Jua, 2005). On the one hand this competition is a stimulus for mobilizing migrants to become engaged, on the other it compounds the sense that politics is a zero-sum game in which one group's achievements must always be at somebody else's expense. Third, declining national economic conditions meant that the state's capacity to deliver development goods was severely constrained. In this context, the kind of self-reliant community development strategies used by home associations became an important means by which the limits of the state could be glossed over. The association is presented not as a rival source of development goods, but a co-worker operating within a governmental framework. So at the present time Cameroonian cultural and development associations find themselves to be a prominent feature on the social, developmental and political landscape.

Conclusions

History shows that Bali and Manyu have been involved in migrants' associations for almost as long as there has been migration. In both places the history of associations is continuous though they flourish, flounder, rest and then re-form. History thus illustrates the way in which ideas about how to organize, what organizations should do, how they should gather money, what they should set as their aims and what they should put in their constitutions have been picked up from numerous sources and experiences over time.

In terms of structure there can be a range of different associations operating within a homeplace, with varying international elements. In the Bali Nyong'a case the international 'branches' are separate organizations with different names. In the Manyu case the international groups took the MECA name but the MECA structure is so highly devolved that they operated largely independently of MECA branches in Cameroon. Furthermore, MECA is not the only association among the Manyu diaspora in the UK. A whole range of associations has been established, which relate to subdivisions, villages and clans in Manyu. There is now a move among the Cameroonian diaspora in the UK to organize in different ways, so associations such as the Young Cameroonians Professional Network, the Cameroon Forum and the Millennium Group all meet on a national or pan-African basis, but these are seen as complements to, rather than replacements for, the home associations that refer to subnational places. The case studies show that the African dimension of these organizations is still much more important than the international dimension. This is particularly evident from the relative amounts of money raised for the development work being done. Bali and Manyu home associations draw heavily on spectacular donations and loans from elite individuals who occupy significant positions in government or business and are based in the main cities. The capacity of the Cameroonian associations to establish a broad membership among the domestic diaspora by acquiring the members of *nda kums* (Bali) or family groups (Manyu) has meant that they can mobilize considerable funds for projects in fairly short spaces of time (see Chapter 9). However this fundraising capacity is limited compared with the ability to raise funds for death celebrations or for political events such as a minister's homecoming.

Notes

1. Much of this financial support was related either to rotating savings and credit associations (Ardener and Burman, 1996) or 'trouble funds' used for medical bills and the costs associated with burial.
2. President, Bali Divisional Council of BANDECA, Bali, March 2005.
3. Interview, Bali diaspora, Douala, April 2005.
4. Kenyang is the language spoken by the Banyang people and has a number of dialects.
5. Chief, Mamfe, 17 February 2005; General MECA President, Yaoundé, 18 March 2005.
6. Divisional Delegate for National Education, Mamfe, 24 February 2005.
7. Manyu elites, Yaoundé, 21 April 2005; London, 24 February 2006 and Cambridge, 27 June 2006. Claims of village-level groups in the UK were heard but only those for larger villages such as Kembong and Ossing seem to be viable.
8. Interview, Manyu elite, Douala, April 2005.
9. Cultural week compares with 'homecoming' events in other parts of West Africa (de Jong, 1999; Trager, 2001).
10. Interviews, Manyu elites, Yaoundé, April 2005; see also Hickey (2004).
11. Western embassy official, Yaoundé, 12 January 2005.
12. Interview, Manyu elite, Yaoundé, April 2005.
13. Traditional council member, Eyanchang, 25 February 2005.
14. Interview, Besongabang elite, London, March 2006.
15. Youth focus groups, Mamfe and Egbekaw, March 2005.
16. From the Director of Le Likumba Club to DO Victoria, 2 October 1929, CNA, Buea, File Si 1935/1.
17. 27 November 1935, File Si 1935/1, CNA, Buea.
18. DO Victoria, 7 July 1936, File Si 1935/1.CNA, Buea.
19. Hon. Sec. Ibo Tribal Union to DO Victoria, 26 September 1937, CNA, Buea, File Si 1941/1.
20. 12 June 1941, CNA, Buea, File Si 1941/1.
21. 1947, CNA, Buea, File Si 1948/1.
22. 1953, CNA, Buea, File Si (1942)1.
23. DO Victoria (HCA Bryant) to Ibo International Union Club, 1939, CNA, Buea, File Si 1941/1.
24. DO Buea to SDO Victoria, 24 March 1948, CNA, Buea, File Si 1941/1.
25. President Victoria Federated Council to Ibo Tribal Union, 27 January 1943, CNA, Buea, File, Si 1941/1.

26. DO Victoria to Ibo Union, 17 September 1945, CNA, Buea, File Si 1942/1.
27. Buea (1943), Mamfe (1943), Bassa in French Cameroon (1948), Bamenda (1949), Mbom Keng (1950), Bangwa (1950), Banyang (1950), Tadkon-Widikum (1950), Bakweri (1950), Kom (1950), Bafut (1951), Ejagham (1952), Mbue (1953), Mamfe Overside (1953) and Mubakoh (the four Mubako speaking Balis) (1954) are all recorded in the archive.
28. The Akum Welfare Movement had branches in Lagos, Ibadan, Kaduna, Enugu and Douala as well as Victoria, Tiko, and Kumba. From Akum Welfare Movement, Yaba Lagos to DO Bamenda, 17 December 1957, CNA, Bamenda, File NW /Si1936/1.
29. Interview, Bali Nyong'a elite, Bamenda, January 2005.
30. Interview, Bali Nyong'a elite, Bali, April 2005.
31. Interview, Bali Nyong'a elite, Bamenda, April 2005.
32. 8 March 1943, File Si/1943/5 CNA, Buea.
33. 3 September 1947, File Si (1939) 2a, CNA, Buea.
34. John Etchu, a former interpreter, was President of the Ejagham Union, and his signature also appears on letters from the earlier Mamfe Improvement Union. 9 September 1947 Police report by Sergeant Fominyen, File Si (1939) 2a. Etchu was President until at least 1952.
35. The Union of Mamfe Natives (Echeme Bo Mmek Mamfe) was formed to defend the interest of 'the indigenous sons' of Mamfe against those of 'strangers' in relation to chieftaincy issues and land disputes in Mamfe Town. 3 June 1950, File Si (1950) 4, CNA, Buea.
36. 9 September 1947, File Si (1939) 2a, File Si (1950) 4, File Si (1948) 1, Si (1951) 3, and missing files recorded in archive index, CNA, Buea. The Bangwa home was at the time in Mamfe Division. After independence it remained in Manyu Division, but since 1992 it has been in Lebialem Division.
37. 3 September 1947, CNA, Buea, File Si (1939) 2a.
38. Bassa Union, French Cameroun Official Gazette of 15 July 1947, CNA, Buea, File Si (1935) 1.
39. Ibo Tribal Union, 1943, CNA Buea File Si (1941) 1.
40. Minute from Enugu, 19 June 1951, CNA Buea File Si (1951) 11.
41. The limited extent of British administration is illustrated by the fact that the British Cameroons 'was staffed in 1945 by an average of 6.7 administrators – about one British official for each 100,000 inhabitants' (Welch, 1966: 156).
42. For example there were the Ossing Development Association (1951), the Ekona Lelu Development Association (1958) and the Akum Welfare Movement (1957).
43. For example in September 1950 the Bangwa Improvement Union (which claimed a membership of 300 people originally from Mamfe District) applied for a permit to carry out a public collection moving from village to village in the Kumba area.
44. 3 January 1951, Mamfe Youths Association to DO Victoria, File Si (1948) 1, CNA, Buea.
45. SDO to Ossing Development Organization Union (Agbor Stephen), 20 June 1951, CNA, Buea, File Si/1951/3.
46. Victoria Improvement Union, October 1956, CNA, Buea, File Si 1957/2.
47. Minute on the proposal for a Widikum State Union, 22 March 1958, CNA. Bamenda, File NW/Si1936/1.

48. 4 June 1958, CNA, Buea, File Si (1958)7.
49. File Td 1951/2, CNA, Buea.
50. File Td 1951/2, CNA, Buea.
51. 24 October 1952, File, Td 1952/37, CNA, Buea.
52. 17 October 1952, Mamfe Improvement Union to Resident Buea, File Si (1952)5 CNA, Buea.
53. November 1953, File Si (1952)4 CNA, Buea.
54. In 1964 the Bamileleke Welfare Union agreed with the SDO Victoria to police the Bamileke community and search for 'undesirable elements'. CNA Buea File Si (1959)1.
55. The law states that it replaced earlier laws of July 1901 and April 1946. These were not enforced in relation to the British Mandate territory.
56. 12 June 1967, CNA, Buea, File Si 1967/1.
57. Bali Social Union application for registration, 3 January 1968, CNA Bamenda, NW/Si/1966/1.
58. August 1968, CNA Bamenda, File NW/Si.1966/1.
59. Special Branch report, 6 September 1969, CNA Buea, File Si 1969/6.
60. Special Branch report, 27 July 1969, CNA, Buea, File Si 1969/6.
61. 17 May 1966, File NW(Si.1966)1, CNA, Bamenda.
62. 24 May 1970, File Si (1970)5 CNA, Buea.
63. 6 January 1971, File Si (1970)4 CNA, Buea.
64. 2 March 971, File Si (1969) CNA, Buea.
65. 30 December 1970, Si (1970)4 CNA, Buea.
66. Special Branch report, 30 December 1970, CNA, Buea, File Si/1970/4.
67. SDO (Victoria) radio message. Reported in Special Branch police report, file Si (1969) 6, CNA Buea.
68. Andrew B. Ashu, 2 March 1971, CNA, Buea, File Si 1969/6.
69. Interview, Bali Nyong'a elite, Bali, March 2005.
70. Interview, Bali Nyong'a elite, Bali, April 2005. In addition to BASCUDA there were two other relevant Bali associations. The Bali Elements Workers Union, founded in the 1960s, represented Bali professionals (for example school-teachers) working elsewhere in Cameroon. There was also a formal (and unsuccessful) political party dedicated to furthering Bali Nyong'a interests called the Bali Aspirant Party, which existed briefly around the same time and paid for a representative to travel to the USA to help 'project' Bali Nyong'a on a wider stage. Bali-Nyong'a elite, Bali, 23 April 2005.
71. Interview, Bali Nyong'a elite, Bali, March 2005.
72. Paul Biya, 22 March 1985, New Deal Congress, General Policy Report, CNA, Buea.
73. H.M. Dr. Ganyonga III, Fon of Bali, 30 December 2004.
74. Unfortunately we were never able to see the library, which was kept locked.
75. Subdivisional association PR Officer, Mamfe, 29 March 2005; MECA-Yaoundé president, 23 April 2005.
76. Freedom of Association, law no. 90/053, 19 December 1990.

5 HOME ASSOCIATIONS AND THE NATION IN TANZANIA

This chapter charts the history of home associations in Tanzania, with a focus on associations from Newala and Rungwe. The templates for home associations have come from a different mix of peoples compared to Cameroon (including Arabs, Asians and Europeans), and, in the colonial period, dance associations were more important for urban migrants than home associations. Nevertheless home associations played an important role in migrants' welfare – indeed they were more focused on this than on developmental activities at home, which were part of the remit of Cameroonian associations from the 1940s. Most crucially though, the home development activities of associations were effectively prevented from evolving in postcolonial Tanzania (until recently) by the state's monopoly over planning social and economic progress and by the more thorough nation-building project with its associated aim of containing ethnic identities. Only in the last decade of the twentieth century has the obligation to take some responsibility for the development of rural homeplaces re-emerged through an efflorescence of state-sanctioned District Development Trusts (DDTs) (Kiondo, 1995).

DDTs are led by a combination of rural elites based in the homeplace and migrant elites based in Dar es Salaam. In their emphasis on development of the homeplace and their linkage between migrants from that place and those at home, DDTs are similar to the standard idea of a West African home association. Very often their urban leaders are prominent politicians or businessmen. DDTs collect revenue from two main sources: the most consistent flow of money comes from a crop tax (or cess) collected from farmers by local government and passed (in varying quantities) to trusts. A more intermittent flow of money comes from the city, where migrants from the district may arrange fundraising events, capitalizing on a culture of public giving associated with weddings and burials. In some cases this external source can exceed the crop cess, but generally whether it does so depends on the profitability of the crops produced in the home district. Occasionally DDTs have been supported by government or international donors, who are drawn in through the domestic diaspora. The money collected is spent delivering services in the district, most commonly in the construction and running of secondary schools (Chapter 8). More recently, and particularly in Rungwe, home associations that appear to be a mixture of DDT and NGO have also become very popular. They are similar to DDTs in their leadership (migrants in the cities) but do not work so closely with local governments. Most of these home associations, which often use the term 'Fund' or 'Foundation' in their titles, rely upon the contributions of the domestic diaspora.

The structure of home associations in Newala and Rungwe

NDF

The Newala Development Foundation (NDF) is the sole DDT for Newala and was registered as an NGO with the Registrar of Societies in the Ministry of Home Affairs in March 1988 under the Societies Ordinance (1954). NDF aims to: 'promote the development of Newala people through formulation and implementation of self-reliant projects by mobilizing resources – human, financial and others – available internally and externally' (NDF, n.d.). In this context 'internally' refers to people living in Newala and 'externally' refers to people from Newala living elsewhere in Tanzania as well as external donors. The constitution prioritizes community-based programmes in education, water, rural transportation, agriculture, cooperative and credit schemes, health, environment, women and child care. The circular symbol of NDF bears the motto *Newala kuchele*, meaning 'Newala is at dawn' in Makonde, together with an open book and a farmer's hoe.

NDF was the brainchild of Newala elites who held social meetings in Dar es Salaam in the mid-1980s, and it has been led by the district's most illustrious sons (women have been very few) since its inception. Prominent politicians including a former Newala parliamentarian and cabinet minister (who became NDF's first chair), other former parliamentarians, former principal secretaries of the Ministry of Defence and the Office of the President, a district and a regional commissioner (one of whom sat on the National Executive Committee of the CCM and is the current parliamentarian and Chair of NDF), together with members of the business and public sector elite, all became involved with NDF. The fact that most elites are either in Newala or Dar es Salaam (including politicians based in Dodoma) means that the only diaspora 'branch' of NDF is in Dar es Salaam. There were formerly branches in Mtwara and Lindi but both became defunct. In contrast to the cases of Bali and Manyu, there are no international branches or affiliated groups overseas. Furthermore, NDF created its own structure and membership – it did not incorporate pre-existing associational forms, as BANDECA and MECA in Cameroon did. Burial societies do exist among the domestic diaspora, but they are independent of NDF.

Despite the wider aims of the foundation, its activities to date have been almost entirely concerned with secondary education. NDF relies on a share of local taxation, local labour and support from the Dar es Salaam diaspora to build and equip secondary schools. In contrast to the Cameroonian associations, and as with RUDET in Rungwe, NDF receives a proportion of local taxation from local government, which is now entirely based on crop cess. The diaspora's role is to top up this local income stream by accessing external support from donors, and by making their own contributions. Indeed the membership of the 'Foreign Relations' committee of NDF (responsible for donor relations) is entirely based in Dar es Salaam.

As with the other case study associations, membership of NDF is vaguely defined. NDF officers claim that everyone from the district, whether at home or outside, is *de facto* a member, but in reality only certain individuals in the district and in the diaspora pay for membership cards. Universal membership for village residents exists insofar as they contribute through crop cess or through other corporate members such as Newala District Council, Newala Cooperative Union, primary cooperative societies, village councils or other affiliated groups. However, according to Seppälä (1998a), the crop cess has been so unpopular among local farmers that some have resorted to 'smuggling' their cashew into neighbouring districts where the cess was not collected. Card-carrying membership thus tends to be restricted to the Dar es Salaam diaspora and NDF officials in Newala. Membership is also limited in Newala itself because, unlike in Bali or Rungwe, those who leave the district for employment rarely return on their retirement. Very few elites have built houses in the district, although the current NDF Chair and Vice-Chair have both done so. As one NDF official put it, 'the moment someone is going to school, he [*sic*] is saying bye-bye to home'.[1]

RUDET

In Rungwe, research focused on the Rungwe District Education Trust (RUDET), formerly Rungwe District Technical Schools Fund (RDTSF). It is the longest-established home association for the whole district, although as in Manyu there are plenty of smaller home associations attached to areas within Rungwe. RUDET was registered as a DDT in 1988 with the Ministry of Home Affairs under the Trustees Ordinance (Cap 375) of 1956, although the constitution refers to the trust as an NGO. Like NDF, RUDET is concerned with improving access to secondary education across the district and is not a broad-based membership association. The trust rents offices and has a paid secretariat in Tukuyu, mostly civil servants or teachers who have retired back home to Rungwe. The lack of a membership base means that RUDET is heavily dependent on the cess on tea, coffee and cocoa, which comes via the district administration but has been cut since 2003. There are no RUDET-associated organizations in the international diaspora, or 'branches' in Tanzania's main cities. In the past, RUDET relied on key elites in Dar es Salaam to act as informal intermediaries with members of the Rungwe diaspora. All the district's parliamentarians since 1981 have been members of the RUDET board of directors. A recent attempt to establish branches in Mbeya and in Dar es Salaam was not particularly successful.

RUDET is not the only home association concerned with education in Rungwe although it is the longest-established and largest, with a mandate over the whole district. Other associations have been established recently that concentrate on smaller parts of the district. In general the role of all of these associations is to transfer relatively small sums of money, often via the local parliamentarian, from the urban elite as 'encouragement' to the people in the village to continue with school construction.

The two largest of these new associations are the Rungwe East Development Foundation (RUEDEFO) and Rungwe West Development Foundation (RUWEDEFO), each attached to one of the two constituencies in the district. These associations, both initiated by constituency parliamentarians, are constitutionally established and registered (RUEDEFO as an NGO, RUWEDEFO as a trust fund). Each association has a chairman, secretary and treasurer, drawn from the higher ranks of Dar es Salaam's civil servants and business community. RUEDEFO has over 50 members, mostly in Dar es Salaam, each of whom pays a Tsh5,000 entry fee, a Tsh60,000 annual contribution plus further donations as required, for example for fundraisers organized by the parliamentarian.

Even smaller associations have also been active in recent years. The Selya Development Foundation (SEDEFO) is an NGO registered with the Ministry of Home Affairs. It is concerned with four wards in the southernmost area of Rungwe East, also described as one of the 'divisions' of *abanyafyale* in the pre-colonial era (Charsley, 1969; Wright, 1972) and which the British designated a 'chiefdom'. It is a membership association for the Selya diaspora in Dar es Salaam, collecting an entry fee (now Tsh10,000), monthly contributions (Tsh3,000) and donations to fundraisers organized by the parliamentarian for development projects in Selya. As a welfare association SEDEFO also makes contributions to members in case of bereavement and sickness. Between 1998 and 2005, SEDEFO contributed about Tsh6 million towards schools in Selya and spent almost Tsh1 million on mutual welfare. When SEDEFO started in the mid-1990s it attracted about 60 members and its advisors numbered high-ranking civil servants. However, as with many other Rungwe associations, membership and contributions have waned in the last few years. The leaders of another small home association in Dar es Salaam, Shirika la Maendeleo ya Busokelo (SHIMABU), expressed similar concerns. Their association is for Busokelo, which in administrative terms is coterminous with Rungwe East; in practice, however, SHIMABU has focused its attention on Mwakaleli ward in the north of Busokelo. Mwakaleli was also designated as a 'chiefdom' under Indirect Rule. SHIMABU started with 100 members but now only a quarter of these are active. Since its capacity to raise money is limited, its activities to date have depended on successful grant applications to donors in Dar es Salaam. In 2003 it was awarded Tsh5 million from the Foundation for Civil Society to undertake training on issues facing the elderly at home in Mwakaleli.

Other associations in the Rungwe domestic diaspora include student associations, such as the Kyela Rungwe Students Association at the University of Dar es Salaam, which sends volunteer teachers to Rungwe and Kyela districts; and the Banyakyusa Cultural Trust Fund, which in 2008 was still seeking registration to 'promote Banyakyusa culture' in Dar es Salaam.

The case study associations within the history of home associations in Tanzania

As in the Cameroonian case the rest of this chapter weaves a national narrative of 'modern' home associations from the beginning of the period of British colonial control together with the specific associational histories of Newala and Rungwe. In particular the aim is to consider how the history of home associations in Tanzania is connected to a history of emerging ethnic consciousness.

The Anglophone literature on associations in colonial and postcolonial Tanzania is better developed than that from Cameroon, partly because colonial sociology and legislation left a more systematic record of associational life in Dar es Salaam and partly because associations have formed a key element in both canonical and recent work on the history of the country and its capital (Ranger, 1975; Iliffe, 1979; Shivji, 1986; Brennan, 2002; Burton, 2005). However, the emphasis has been on dance associations and those formal associations that were central to the emergence of national political history, for example nascent political parties, trade unions and cooperatives. There are already detailed accounts of the history of the African Association (Iliffe, 1979: 405–35), which was a key precursor to the Tanganyika African National Union (TANU), the political party that emerged in the last years of colonialism and led the country to independence. The literature on dance associations is also rich (Ranger, 1975) and draws out their social, welfare and political functions. In contrast the account here pays attention to home associations (in the form of 'tribal associations' in the colonial period and DDTs in recent decades). Tribal associations tend to have been in the background (but see Iliffe, 1969: 145–7, and 1979: 389–91) because they were less significant to nationalist politics, though they are an important part of the story of the crystallization and internalization of ethnic identity in late colonial Tanganyika. Indirect Rule was central to this process: 'The British wrongly believed that Tanganyikans belonged to tribes; Tanganyikans created tribes to function within the colonial framework' (Iliffe, 1979: 318). Tribal associations were both a means through which tribes were created and subsequently a symptom of the process of creating tribes. After independence such associations were effectively erased from the social landscape. More recently a different version of home associations has emerged through DDTs but these too have received less attention than other aspects of civil society such as NGOs.

Early templates

Two groups of migrants in Dar es Salaam had prominent associations in the early 1920s: European colonial employees and Asian colonial employees. The former organized the Tanganyika European Civil Servants Association, one of whose stated aims was 'the promotion of the interests and welfare of civil servants of the Tanganyika territory as a body'.[2] Similar versions of this aim were subsequently used by many other associations such as the Indian Association (founded in 1918), the Non-European Civil Service Association and the Railway Asiatic Union (Iliffe, 1979: 264). These clubs were models for the Tanganyika Territory African Civil Services Association (TTACSA), formed by African clerks in 1922 (Iliffe, 1979; 267), which defended African interests relative to Indian clerks in government service. There was a branch of the TTACSA in Tukuyu (Rungwe) up to 1932 (Iliffe, 1979; 268) and in its branch structure this association was in turn an early African model for some of the later 'tribal unions'.

The Indian Association provides a good example of the ambivalence the colonial authorities felt about such organizations mimicking equivalent European clubs. On the one hand the state recognized their economic value as a means of supporting businesses but on the other they were uncomfortable about the way such groups provided a platform for individuals whom they did not fully trust. Writing about the Indian Association in 1924 the British Provincial Commissioner in Dar es Salaam commented:

> the association serves a very useful purpose ... unfortunately there is a tendency for undue weight to be carried in its council by shallow individuals who mistake instruction for education and memory for character; a simian facility enables them to ape the mannerisms of men of ability ...[3]

The colonial anxiety about the agency of the mimic-men shows in the racism of the primate metaphors (Bhabha, 1994). From the administration's perspective the dilemma was that associations like this aided the process of government by developing a business class and lubricating commerce, but simultaneously enabled colonial subjects to articulate aspirations different from those they had been assigned by the colonial state. This ambivalence runs through the historical record for both Asian and African associations in Tanganyika.

In 1921 Dar es Salaam District, with a population of 110,000, contained a diverse African population including 92 different tribal categories.[4] Immigration was driven by the preferences of the European employers in the coastal plantations who regarded the local people to be 'lazy and of poor physique'[5] and therefore recruited labour from further afield. Indeed the British interpretation of the city's attraction to Africans was that it was 'free from family or tribal ties', and at the time they discerned no tribal organizations in the city.[6] At some times individuals were appointed to take responsibility for specific groups of migrants, for example Saidi Litewa represented Ngindo, Nyasa, Makonde and Makua migrants from the South as well as the local Shirazi in the town council of 1933 (Leslie, 1963: 34). However, the overall story of urban administration was of a failure either to enforce the colonial will or to satisfy the needs of Africans (Burton, 2002: 98–118). Given the lack of effective urban administration and services, urban residents were forced to produce their own systems of support. Under both German and British rule each 'tribe' was expected to take their own dead from the hospital, bury them and register their death. For this to happen there needed to be recognized leaders who organized these tribal communities, and retrospectively this task is often seen as the origin of home associations.

The associations of which the British colonial officials *were* aware from the 1920s were the urban dance and music clubs often referred to generically as *ngoma*. Though *ngoma* literally means 'drum' or 'dance' the term can also describe an association and it has an extensive geographical reach across southern Africa. *Ngoma* in Tanzania have a long, complex history. For example *beni* societies, which originated on the Kenyan coast, were spread through the territory by soldiers discharged after the First World War. They were organized by status rather than ethnicity (Iliffe, 1979: 248), and in the 1920s they were interpreted teleologically by officials as a move away from African or tribal forms of association: 'the whole movement may be regarded as the natural evolution from a savage tribal *ngoma* brought about by civilization and Western lives'.[7] However, Terence Ranger's work on the *beni ngoma* has shown that 'the music and the dance were merely one part of the activity of Beni members' (Ranger, 1975: 5). *Ngoma* members use the association to help create group identities, negotiate differences between identities, create welfare support networks and advance their social status (Gunderson and Barz, 2000). The retraditionalization of these dance associations after the Second World War has been closely associated with the rise of nationalism in Tanzania, and in some accounts *ngoma* are presented as the glue that bound TANU together (Geiger, 1997; Edmonson, 2001; Askew, 2002).

The relationship between *ngoma* and ethnicity is not straightforward. On the one hand a *ngoma* may be associated with an ethnic group – for example, the Makonde from Newala are associated with the *sindimba* dance – but historical studies show that actual *ngoma* group members were not always ethnically homogenous. Iliffe claims that it was through dance that diverse groups became agglomerated into tribal categories: 'as men of many origins interacted in town or workplace, so they became identified by tribal names, and often one of the many dances which each group performed at home became known as its tribal dance' (1979: 238).

In Rungwe, Ellison (1999) argues that Nyakyusa ethnic identity was partially created through *ngoma* learned by migrants while away from home. However, British administrators considered that *ngoma* were tending 'to regroup society into guilds rather than tribes' (Baker, 1931, in Brennan, 2002: 111). As Askew writes of the postcolonial period, '*ngoma* societies incorporated people from a variety of ethnic backgrounds and created communal ties that nicely paralleled government objectives' (Askew, 2002: 66). Indeed as dance became professionalized, performing arts schools such as that in Bagamoyo ensured that though a dance was ethnically marked the dancers were not. Yet at the same time since particular *ngoma* were still associated with particular ethnic groups they have been interpreted as 'an attempt to channel ethnic identities into carefully contained modes of expression' (Edmondson, 2007: 78) within the nation. Dance groups, then, were a far more prominent form of association in colonial Tanganyika than home associations.

Detribalization and tribal associations

By the mid-1920s there were clear signs in administrators' reports of the concept that would come to frame discussions of social identity in East African cities: detribalization. This was the idea that outside the sanctions of the tribal framework and the rural homeland Africans were inclined to become demoralized and degenerate: 'The breakdown of tribal custom and former control is responsible for a great lack of discipline. The women themselves have obtained freedom from the old salutary restraints without having built up any character of self-respect to fortify their own conduct, and the result is deplorable'.[8] Over the next four decades this concept was key to the way administrators understood African associational life in Tanganyikan cities.[9]

The concept of detribalization is central to the interpretation of colonial attitudes to home associations, though it also brings out the multiple contradictions inherent in colonial attempts to manage urban populations. Before independence a distinction was drawn between 'stabilized' urban citizens and their families who had left behind their tribal roots (in a positive sense), and mobile unemployed detribalized migrants who formed an urban underclass that should really be sent 'home' to 'tribal' areas. From the 1930s onwards the latter group was known as the *wahuni* (Burton, 2005: 5). An imagined geography divided the colony into two: modern cities where citizens were free from tribal obligation (with the exception of the indigenous inhabitants), and traditional rural homelands, which were understood in tribal terms and governed through tribal laws using the policy of Indirect Rule. In this context associations that crossed this rural–urban divide must have been hard to imagine – Iliffe talks of an 'innate fear' (1979: 415) among administrators of urban–rural communication. Yet tribal associations in the city were a potential means of managing the *wahuni* or at least of devolving responsibility for their welfare. Some of these associations (for example the Nyamwezi Association) also effectively enabled the repatriation of labour from the city once it ceased to be useful. In the colonial imagination home associations were seen as evidence of the inherently tribal character of Africans and were interpreted as evidence of continuity with a tribal past. But officials must also have known that these same tribal categories had previously been relatively porous, becoming meaningful quite late during the colonial period. Elsewhere in Tanganyika in the 1920s (for example in Rungwe) colonial officials were undertaking a process they literally called 'tribalization'[10] – consciously amalgamating different groups together under a small number of labels to facilitate the operation of Indirect Rule.[11] Far from being evidence of continuity with a timeless tribal identity, home associations (along with other institutions such as *ngoma*) were actually integral to translating a 'fluid ethnonym into a hard "clan" identity' (Brennan, 2002: 195). So home associations were welcomed precisely as a brake on detribalization and a means of managing its consequences, yet simultaneously they offended the colonial separation of town and countryside. They were 'evidence' of the inherently tribal character of Africans, yet were actually a symptom of the invention of tribalism.

Among the early examples of African associations concerned with the interests of their homeplace were the Bukoba Bahaya Union of 1924 (Iliffe, 1969: 139–40) and the Arabu-Congo Association and the Tanganyika Association in Ujiji later in the 1920s and into the 1930s (McCurdy, 1996). The Bahaya Union was limited to wealthy cash-croppers in Bukoba (Bates, 1974; Curtis, 1992) but the two Ujiji associations had wider membership and began to develop a more extended geographical structure. Each represented communities associated with homes on different sides of Lake Tanganyika and they were highly competitive. They were concerned with community improvement and were 'interested in promoting their communities by assisting their members in trade, marriage and burial arrangements' (McCurdy, 1996: 12). By 1932, both associations had meeting halls, significant savings, and affiliated groups in Tabora. The Arabu-Congo Association had 450 members and the Tanganyika Association had 1,300 members (McCurdy, 1996: 13). Once people from Ujiji were in Dar es Salaam the antagonisms of home seem to have been less important so that they were able to cooperate within the Manyema Association.

The African Association was founded in 1929[12] (Iliffe, 1979: 405–35) by members of the urban, educated elite 'to safeguard the interests of Africans, not only in Tanganyika but in the whole of Africa'.[13] Though settlers and government officials initially took very different attitudes to the African Association (the former antagonistic, the latter cautiously sympathetic) both groups saw that it was outside a framework of tribes. An anonymous letter published in the Tanganyika Standard in 1930, for example, says of the leadership, 'I doubt whether any of them have any status in any tribe whatsoever.'[14] In contrast there was an implicit tolerance of the tribal associations. We know for example that the 'Manyema Community'[15] made successful representations to the Governor to be allocated land for a cemetery in Dar es Salaam in 1930.[16] The tribalization of urban associational life was in effect also its naturalization in the eyes of the colonial state and settlers. The African Association sought official registration[17] as the sole voice of Africans in the territory but (as in Cameroon) this was initially refused by colonial officials. They argued that the African Association was 'not representative of the African community as a whole, e.g. there is also the African Welfare and Commercial Association and thousands of Africans in the town who do not belong to either association'.[18] The African Association then sought registration as a cooperative, which was also refused.[19] In contrast the tribal associations were officially government-approved even in 1956; some of them still knew their registration number from the 1930s (Leslie, 1963: 54).

In the 1940s, associations that sought solidarity through 'racial' categories seem to have lost influence relative to tribal unions in Dar es Salaam (Iliffe, 1979: 408–10; see also Brennan, 2002). The continuing presence of the Pogoro Association (1912), Chagga Association (1919), Sudanese Association (1921), Congo Natives Union (1930), Wanyamwezi Association (1938) and Wazaramo Union (1938)[20] reflects the inability of either the African Association or its later (1934) rival the Tanganyikan African Welfare and Commercial Association (TAWCA) to sustain a broad-based organization that rested on identifying as 'African'. However, the main reason for this is that by the 'late 1930s both the African Association and TAWCA had become vehicles of personal advancement at the expense of viably representing Dar es Salaam's Africans' (Brennan, 2002: 118). To see the relative waning of these associations in Dar es Salaam and the rise of the tribal associations at this time as related not only excludes the possibility of multiple forms of identification but also ignores the specificities of the history of these associations with their very particular memberships, interests and problems. However, the failure of either the African Association or TAWCA to enrol large numbers of those Africans categorized as *wenye mji* (owners of the town) in Dar es Salaam certainly opened the way for the most significant of the tribal associations in the inter-war period.

The Wazaramo (later the Zaramo) Union was founded in July 1938.[21] According to the Provincial Commissioner at the time 'this body is not of a political nature but has been formed with the main object of assisting members of the Zaramo tribe who may be in distress'.[22] The echoes of colonial interpretations of tribal unions in Cameroon are obvious. According to its first president the Union sought to unite all the Zaramo, both those living in Dar es Salaam and those living in the Uzaramo districts around the city's periphery (Brennan, 2002: 176). The reorganization of the government of Dar es Salaam and neighbouring districts in 1942 reinforced the links between urban and rural Zaramo and enabled them to exploit their unique economic opportunity of access to land on the edge of the growing city through food production and marketing. This economic growth underpinned the politicization of the Union, which after the Second World War became 'the most independent and important political organization in Dar es Salaam, and perhaps in the entire territory' (Brennan, 2002: 186). Membership was measured in tens of thousands and there was a network of at least nine branches throughout the Zaramo district.

The Wazaramo Union was concerned with 'rural improvement' in a way more akin to hometown development than were the activities of many Tanganyikan tribal organizations. It explained the relative weakness of the Zaramo in the past as a result of lack of tribal unity and it aimed to bring education and prosperity to the tribe through uniting their efforts and developing a stronger sense of competition with other tribes.[23] The Union positioned itself not only against the Indian traders with whom the Zaramo competed economically but also against the *jumbes* who officially represented the tribe and whom it described as government 'yes-men'.[24] Particular resentment was developed towards the lorry owners who transported people and goods from the hinterland into the city, and by 1946 the Union had purchased its first lorry to capture some of this trade.[25] After 1948, however, the Wazaramo Union declined as it suffered problems with embezzlement of funds by Union officials.[26] The story of this Union is unique because of the particular opportunities provided by the proximity of Zaramo land to Dar es Salaam but the initiation of this 'tribal' movement, which challenged 'foreign' elements, whether Indian traders or non-Zaramo appointees in their 'home', is not.

By the late 1940s the colonial state considered that, 'of the odd fifty thousand Africans living in Dar es Salaam, a considerable proportion have strong tribal loyalties, even though remote from their own tribal areas' and it identified 'a resurgence of tribalism at present'.[27] This crossed the divide between the educated and uneducated by bringing them together in tribal unions, which though they were perceived to have emerged from dancing clubs were by this time aimed at the welfare of the tribe as a whole. These unions reflected a limited degree of ethnic social segregation in Dar es Salaam and ensured the 'maintenance of tribal language and customs and full tribal consciousness and pride'.[28] However, though it was suggested that the detribalized were more difficult to administer, there was scepticism that detribalization was the cause of a growing urban underclass. Several officials commented on the 'advantages' of tribalism 'for our primitive Africans' but also predicted that 'the modern trend of events will undoubtedly break down the tribal system, and it will ... be replaced by a healthy nationalism'.[29] It was agreed that 'while no particular encouragement should be given to such manifestations of tribalism they should be sympathetically handled as and when they arose'.[30] On plantations and agricultural schemes, however, the active organization of tribal associations with elected tribal representatives (as happened in the Rhodesian mines) was felt to be essential.

During this time labour migration within and outside of Tanganyika provided the conditions under which migrants' associations were formed among people from Rungwe. Indeed these associations were central to forging Nyakyusa identity during the colonial period. One of the first 'tribal unions', the Umoja wa Wanyakyusa (Nyakyusa Union), was established among migrants at the Lupa goldfields in 1942 as a welfare organization to 'preserve the good customs and habits of the tribe' (Iliffe, 1979: 332). The Wanyakyusa Association registered in Mbeya in 1954 but claimed to have been operating there since 1942.[31] A Wanyakyusa Union registered in Tanga in 1959 (Askew, 2002). In Mbeya, the association declared its aim was 'to promote tribal welfare, sympathy, understanding and culture'.[32] Membership was restricted to Nyakyusa tribesmen and the association claimed that there were 60 members. Iliffe also reports the establishment in the 1950s of the Mbeya District Original Tribes Association to 'resist control by Nyakyusa immigrants' (1979: 489). In 1957 there is correspondence between branches of a society registered as the Banyakyusa Union with branches in Iringa, Ifunda, Tabora, Dar es Salaam, Dodoma and Mbeya.[33] The Dodoma branch appears to have been the most active.[34] This is probably also the association that was surveyed by J.A.K. Leslie in Dar es Salaam in 1956.

He likened it to the Pare Association since it was made up of a small number of young, educated men. It held elections and aspired to run an employment advice bureau and a repatriation organization. Leslie concludes, 'the association is more of a club of like-minded members of the tribe in Dar es Salaam, which would perhaps have passed away like so many products of a temporary enthusiasm were it not that the necessity for registration of the association periodically reminds them of its existence' (Leslie, 1963: 52). In addition there is a registration from July 1958 of a Banyakyusa Students and Ex-Students Association, which met in Tukuyu.[35]

Tribal associations were established throughout the Nyakyusa labour diaspora in eastern and central Africa, earning the Nyakyusa a reputation as one of the most 'clubable and pushiest tribes in Tanganyika' (Roosegaarde-Bisschop, 1982: 167, in Ellison, 1999: 228). Such associations were encouraged by mine owners as they provided some welfare for their workers. In Northern Rhodesia in 1956 there was an Abanyakyusa United Association based in Nkana, Kitwe. Membership was open to 'all Nyakyusa and kindred Tanganyika tribes' and required a five-shilling entrance fee plus monthly subscriptions. The aims of the society were '(a) to secure the complete unity of all persons of Abanyakyusa and other Tanganyika tribes working in Northern Rhodesia. (b) To protect and promote the interests of Members'.[36] In addition it hoped to provide hospitality to recruits from Tanganyika, relief for the sick, injured or unemployed, funeral expenses and repatriation costs.

In contrast the evidence for Makonde tribal associations during this period is scant despite large-scale labour migration from the Makonde Plateau in the 1920s and 1930s. Askew (2002) reports the existence of the Wamakonde Association of Tanganyika, Tanga Province, which registered in Tanga in 1960, but no further information on its membership or activities is available. An attempt in 1951 to establish the Wamakonde Union among the Makonde of Lindi District was quashed by the British who in this corner of the colony had by this time become suspicious of 'ethnic parochialism' (Liebenow, 1971). The Makonde are, however, frequently mentioned within the lists of ethnic groups who came together to form the southern tribal associations.

In Dar es Salaam the Manyema seem to have been among the leaders in forming tribal associations, even though theirs was an obviously assembled tribal identity. McCurdy (1996) suggests that there were Manyema associations in Tabora, Dar es Salaam and Zanzibar by 1930. In 1939 eighteen 'tribes' of the Manyema formed an umbrella organization, the Umoja wa Wamanyema (also known as the Congo Union

Association), in Dar es Salaam.[37] In the 1930s the association had membership rates and fixed levels of financial support for members who needed help, particularly in the case of burials. In 1941 the Wakusa Society Association made up of 21 Manyema tribes reconstructed a mosque in Dar es Salaam.[38] The Nyamwezi Association (and its offshoot the Sukuma Association), Ngoni Association, Pare Association and Chagga Association were also prominent. In 1944 the Bondei Welfare Association and Digo Association, both with headquarters in Tanga, represented migrants from northeast Tanzania.[39] Their main functions were to resolve disputes between members and help with the cost of burials for members. As in Cameroon some of the strongest unions seem to have been those whose members were from outside the Tanzanian territory – for example the Comorians and the Luo formed Unions in 1946.[40]

Another 1940s phenomenon was the formation of tribal associations that represented federations, bringing together the interests of several smaller groups, particularly those from the south. In 1938 a federation of Luguru groups formed the Ukami Union (Leslie, 1963: 41). In 1946, 15 communities from the south – including Makonde, Yao and Makua from Newala – announced the formation of Umoja Kusini.[41] Later in the same year the Southern Upcountries African Association was formed bringing together 13 groups, many of which were already in Umoja Kusini. Their aim was 'to follow our various tribal rites and custom, and to help each other in time of need and to avoid any troubles which may arise to hinder our progress … We shall always be bound to follow Government Orders, Rules etc. and we are not against government orders … We pray god that the British Government may rule on us for ever.'[42] In 1948 the Younger Southern Aggregation was formed as a specific youth federation.[43] The migrants forming these federations had less success in education and commerce than those who had been in Dar es Salaam longer and in greater numbers. The welfare aspects of the tribal associations representing less well-established groups were correspondingly more important, particularly in relation to burial. However, these federations meant that it was hard for associations to connect to a particular homeplace outside Dar es Salaam.

In the last few years before independence two sources provide a good picture of home associations: the 1954 Societies Ordinance, and J.A.K. Leslie's social survey of Dar es Salaam. According to the Report of the Ndola Conference on Urban Problems in East and Central Africa (1958), 'urban dwellers are kept in touch with affairs in the more distant rural areas through the medium of tribal associations, of which for example there are one hundred or more in Dar es Salaam'.[44] Yet the general sentiment was that the significance of these associations was in decline.

The introduction in 1954 of the Societies Ordinance revised the colonial government's relatively liberal attitude towards associations (Iheme, 2005: 54). In response to rising nationalist sentiments the Ordinance required all associations across Tanganyika to complete a formal registration process. This was carried out in all districts but the final forms were deposited with a central Registrar of Societies in Dar es Salaam, now part of the Ministry of Home Affairs. By the end of 2004 over 13,000 applications had been lodged, of which 708 associations were successfully registered in the first year of operation. Critics of the Societies Ordinance view it as a repressive tool for the control of civil society (Lissu, 2000), and the Registrar certainly had the capacity to refuse associations' registration and to punish with prison terms those who did not comply. However, few applications were actually refused (just one in 1954) and the granting of permission to branches of TANU was under-taken with slightly surreal civility on both sides. The records present only a very limited amount of data, so categorizing them is a subjective exercise. However, they suggest that in 1954, 210 associations were sports or social clubs and 156 were religious groups. There were 74 associations with names relating to an ethnic group. It is clear that some home associations were registered at home and some in Dar es Salaam, so it is difficult to say with confidence how many of these 74 connected migrants to their home area and how many only operated at home. Of the remainder, 66 were connected to dance or music, 61 were affiliated to professions, 40 were general welfare organizations, and 38 were concerned with agriculture.

A more nuanced sense of associational life can be gleaned from the publication of a 1956 social survey of Dar es Salaam undertaken by the government sociologist, J.A.K. Leslie. He positioned urban Tanganyikans in the 1950s within a web of obligations to tribe, area group, kin and strict family as well as to their employer, urban neighbours, social clubs, dance bands and football clubs. He also drew attention to groups of tribes that cooperated because they shared a route to Dar es Salaam. At the apex in terms of significance was the kinship group of cousins, uncles and nephews. Indeed he argued that 'The real bond is not tribe, but kinship.'[45] Area groups (referring to a geographical place or village within a tribal territory) were, he suggested, often a more meaningful scale of belonging than tribe. Indeed for larger groups the tribal scale was of decreasing importance. In arguing that tribes had 'lost much of the loyalty they once inspired' (Leslie, 1963: 37), he perpetuated the erroneous view that tribes had at some point in the past governed an individual's identity.

Leslie devoted considerable attention to tribal associations. His basic narrative was that new small groups of migrants needed associations, but that over time the subsequent generations did not and so the associations were withering away as families took on the jobs for which associations previously had responsibility. Where they still existed they were generally the preserve of elderly first-generation migrants. He argues that there were three reasons why these associations came into existence. First, there was the obligation placed on tribes by government to bury their own dead. This required a network of messengers who passed information around to organize funerals. Second, there was the appeal of the dances, and third there was the value of resolving disputes within the community through tribal elders and thereby avoiding going through the courts. Unlike most other sources Leslie argues that if associations had a welfare role outside funerals it was only in enabling an individual to identify those of their clan to whom they could turn for help (for example in finding work or accommodation or with healthcare). Given the continuing assumption that many urban migrants were glad to escape tribal authority he also points out that there was always a process of individuals actively avoiding registering with the association. By the 1950s he claims that for young people the tribal associations had little to offer and were an economic burden, while for their existing older participants membership primarily offered status. Many associations, he claimed, were mired in scandals over their common funds (1963: 57). Nevertheless the associations remained active in relation to funerals, repatriation of tribal members to rural areas, and payment of fines. They also acted as 'postal distribution centres', with the associations' leaders transmitting letters between town and home. Members donated money for funerals publicly within the group and helped those who were inexperienced to bury their relatives. However, burial was primarily the responsibility of the family, not the association. Association meetings were rare, and it was only at funerals, weddings or other rites that the association members assembled.

Even as the city grew and their influence declined, the associations' leaders still had effective networks across town. These were based on identifying senior individuals who would represent geographical sub-divisions of the homeplace (known as 'area group representatives') through whom announcements could be disseminated across Dar es Salaam. Leslie regarded the area group representatives of the tribal asso-ciations as among the 'most valuable and satisfactory kind' (Leslie, 1963: 46) because they had emerged organically from within the community.

Against the general story of perceived decline there were also examples of thriving associations in Dar es Salaam in 1956. The Pare,

Chagga and Fipa Associations (which included wives) met regularly, spoke in the vernacular and registered a significant proportion of the total population of these groups. The Nyakyusa Association was similar in type but less dynamic than the others (Leslie, 1963: 39, 50–53). These associations had constitutions, written registers and monthly subscriptions. Their members had good jobs, were relatively young and well-educated though small in number. Unlike other associations they had not had to organize funerals, chose not to organize dances or education in tribal lore for their children and did not run a community postal service. Instead they provided 'mutual sympathy and understanding … [because] they are an exclusive group, apart from the bulk of the population' (Leslie, 1963: 50–51).

Unlike the associations in Cameroon there appears to have been little or no involvement in explicit 'development' activities at home. Nevertheless tribal associations were part of a process of 'rural improvement' through the transfer of remittances and people from town to countryside. Some ethnic groups preferred to educate their children in the country rather than the city believing the quality of schooling was better and this, along with the health needs of family members, ensured a steady stream of money from town to country within families. Some people retired to the countryside, which was also effectively a transfer of capital from town to countryside. Whilst all of these transfers are one degree removed from the activities of the associations, they are connected because the associations were one means of preserving the link. In addition to the communities' sizes and values, Leslie noted (1963: 11) that these linkages were shaped by the distance and difficulty of the journey between town and country.

The delegates to the 1958 Ndola Conference on Urban Problems in East and Central Africa concluded that ties between urban and rural areas were to be deliberately encouraged and fostered because they enabled migrant labour to move between town and country more easily. For this reason they advocated active government support for tribal associations alongside urban tribal courts, visits by chiefs and notables from other districts, tribal newspapers and broadcasts as well as liaison officers.[46] However, by the time this report was published in Tanganyika, the role of tribal associations had been swept aside by the rise of TANU and nationalism.

The post-independence era

After independence in 1961 tribal associations disappear from the record for two decades. Joan Vincent claimed that 'immediately prior to independence, most ethnic and voluntary associations seemed to disappear overnight' (1970: 155). The Tanzanian nation-building project explicitly condemned tribal loyalties (or 'factionalism'), and tribal organizations were banned as a consequence. The 1954 ordinance was amended in 1962, widening its scope to give the government the capacity to dissolve any society if the Minister for Home Affairs concluded that it was conducting activities predominantly for a purpose other than lawful trade (Iheme, 2005: 55). Of the 169 applications made to the Registrar of Societies in 1964, for example, 33 (many of which were for ethnic mutual aid or burial associations) were refused. By 1970 there were only 81 applications, of which 6 were refused. President Julius Nyerere sought to undermine politicization of ethnic affiliation by ensuring that 'tribe' was not a platform used by politicians. Chieftaincy was abolished in 1962 as part of the transformation of local government, which aimed to establish elected local councils, and a number of traditional organizations disappeared with it. Many chiefs had by this time a firmly secured economic advantage over other citizens and they were often compensated with civil service posts, so they managed to retain elite positions (Lange et al., 2000: 5). School curricula established both a national and a pan-African sense of history, and above all the near-universal use of the Swahili language muted discussions of ethnic attachment, which effectively became taboo in public discourse. After 1963, associations such as the Mbeya Cultural Society, which had previously used Safwa and Nyakyusa alongside English, were instructed that all meetings should take place in Swahili. As the new Regional Commissioner told the committee, 'the society's committee should … invite TANU representatives to decide its new form of constitution … every society was an agent of the government … If the society followed this principle … then government would view its existence with interest and would regard it as a useful arm in building the nation'.[47] The state effectively regulated and emasculated the association in this way.

After the Arusha Declaration of 1967, when the government's policies took a more radical turn, the state absorbed formal associational life. This was achieved through the expansion of the state machinery into all aspects of economic and social organization, particularly the provision of social services. Trade union autonomy was destroyed in 1964, one-party rule was introduced in 1965, the powers of cooperatives were reduced in 1968 and they were banned in 1976 (although they were reintroduced in 1982). Autonomous organizations such as the Dar es Salaam University Student Organization, Umoja wa Wanawake wa Tanzania (UWT), the Tanzanian Parents' Association, and the national youth organization were all brought under the wing of TANU. While small informal associations may have continued to be important at the grassroots (and particularly urban) scale (Tripp, 1997), the formation of formal organizations was effectively curtailed. Some associations survived (often charitable religious bodies) but even these could fall foul of the state as the examples of the East African Muslim Welfare Society (founded in 1945) and the Ruvuma Development Association showed. The former, an international organization partly funded by the Aga Khan, built schools and mosques in Tanzania and was banned from using the Societies Ordinance in December 1968. The latter (founded in 1960), a high-profile resettlement scheme, was dissolved in 1969 as the state shifted away from popular participation (Jennings, 2002: 517–25). Table 5.1 illustrates the dramatic dip in applications from associations to the Registrar of Societies during the first three decades after independence; Table 5.2 shows that this dip was particularly marked among ethnic and place-based associations.

The paradoxes inherent in the policies of the 1960s came to the fore in the 1970s. On the one hand, government policy encouraged peasant participation, egalitarianism and democracy, while on the other it blocked off avenues for popular engagement and obliged participation to be directed through state organizations instead (Tripp, 1994). As late as 1966, self-help organizations with explicitly ethnic affiliations such as the Unyakyusa Development Committee were operating successfully in the construction of schools,[48] yet officially rhetoric opposed such ethnic loyalties even as it encouraged self-reliance. The state sought to abolish all

Table 5.1 Successful applications to the Registrar of Societies, Tanzania, selected years

Types of association registered	1954	1964	1970	1984	1995	2004
Religious groups	156	16	10	17	70	75
Place-based groups	74	2	2	8	74	166
Sports groups	210	15	30	22	8	2
Business and professional groups	61	14	13	20	63	55
Agricultural groups	38	4	1	3	11	134
Music and art groups	66	21	9	1	0	0
International NGOs	1	1	2	4	16	12
Others/unclassifiable	102	64	5	8	106	219
Total	708	137	72	83	348	663

Note: Over time, societies have been explicitly defined to exclude sports clubs.
Source: Registrar of Societies archive, Dar es Salaam.

Table 5.2 Successful applications from place-based groups to the Registrar of Societies, Tanzania, selected years

Place-based groups	1954	1964	1970	1984	1995	2004
Registered away from 'home'	16	0	1	1	19	19
Registered at 'home'	58	2	1	7	55	147

Source: Registrar of Societies archive, Dar es Salaam

possible forums for opposition and, with this, to bring civil society under its direct control.

From the mid-1970s the state's capacity to provide effective social services declined dramatically. Real wages fell, unemployment rose, and progress in education and healthcare was reversed (Lugalla, 1993). In response many people started to organize themselves in welfare associations. The government's increased tolerance for such autonomous groups reflected both the successful inculcation of a national identity (Kelsall, 2000: 546) and its recognition of the lack of state capacity to deliver services (Kiondo, 1995).

Although formal associations were officially proscribed, people continued to organize around their homeplace. Rungwe migrants in Iringa, Dodoma, Morogoro and Moshi in the 1970s and 1980s formed associations that brought together migrants from the Southern Highlands including Ruvuma, Rukwa, Iringa and Mbeya. In Dar es Salaam, burial associations were formed in different residential areas of the city, such as the Umoja wa Kuzikana wa Nyanda za Juu, established in Keko among Southern Highlands' migrants in the 1970s. So although there is no evidence yet of a Nyakyusa Union or Makonde Association in postcolonial urban Tanzania, people in the domestic diaspora did, however, find ways to meet, support each other and channel support to their home areas, as the early meetings of NDF and RUDET show for Newala and Rungwe.

This opening up of a space in which associations could again operate outside the ruling party was particularly clear from the education sector in the 1980s. Here the government started to encourage local groups to take a role in constructing and running schools: 'In less than ten years (1984–1992), the number of NGO-run schools tripled from 85 to 258' (Lange et al., 2000: 6). This expansion of the NGO sector continued through the 1990s: 'In 1993, there were 224 registered NGOs in Tanzania. Seven years later, in 2000, the number is 8,499' (Lange et al., 2000: 6). A 1993 study found that non-government actors were running 61 per cent of the secondary schools and 87 per cent of the nursery schools (Kiondo, 1993: 160; Ishumi 1995). It would be wrong to think of this expansion as uniformly an expression of local grassroots activity. Many of these NGOs were closely associated with the state and were a means of tapping into new international donor funding channels that set out to support civil society (Mercer, 1999, 2002). Furthermore the protracted debate over the NGO law (see below) illustrates that the politics of associations remained contentious. Yet the basic point still stands: local associations returned to Tanzania in force in the late 1980s and 1990s. But how many, if any, of these were home associations (Table 5.2)?

One of the main forms of these new associations was the District Development Trusts (sometimes called District Education Trusts or District Trust Funds; generically referred to in short as DDTs). According to Lange et al., 'eight hundred and fifty District Development Trusts ... were formed between 1960 and 1991, the most active period being from 1980 onwards' (2000: 9; see also Baroin, 1996; Ishumi, 1995; Kiondo, 1995). DDTs have often been discussed in the context of NGOs yet definitions are imprecise. Legally, DDTs are dealt with separately from NGOs. Any trust must register under the Trustees Incorporation Ordinance (1956) via the Administrator General at the Ministry of Justice and Constitutional Affairs, and the application must also pass through the relevant District Commissioner and the Ministry of Education and Culture.[49] In contrast NGOs apply to the Registrar of Societies, although this is under revision following the NGO Act of 2002 (REPOA, 2007). In practice, however, many of the DDTs included in this research describe themselves as NGOs; some were registered as trusts and some as NGOs under the Societies Ordinance. The records at the Registrar of Societies suggest that many associations that have the term 'Trust' in their name were also registered as societies.

Several authors have likened DDTs to West African home associations (Kiondo, 1993, 1995; Gibbon, 1998, 2001; Kelsall, 2000):

> Tanzanian District Development Trusts closely resemble West African home town associations, in that they involve an alliance between resident district elites, mainly found in local government and private business, and the local elite diaspora – basically professionals, businessmen and politicians in large towns. (Gibbon, 1998)

The most extended discussion of DDTs is based on a 1993 survey undertaken by Andrew Kiondo. He argued that DDTs are interesting because they 'combine the genuine interests of the masses with self-serving elite initiatives and involvement' (Kiondo, 1993: 178). As service providers, he suggested, they achieved more than the state. However, he identified what he described as 'the privatization of local government' (1995: 163). Some trusts had expanded from education into other sectors, to the extent that they were not so much supplementing the state as replacing it. This privatization is not merely economic but also involves the privatization of decision making, which Kiondo argues is limited to a few unaccountable elite individuals. Taking this critique a step further, Gibbon argues that the collapse of the state in the 1980s meant that the middle class could no longer reproduce itself on the basis of educational achievement and bureaucratic competence. Instead it used DDTs to mobilize resources in homeplaces as a means of ensuring the education of its children. The result was a stronger link between the middle classes 'at home' and those in the domestic diaspora; 'The consequence is that the middle class ceases to be reproduced as a socio-economic category on the national plane, but becomes vertically fragmented through a process of "balkanization"' (Gibbon, 1998).

The extent to which DDTs are ethnic associations is a moot point. For Gibbon the middle classes 'mobilize resources (private and public) from ethnic, subethnic and clan sources' (Gibbon, 1998). The officials who undertake the registration of societies maintain that DDTs with explicit tribal names would have their applications rejected, yet government officials also argue that ethnic groups are encouraged if their aim is to protect heritage and promote the cultural values that make a positive contribution to development.[50] DDTs that are organized around a district are acceptable, even if it happens that the district is dominated by a particular ethnic group.[51] Tanzania is divided into 26 regions, each of which is subdivided into a number of districts. There are currently 127 districts, each of which is in turn divided into wards. The correct assumption is that a map of ethnicity in rural Tanzania and a map of rural districts would not overlap perfectly and this enables the language of political geography to hide what is effectively a vehicle through which ethnic patronage operates. If the numbers of trusts given by Lange et al. is correct then it is clear that there are many more trusts than there are districts, and this would certainly be supported by our evidence from Rungwe.

This process has played out differently in the two case study areas. In Newala there is little evidence that NDF is used as a vehicle for ethnic mobilization, even though the majority of members are Makonde. In contrast to Rungwe, the decentralized nature of pre-colonial and colonial political organization of Makonde society on the Makonde Plateau has fostered neither a strongly ethnically homogenous home association in

NDF, nor a series of subethnic offshoots.[52] However, there is evidence that associational life is mirroring the regional blocs that have begun to emerge in national politics recently (Kelsall, 2002). The newest home association connected to Newala is a multi-ethnic pan-southern-districts group called LITANEMA (Lindi Urban and Rural, Tandahimba, Newala, Mtwara Urban and Rural, and Masasi). Echoing those associations that amalgamated southern tribes in the 1930s and 1940s, LITANEMA is an urban welfare association, registered with the Ministry of Home Affairs, which also plans to undertake development work at home and to 'remind government' that the South needs to be developed.[53] There have also been attempts to unite people from the Southern Highlands, such as the unsuccessful launch of the Mbeya Bank. Among the Rungwe domestic diaspora, however, it has been the smaller associations with a degree of ethnic or subethnic homogeneity that have flourished. With the exception of the Banyakyusa Cultural Trust Fund, and in contrast to the migrants' associations that existed during the colonial era, none of the contemporary home associations describes itself as a Nyakyusa association. Yet all of them depend on the domestic diaspora identifying with a particular 'homeland', however small, and its people. In fact the smaller home associations have proved more popular than RUDET because contributors in the domestic diaspora want to know that their money is going to benefit their close kin at home rather than being spent in another part of the district. The various Rungwe associations bring together members of clans, villages, and wards; people from areas associated with particular ancestry, *abanyafyale* or groups of *abanyafyale*; as well as the diaspora from contemporary administrative divisions and parliamentary constituencies. The fact that the Nyakyusa diaspora has fractured into many smaller groups suggests the continued salience of pre-colonial and colonial forms of identification, and that such identities continue to have meaning for people. In several cases, the association chairman claimed to be descended from the lineage of an *umalafyale*, implicitly claiming the authority of traditional leadership.

Yet in other parts of Tanzania ethnic mobilization is causing more concern. Writing about the northern highlands, Kelsall observes:

> The search for new sources of wealth is manifested in struggles for control of local non-state institutions which have comparatively large resources. Such struggles mobilize the support of local forces and are commonly couched in an ethnic or religious idiom ... [I]nstead of an elite co-opted to the secular, modernizing ideology of the centre, they are seen increasingly as articulations of an invigorated ethnic identity. (2000: 550)

Ethnic competition is regarded by most Tanzanians as dangerous, and both state and media are quick to condemn tribalism and move effectively to shun those whose public comments suggest they are partisan. It would be wrong to overstate the risk posed by trusts and home associations to the nation. Nevertheless, by providing a space through which local and national politics can be linked through a form of ethnic patronage these associations have allowed one of the features that was key to Tanzania's success (the absence of national leaders who relied on a strong local client base) to begin to be removed.

Conclusions

Twenty-first-century home associations are modelled on a melange of different pre-colonial, colonial and postcolonial templates. Their activities, structures and membership are often also a response to the national policies of the colonial and postcolonial state in Africa. They are hybrids, both in the sense that they are a mix of other forms of associations and in that they meld the policies of governments with the actions of multiple individuals with different interests. Home associations have always provided mutual welfare for members, sought cultural preservation and provided a means of managing labour, whether in the colonial plantations, mines and domestic cities, or in the cities of the global labour market. In the last two or three decades they have started explicitly to deliver the kind of social programmes that are generally described as 'development'. This has been a response to the limits of state-led and donor-led projects and to the opportunities provided by relative prosperity among some community members, whose motivations for involvement vary widely. In order to become development organizations the home associations have appropriated the practices of community development in rural Anglophone Africa, which date back to the early 1950s and rhetorically into the pre-colonial period. The recent addition of this developmental remit to the work of home associations follows the expansion of the idea of 'development' to a point where it is now all-pervasive, if not quite hegemonic, among African societies (Ferguson, 1990; Crush, 1995; Escobar, 1995).

In contrast to Bali and Manyu in Cameroon, the historical perspective in Tanzania reveals different histories and geographies of home associations. There is a patchier record of associational life in the two homeplaces, particularly in Newala, even though both have long been sites of out-migration. In the Tanzanian case there is also a significant rupture in associational life during the 1960s and 1970s, but even then there was some covert continuity. The history of associations recounted here shows that home associations are involved in a dynamic process of mixing association templates drawn from different sectors of society, and mutating practices of organization, regulation and activities. Most recently there has been a proliferation of associations that appear to be a mixture of DDT and NGO.

Both the Newala and Rungwe home associations rely on donations and loans from elite individuals, often the urban leaders of the associations, who are well-established in government or business. However, there is a major difference in Tanzania since DDTs receive some funding from local government taxation. This does not necessarily shore up their position: NDF, for example, is less secure financially because it relies on a small domestic diaspora and a cess on a particularly unpredictable crop (cashew). In contrast the Bali and Manyu associations are more secure since they have a much broader membership in the domestic diaspora, which has enabled more successful fundraising. In all cases, but especially in Tanzania, there is a sense among leaders that these associations are missing many potential members in the city.

Again in contrast with the Cameroon cases, there were no international elements to the Tanzanian home associations. When Tanzanians associate in the UK the 'home' that brings them together is the nation, whereas when Cameroonians associate in the UK the 'home' that brings them together is a subnational space such as Manyu Division or Bali Nyong'a Fondom. Tanzanian groups in Britain might bring together a group of Tanzanians living in Slough or Reading, so people do not travel too far and therefore reflect more closely the geography of Africans in Britain (Daley, 1998). However, there are separate associations for people from the Isles, such as the Zanzibar Welfare Association, based in east London. In Part Three we look at the work of these associations in more detail.

Notes

1. Interview, NDF Vice Chairman, Dar es Salaam, July 2005.
2. 3 August 1920, File AB385, TNA, Dar es Salaam.
3. 1925, '1924 Report of the Provincial Commissioner for Dar es Salaam District', TNA, Dar es Salaam.
4. 12 May 1922, '1921 Report of the Provincial Commissioner for Dar es Salaam District', TNA, Dar es Salaam. The census included 89,000 Wazaramo but also 2,200 Wanyakyusa from Rungwe.
5. 1924, '1923 Report of the Provincial Commissioner for Dar es Salaam District', TNA, Dar es Salaam.
6. 12 May 1922, '1921 Report of the Provincial Commissioner for Dar es Salaam

District', TNA, Dar es Salaam.

7. 12 May 1922, '1921 Report of the Provincial Commissioner for Dar es Salaam District', TNA, Dar es Salaam.

8. 1925, '1924 Report of the Provincial Commissioner for Dar es Salaam District', TNA, Dar es Salaam.

9. 1959, 'Detribalization', M.J.B. Molohan, Senior Provincial Commissioner, TNA, Dar es Salaam.

10. 6 January 1927, Captain H. MacAllen, '1926 Rungwe District Annual Report', TNA, Dar es Salaam.

11. The explicit and arbitrary character of this process is well captured in R.A. Thompson's Rungwe District Annual Report for 1925 in which the people of Waseria (Selya) are given the choice of paying tax either via the Banyakyusa treasury or via Mkukwe. They opted for the latter though the administrator felt them to be more closely associated with the former. Within a year they were requesting the opportunity to change their minds – a request that was refused. Yet in 1935 the British amalgamated both groups into a single Nyakyusa tribal group (Ellison, 1999).

12. Brennan (2002) argues for an earlier date, 1926 or 1927.

13. *Tanganyika Standard*, 21 October 1930, File 61/385/Vol. 2, TNA, Dar es Salaam.

14. *Tanganyika Standard*, 20 October 1930, File 61/385/Vol. 2, TNA, Dar es Salaam.

15. 'Manyema' is a term used since the mid-nineteenth century to describe people from the northeast Congo basin. It is an assimilative term that is used as an ethnic label to describe an amalgam of different people who gathered in the settlement of Ujiji. For more on the history of the Manyema diaspora and associational life see McCurdy (1996).

16. 1930 report for Dar es Salaam District, TNA, Dar es Salaam.

17. 3 August 1939, File 61/385/Vol. 2, TNA, Dar es Salaam.

18. 17 November 1938, Provincial Commissioner (A.V. Hartnoll) to African Association, File 61/385/Vol. 2, TNA, Dar es Salaam.

19. 6 January 1940, Provincial Commissioner's Minute (Longland), File 61/385/Vol. 2, TNA, Dar es Salaam.

20. July 1938, File V26027, The Wazaramo Union, TNA, Dar es Salaam. J.A.K. Leslie (1963: 51, 52 & 48) gives the dates for the other associations except for the Congo Union, which is taken from McCurdy (1996).

21. 1938, Acting Provincial Commissioner to Chief Secretary, File V26027, The Wazaramo Union, TNA, Dar es Salaam.

22. 1938, Acting Provincial Commissioner to Chief Secretary, File V26027, The Wazaramo Union, TNA, Dar es Salaam.

23. 6 June 1948, File 26027, TNA, Dar es Salaam.

24. President Wazaramo Union, 31 July 1946, File V26027, The Wazaramo Union, TNA, Dar es Salaam.

25. Hon. Gen. Sec. Wazaramo Union to the Administrative Officer Pugu, 29 June 1946 and 31 July 1946, File V26027, The Wazaramo Union, TNA, Dar es Salaam.

26. 29 May 1948, Police report on dispute between treasurer and president of the Zaramo Union, File 26027, TNA, Dar es Salaam.

27. 2 April 1948, Memorandum on detribalization, File 37520, Detribalization, TNA, Dar es Salaam.

28. 2 April 1948, Memorandum on detribalization, File 37520, Detribalization, TNA, Dar es Salaam.
29. 24 April 1948, Secretary for African Affairs (Mr Cheyne), Memorandum on detribalization, File 37520, Detribalization, TNA, Dar es Salaam.
30. 15 December 1948, File 38638, Effect of Industrialization on Africans, TNA, Dar es Salaam.
31. 30th June 1954, Registration Form. File 327/a/6/34/ Vol. II, TNA, Dar es Salaam.
32. Ibid.
33. 23 April 1957, Secretary and President of the Banyakyusa Union (Iringa) to Rungwe African District Council, Tukuyu A6/16, TNA, Dar es Salaam.
34. 18 March 1959, Mr Mwasumbi was President and Mr Mwakasepe Vice-President of the Dodoma Branch, File A6/8/vols 1 and 2, TNA, Dar es Salaam.
35. 4 July 1958, File 18/A6/16 Misc. clubs and Associations, TNA, Dar es Salaam.
36. 4 April 1956, File A6/16 Misc. clubs and Associations, TNA, Dar es Salaam .
37. 23 March 1945, File 3/32/4, TNA, Dar es Salaam.
38. 26 August 1941, Wakusa Society (Fikirini Msanga) to Hon. Chief Secretary, File 61/275(1), The Wakusa Society, TNA, Dar es Salaam.
39. 14 July 1944, File 782, TNA, Dar es Salaam.
40. 15 February 1946, Young Comorian Association, 21 August 1946, Luo Union File 540/3/32, TNA, Dar es Salaam.
41. 30 April 1946, Umoja Kusini to District Commissioner, File 540/3/32, TNA, Dar es Salaam.
42. 10 September 1946, Amrani Masudi, President, File 3/32/4, TNA, Dar es Salaam .
43. 30 March 1948, File 3/32/4, TNA, Dar es Salaam .
44. 1958, Ndola Conference report, p.70, File 10/49/02, TNA, Dar es Salaam.
45. 5 June 1958, File 183/10/49/02, TNA, Dar es Salaam.
46. 1958, Ndola Conference report p.72, File 10/49/02, TNA, Dar es Salaam .
47. 28 September 1963, Regional Commissioner (Waziri Juma) to Mbeya Cultural Society, File 181/MB/CS, TNA, Dar es Salaam .
48. File 7/101/RDI/16, TNA, Dar es Salaam .
49. Director NGO Division, Vice President's Office, Dar es Salaam, 8 September 2005; and Legal Officer, Ministry of Home Affairs, Dar es Salaam, 6 September 2005.
50. These comments were made during the launch of the Nyakyusa Cultural Festival at the Village Museum in Dar es Salaam, 1999 (former Commissioner of Culture, Dar es Salaam, August 2005); also Legal Officer, Ministry of Home Affairs, Dar es Salaam, September 2005.
51. Interviews, Director NGO Division, Vice President's Office, Dar es Salaam, September 2005; and Legal Officer, Ministry of Home Affairs, Dar es Salaam, September 2005.
52. The fact that the majority of members (and leaders) are Makonde helps cohesion even though there may be no 'ethnic mobilization' as such. While the nature of flat societies is such that it may seem to work against broad-scale mobilization, it can (under the right circumstances) promote the opposite as small groups can come together at any level around a common project.
53. LITANEMA officer, Dar es Salaam, September 2005.

PART THREE

The developmental and political work of home associations

....

6 WELFARE AND SOCIAL SUPPORT IN THE DIASPORA

··

In times of problems we can help each other, in times of joy we can celebrate together … first of all you turn to your family people, to your tribespeople, they are the people who can support you financially.[1]

This chapter looks at the primary function of home associations, which is to look after the welfare of members. Welfare is broadly defined here to include sociality; moral and material support at key life stages or times of distress; financial services; and help with housing and employment. These activities are all considered to be forms of welfare because they are concerned with providing social support for people away from their homes in unfamiliar and sometimes uncongenial surroundings. The chapter weaves discussion of the welfare work that the associations do in Cameroon, Tanzania and the UK together in the analysis because home associations provide broadly similar services to diasporas wherever they are. However, there are some differences in the welfare needs of domestic and international diasporas, which are determined by the different contexts in African and Western countries. The chapter considers how home associations' services are regulated and maintained as well as instances where they are limited or fail, and it addresses the question of whether their welfare provision brings deepening parochialism or promotes integration.

Three arguments are made. First, the most important function of home associations remains the provision of welfare to migrants, or at least to members and their close relatives. Second, however, drawing a distinction between welfare and development may be a false dichotomy because welfare provision can also be seen as 'developmental' through its delivery of social benefits. Not only is looking after the people of the place strategic in the long-term development of the place, but improving the services and ceremonies associated with key rites of passage is also development in itself. And third, welfare is a means through which a 'progressive sense of place' (Massey, 1993) can emerge because, as with development, place is the locus for mobilizing the mutual support described. The effective delivery of welfare is part of the practice of moral conviviality insofar as it is about establishing fair rules of living together and helping one another. Whilst this may entail establishing the boundaries of obligation, the overall tenor of the exercise is quite different from the politics of belonging since it is about cooperation and collaboration.

Sociality

Welfare provision by home associations emerges from and is intimately linked to their role as sites of sociality. Indeed, discussions with members about the history of their associations in both the domestic and the international diaspora indicated that informal socializing commonly preceded formalized association. The founder members met socially in domestic cities or overseas, often already knowing each other directly or indirectly from home, school, university or family connections, and such gatherings led to the inception of the home association. The associations continue to provide a space where people sharing a common loyalty to a particular place can meet, relax and talk in their vernacular, get news of their homeplace and of people from it, and enjoy food and music from home.

Individual migrants' desire for this sociality is driven by various factors. In the domestic diaspora, people generally spoke of the alienating and potentially threatening environment in which they found themselves. African cities, like all cities, can be disorientating for new arrivals; the familiar mores and rules of home do not necessarily apply. Predatory and sometimes hostile urban authorities and bureaucracies have to be faced, and migrants often find themselves in competition with other migrants and locals for jobs, housing and other resources. In this setting, people find comfort and security mixing with others from home who face similar problems. As one man in Dar es Salaam explained:

> The Makonde come here to find a better life and, when they are here, they come together. It feels okay being together with fellow Makonde, so he [the migrant] tries to find them. He hopes he won't be left alone if there is another Makonde there.[2]

Such needs are evident in the international diaspora, too. One Cameroonian woman said that she attended home association meetings when she first came to the UK as a student because 'it was important to know that there are people there and that they care for you'.[3] Another said: '… it is important to belong to a group for a sense of encouragement. You know that you have people behind you. And also if you get problems you know where you can turn.'[4] Some interviewees saw such sociality as especially pressing in the UK, to avoid social isolation in a context where people from home may be thin on the ground and where new arrivals may need considerable 'mentoring'. Again, this heightened need is bound up with the idea of mutual support, with an ethos of '[h]elp me, then I will help you; be close to me, then I will be close to you'.[5]

For Africans in the UK there is the added strain of coping with racialized labour markets and unfamiliar and sometimes hostile social contexts (Mohan and Zack-Williams, 2002), while simultaneously dealing with the expectations of those at home. Members of home associations were often ambivalent and sometimes contradictory about their diaspora identity in Britain. Depending on their experience, some felt a provisional or grudging acceptance of their position, while others saw the UK as a 'second home'. So for example one Cameroonian man explained, 'I feel British because I trained and settled here throughout my active life. My children were mostly born here and I want them to feel British and enjoy all the opportunities that Britishness provides.'[6] On the other hand, this reflection by a Cameroonian woman was also very common: 'I live here, I'm naturalized here, but I belong to Africa. Because with all fairness I can't be accepted here as British.'[7] In this context home associations are able to play a small part in making the experience of being in the diaspora easier, as the following exchange with a Cameroonian couple in London shows:

> Researcher: Do people feel excluded from British society, is that why it's important to be a home association member?
>
> Male interviewee: Yes, to a certain extent. That's why you want to join, because you know these are my people, and you feel you belong.
>
> Female interviewee: I couldn't have talked to you like this 15 years ago – I myself have gained in confidence over time being here – but there are times you feel you don't really belong. Like when I go to the pub with my work colleagues and they are spending money on drink just like that! And I kind of have to participate but I'm thinking, they don't have to send money home to their families. They just have all this money to spend on themselves. It's very different. How many Africans do you see in British pubs? Okay there are some Cameroonian pubs in east London and we go there, but it's different to going to British ones. There are financial constraints. We don't belong in that aspect of British society. We go to

Cameroonian pubs, and to our meetings, and we feel safe and secure there.[8]

Similarly, a young Cameroonian who worked long hours as a trainee doctor described membership of his home assocation as central to his emotional well-being. Ejagham South UK, a Manyu subethnic association, was somewhere to escape to, where he could be among people from home and unwind from the stresses of everyday life:

> If I have to be useful here, I have to imbibe some Britishness. I've been trying to do that in my two years here, but not at the expense of my Cameroonian identity – I don't feel it detracts from that. I guard my Cameroonian roots here jealously. When I was doing my PLAB [the UK General Medical Council's Professional and Linguistic Assessments Board test for medical graduates from overseas] I associated mainly with Cameroonians. I spoke in Pidgin and could open up with them. The shock after that was enormous: I had to fine-tune my accent, body language, etc. I had sleepless nights … I just felt that it was important to join something so that if I had a problem, I wasn't living in isolation; and I don't identify with the British. What if, God forbid, I drop dead – how would my corpse get home? The [Cameroonian] embassy is not very good in this respect. I was not impressed with the reception I got there when I had to get a form: I had expected it to be like going home but I was disillusioned … Personally I see ESUK as an opportunity to meet people from the same area and offload. I tend to work twelve hours some days and want to share my innermost thoughts, to be myself … I need somewhere I can go once in a while and talk about home.[9]

In some cases the need to escape means getting away from their own families, if only temporarily. Members of the Bali Women's Association in London were asked by their president to bring their families to a social event but some were reluctant, arguing that they would not be able to relax if their children and husbands were with them.[10] Another informant saw his home association literally as a space of refuge, claiming that '[i]f you come to England from Africa, you're a refugee unless you're on a temporary business trip or a diplomat'.[11] He argued that MECA-Birmingham, of which he was a founder, should register itself as a 'refugee community organization' – legally recognized and able to apply for support from government and NGOs. This view was rooted in an extreme personal experience as he had once been a destitute asylum seeker. But it serves to illustrate that welfare concerns are probably more diverse among Africans in the UK than in their home countries, reflecting very different migration histories.

Structures for mutual support

Social meetings among people with common experiences and backgrounds may seem unremarkable but, as the quotations indicate, they are strongly bound up with a moral sense of mutual support at key life stages or at times of crisis – in particular when there is a newborn, a wedding, a burial or a death celebration and when people need money quickly for healthcare or education. This mutual support can translate into material benefits to those affected although these are usually relatively more significant in Africa than in the international diaspora.

In the context of the case studies, such benefits were in Africa most often delivered through the smallest units of home association identified. In Cameroon this generally meant *nda kums* for Bali and family groups for Manyu. However, other levels of association were often also involved to varying degrees. Subgroups of home associations may deliver specific welfare benefits: for example women's groups or people organized into *njangi* (rotating credit groups). In Tanzania there is a strong tradition of 'burial societies', which may be home-based (at whatever level: village, ward, district, region, clan or ethnic group), for example for Nyakyusa living in a particular neighbourhood of Dar es Salaam. Alternatively they are sometimes organized along other lines such as among colleagues at a workplace. While they are generally not formally registered, they do have the usual associational trappings such as a constitution, financial records, a committee and monthly meetings. As with other home associations, each member contributes monthly into a standing fund, which is used to provide a fixed benefit on bereavement or sickness. Burial societies may also provide support to their members for weddings and school fees. However, some low-income members of burial societies interviewed in Dar es Salaam still identified their extended family in the city as their main source of support – just as they did in J.A.K. Leslie's survey some fifty years ago (Leslie, 1963). Unlike associational support, such help was not fixed in scope or amount and could be used to help grow a business as well as in times of crisis. Others in Dar es Salaam spoke of wider informal networks for the repatriation of corpses and burial support, encompassing family, people from home, friends and colleagues.

Home associations, then, are not the only bodies providing welfare. African cities are usually rich in associations delivering various services in the absence of adequate public sector provision (Tostensen et al., 2001). Migrants may therefore choose to rely more on other, urban-based support systems such as their immediate family, work, trade or neighbourhood associations, church or mosque, even if they maintain their

Table 6.1 Membership of home associations (survey data, percentages)

	Bali residents	Manyu residents	Newala residents	Rungwe residents
Member of an association	58	37	21	9
Member of BANDECA/MECA/ RUDET/NDF	38	2	6	0
	Bali domestic diaspora	Manyu domestic diaspora	Newala domestic diaspora	Rungwe domestic diaspora
Member of an association	71	66	13	13
Member of BANDECA/MECA/ RUDET/NDF	62	14	5	1

Note: 2,240 people were asked (in English, Pidgin English or Swahili), first, if they were a member of an association; and, second, if they were a member of the named home association identified in the relevant case study.

home association membership. The leadership of MECA-Yaoundé estimated that only around one third of Manyu people in the city are members; in Douala, the MECA president estimated less than one fifth.[12] This was a common problem across the home associations (Table 6.1).

International diasporas seem to exercise even greater choice in their associational lives and hence where they derive welfare support; and there are those in the UK who may be so financially secure that they do not need the support of any group. The predominant level of association among Cameroonians is more fluid than in the home country, depending on both context (for example the size of the relevant diaspora population in the British city or town in question) and individual preference, while Tanzanians tend to associate more informally at a national level of identity. Some in the UK identified churches, particularly black-majority churches, as a strong and growing site of welfare among the African diaspora. For example, one older Manyu elite in London had found support in a black-majority Pentecostal church following his divorce.[13] Another had recently started attending a 'healing ministry'.[14] At the 2007 African Diaspora and Development Day (AD3) in London run by the pan-African diaspora group AFFORD, those trying to promote development at home asked what they could learn from churches in both Africa and the UK.[15] In contrast in a similar forum, concern was expressed that social support fostered within black-majority churches sometimes replaces engagement with home.[16] One interviewee argued that this was a generational shift, observable particularly among African students in London.[17] However, such churches have a longer history than this claim would suggest (Harris, 2006). Furthermore, the distinction between home associations and church activity is not always clear: black-majority churches sometimes have a home affinity at some level, usually ethnic or national. A number of Tanzanian Christian interviewees in the UK, for example, were or had been members of the Swahili Congregation at St Anne's Lutheran Church in London.[18]

Death and burial

Broader contemporary changes in customs around death including mortuaries, burial at home, funerals, commemoration of the deceased and the treatment of widows are discussed in Chapter 7 in terms of attempts by the diaspora to 'modernize' practices at home. Here, however, we are concerned with the social and economic elements in the diaspora. The repatriation of bodies of migrants who die in the city and support to the bereaved have been and remain the primary function of most home associations in sub-Saharan Africa, and the case studies mostly supported this.

In Cameroon and among Cameroonians in the UK, such practices are based on a generally strong desire to be buried at home even if people do not intend to retire there. Feelings in Tanzania seem more mixed: well-established migrants in Dar es Salaam and other cities are sometimes less concerned to be buried at home. As one Newala woman in Mtwara with a long career in the diaspora asked, '[I]n Newala, who will cry for me?'[19] Interviews in Tukuyu also bore out this anxiety. Those living at home said that they buried those whose corpses came home in the correct way, but if they did not know the person it was a more empty process of going through the motions. Whilst they emphasized that they would show respect to any corpse, they put more effort into the burial if it was someone who had regularly come home and particularly if he or she had contributed to development at home. Some Tanzanians in the UK were also content to be buried in Dar es Salaam rather than in their home areas. Contrary to some claims made by Tanzanian informants, such wishes did not necessarily fall along Muslim–Christian lines, although the Islamic imperative for burial to take place as quickly as possible after death was evident. Rather, it was a complex, personal calculation based on the length of residence away from home, the presence (or not) of family members at home to receive the body, personal preference and the means available. However, even if the burial was in the city rather than back in the place of origin there were still considerable costs and so there was still an incentive to participate in burial societies.

Typically, the benefits given to home association members on the death of one of their family members are prescribed in the constitution or rules. The money provided is intended to pay or contribute to the costs of repatriating the body to the home village and the funeral there, or to pay for funeral costs in the city. In Cameroon, a prescribed lump sum (in most cases measured in tens of thousands of CFA francs, though it can be more) is provided out of the home association's 'trouble fund', which is maintained by monthly contributions from members. Similar procedures apply in burial societies in Tanzania: a set contribution from the standing fund is paid plus whatever is collected on the day. Home associations in Cameroon usually make a distinction in benefits according to the relationship of the deceased to the member receiving them, so there is a 'first-class death' (usually a spouse, child or parent); a 'second-class death' (usually a sibling, uncle, aunt or grandparent); and sometimes even a 'third-class death' (a more distant relative). If it is a member him/herself who dies, the benefit goes to the next of kin. This benefit is supplemented by an additional sum provided ad hoc from contributions by members. The latter sum is therefore variable: a set amount per member; or per member attending the vigil, service or other rites prior to repatriation or burial; or a purely voluntary contribution of any amount.

The situation is different in the international diaspora. The costs of repatriating the body of someone who dies in the UK and the formalities involved are greater, but home associations generally still manage to provide some level of support to their members. Again this usually includes prescribed and ad hoc elements. Tanzanians in the UK, with their informal networks generally formed at the national level of identity, seem particularly effective in bringing forward people to console the bereaved and make financial contributions, even when the deceased is not known to them personally. Again, a strong moral sense of reciprocation is at work: as one Tanzanian said, 'death here, it is everyone's fear, and if you don't contribute today, people won't contribute for you tomorrow'.[20] An important consequence is that the contributions raised through such systems can depend considerably on the profile and popularity of the deceased: those who were active in their diasporic communities will, on their death, attract more contributions than those who were less engaged.[21] For example the 'disaster fund' of the Tanzanian Association of Seventh Day Adventists in the UK collects monthly contributions of

£10, and the association is able to donate between £100 and £300 in the event that a member loses a spouse, child or parent, but additional collections for popular people have raised up to £5,000.[22] One association has been formed among Tanzanians in the UK partly to overcome such unpredictability, paying funeral costs for 'first class'-type deaths only.[23] In many cases, however, the financial contribution made by home associations cannot cover the costs of repatriation, which remain fundamentally the responsibility of kin and sometimes close friends. The support from the association is then a gesture of solidarity and a material demonstration of sympathy for the bereaved, rather than a means of covering the full burial costs.

In both the domestic and international diasporas, participation in rites and collection of contributions depend on rapid dissemination of news of a death. Home associations or other home-based networks are key to this, contacting their members in person, by mobile phone (voice or text message, sometimes using 'cascade' methods) or by putting an announcement on local radio. At international level, particularly, internet discussion groups commonly demonstrate a high level of solidarity and solemnity when it comes to death announcements and postings in reaction to them.

Support during other key life stages and sickness

Home associations also provide support to members at times of sickness and other key life stages. In the domestic diaspora, on the birth of a child a member is given benefits in the form of cash and sometimes soap; in the international diaspora, money and/or another appropriate gift, such as a pushchair, may be given. Cameroonians commonly hold 'born house', a set time when the new parents welcome all-comers to their home and such contributions may be made. Home associations may also help prepare people in the diaspora for initiation, circumcision or other ceremonies, usually at home, particularly through teaching younger members how to do traditional dances. This is a long-standing role for home associations in parts of Africa (de Jong, 1997). Marriage is another rite of passage in which home associations may be involved, giving cash and/or gifts to the member(s) concerned and with other members attending the wedding or associated celebration. In Dar es Salaam, people from a particular homeplace or clan often come together to provide such support, not necessarily through a formally constituted association even though the trappings of formality, such as posts of Chair and Secretary, are usually evident (Sherrington, 2007). As one Rungwe elite tellingly noted about such get-togethers, 'it's kind of informal, but expected'.[24] In the UK too, Tanzanians use their informal social networks to set up wedding organizing committees in much the same way. One such committee was set up in Slough among a small group of extended kin and friends who undertook to raise £1,500 for a member's wedding, which was to be held in Dar es Salaam. During a meeting at the house of the groom's brother, the group decided that each single member would contribute £100, while couples would contribute £150. In addition each member would collect small contributions from their networks among other Tanzanians, many of whom would not know the groom personally but could nevertheless be relied upon to contribute towards the wedding of a fellow Tanzanian.

Clearly, then, home associations have the capacity to provide welfare, in all its forms, to members throughout their lives. This is the main means through which the rhetoric of cooperation and collaboration so often found in home association constitutions is manifested, but welfare provision is not just a social nicety between people who know each other. It is a means by which a sense of conviviality is rehearsed and reinforced through the affirmation of social ties among people sharing an affinity to a homeplace. Literally from cradle to grave, members are embedded and acculturated in their home community through welfare structures, imbued with an idea of 'home' even if they were not born there but raised in the city or abroad. This is perhaps particularly true for some migrants who came to the UK relatively young, or for the second generation, with home associations providing a way of becoming more acculturated to the language, dress, dances and mores of 'home' from a level of relative ignorance and inexperience.[25] Such practices are a key means through which a 'progressive sense of place' (Massey, 1993) emerges.

Financial services

The provision of financial services is another common role for home associations, particularly in the domestic diaspora. Structures such as credit unions and ROSCAs (rotating savings and credit associations) have a long history in the associational landscape of Africa. They are commonly found in home associations, either as a service offered from within their own structures, or more informally among a subset of members. Examples include ROSCAs, exemplified by *njangi* in Cameroon, or *ntchinyingdab* for the more wealthy (from Bali); savings banks; and thrift-and-loan schemes. These structures should also be seen as forms of welfare. Given the poorly developed financial services sector in much of sub-Saharan Africa, and the difficulties of accessing it for those on low or irregular incomes, these structures provide their members with services unavailable elsewhere, enabling them to save, borrow or just manage their finances more efficiently for social needs. These forms of saving are used for various kinds of expenditure including house maintenance and construction, school fees and other costs associated with education, and emergency expenditure such as medical bills.

Attempts to connect these trouble funds to formal financial products within Africa have generally been unsuccessful. For example, an attempt by MECA-Douala to introduce a commercial insurance scheme to cover funeral costs met with resistance partly because of the high premiums charged by the insurance company in question and, more generally, because it seemed that people would rather wait for a death to occur, and then pay.[26] Explanations for such resistance can perhaps be found in the way that home association financial services operate. As dynamic, collective pools of money from which benefits are frequently drawn, trouble funds depend largely on contributions made around the time of crisis rather than comprising a long-term, individualized form of saving or investment. Another issue is trust: home association collections, made during meetings, are highly transparent and conducted by people known to participants. Cameroon in particular has a painful recent history of the government plundering banks in which it owns stakes. As far as savings groups such as *njangi* are concerned, members are self-selecting so they tend to be people of similar financial capability and the amount of monthly contributions varies accordingly. These reasons may be why there is little enthusiasm among domestic diasporas for moving to privatized systems of insurance or saving with a faceless bank or other institution.

However, there are sometimes problems with home association services. Misappropriation by people in positions of trust is possible. Temptation may be particularly high when contributions outweigh withdrawals and a substantial surplus is built up. Such a situation may also prompt debates within the home association over whether the money should be used for other purposes, such as development. One informant in Dar es Salaam cited his experience with a burial society that ran into problems because no one died for six months, causing a divisive dispute over whether the contributions accumulated should be diverted to other purposes.[27]

Even in the British context, such services may be important. Banks are sometimes chary of giving accounts (at least accounts with full privileges) and loans to new arrivals from abroad. One Cameroonian who had not been allowed to work legally in the UK for some years after completing tertiary studies there said that the *njangi* he joined in London provided him with an important means of saving.[28] Examples of formalized financial services are more commonly found in the international diaspora than in the home country, probably because of the better-developed financial services sectors in host countries, higher and more regular incomes among members, and a wider culture of formal insurance in the West. For example BCA-USA has done a deal with an insurance company to provide cover for the cost of repatriating a corpse to Cameroon (Jua, 2005). They were able to negotiate this policy because they form a large lobby, although the market for this policy presumably extends well beyond the group concerned. Individual members of home associations may also choose to take out personal insurance for having themselves buried back in Africa.[29] A further example of formalization involving the international diaspora is the establishment by the Tanzanian bank CRDB of the 'Tanzanite' bank account, into which a family member can make deposits in the UK and from which nominated family members can make withdrawals through the bank's branches in Tanzania: this is not only cheaper than money transfer, but safer.

Housing, jobs and urban life

There is a long-standing debate in the literature about the extent to which home associations help integrate new arrivals into the urban or foreign environment. Some claim that home associations are an important means of delivering such assistance while others (e.g. O'Connor, 1983) challenge this, arguing that migrants only get involved in home associations once they are established in town, if at all. The latter view seems convincing. There is little evidence of home associations helping migrants to secure housing or jobs in either the domestic or the international diaspora. In contrast to the many discussions about death contributions and benefits at meetings, little if anything was heard about housing or jobs. Only one interviewee claimed that new arrivals were actively helped with accommodation through a home association.[30] Rather, it is family or friends already known from home who put up new migrants for the first few weeks or months after they arrive. One leader of a diaspora group described frequent calls from Heathrow airport where new arrivals from Cameroon had arrived with just his name and telephone number as a point of contact. The obligation to go and pick the newcomers up was clearly perceived as an unreasonable burden, but he still fulfilled it. It was often through the family and friends with whom they first lodged that interviewees came to be involved in home associations. In other instances they met fellow nationals through study, work or church and became drawn into diaspora networks that way. The primacy of kin is again evident: migrants' primary responsibility towards their families at home (usually fulfilled through sending remittances) is mirrored in the support that they get from family members when they first arrive in an African city or the UK.

But contradictory evidence about the role associations play in supporting new migrants may actually reflect changing circumstances in both African cities and the international diaspora. For much of sub-Saharan Africa, Potts (2000, 2005) claims that material conditions in cities are deteriorating: there are fewer formal-sector jobs, falling real urban incomes, increasing urban poverty, and declining urban welfare provision by the state. In such an environment, she argues, the increased hardship of urban life causes new migrants to return to their rural homes sooner if they are unsuccessful. Established urban migrants can no longer offer the same assistance with jobs and housing that they could in the past. New migrants must either quickly become financially self-reliant, or go home.

In the international context, too, circumstances seem to have shifted. The earlier generations of African migrants from Cameroon and Tanzania who established home associations in the UK in the 1960s were fewer in number and usually benefited from support from their home governments, particularly in the form of scholarships. They comprised a smaller group and were materially more secure. Established migrants in the UK were therefore in a better position to know and help new arrivals who were identified through official lists at the Cameroonian Embassy or Tanzanian High Commission. With deepening economic crisis in Africa, however, subsequent migrants used other sources of support. And with the decline in scholarships, the Cameroonian Embassy (now a High Commission) lost its role as a nucleus for association. Relationships between established diaspora groups and new arrivals also reflect differences in class and generation. For example, established migrants may prefer to distance themselves from new migrants from home with whom they feel they have little in common – and this may be another reason why the most comfortably off migrants avoid home associations. Younger people also are rarely active in home associations, which strike them as 'parents' associations', which can be 'oppressive'.[31] One British-born Yoruba expressed surprise at the social pressure sometimes put on people to attend and contribute to home associations, in contrast with the more relaxed ethos of the mainstream British voluntary sector: '[t]hey always come to the meeting and always tax themselves'.[32] Such attitudes were reflected in the demographics that were seen at home association meetings attended in the UK, where those present (particularly the leadership) are predominantly middle-aged. Even if members sometimes bring their younger children, teenagers are generally absent, although they are more conspicuous at pan-African meetings such as those organized by AFFORD and AfricaRecruit.

Beyond housing and employment, home association projects can be identified that engage with other aspects of urban life that are problematic for members. Both MECA-Yaoundé and MECA-Douala have run HIV/AIDS awareness campaigns in recent years. In Douala MECA worked with a local NGO, which visited every family group; MECA also paid for HIV tests for any member wanting one and subsidized the provision of anti-retrovirals to those needing them.[33] MECA-Yaoundé has researched and engaged with the problems of criminality among members in the city, discipline among its young people, and generally falling standards of education among Manyu people.[34] Education also is the main concern of the Manyu Solidarity Foundation, based in Yaoundé and associated with MECA, which awards scholarships to the best Manyu students in secondary and higher education in a grand annual ceremony.[35]

Regulation, limits and failures

Sanctions are applied to association members if they fail to keep up with their financial contributions, particularly in the domestic diaspora. It may seem easier for individuals living in cities to evade the 'enforced voluntarism' of home association activity compared with those at home (who are more easily dragooned into contributing labour and sometimes money to development projects). However, those in the diaspora still risk the power of 'home' being turned on them if they do so. Typically, unpaid dues to the 'trouble fund' are deducted from any benefit given – sometimes to the point that no payment is actually made to the recalcitrant or s/he still ends up owing money to the home association. Non-payment can also expose the defaulter to sanctions, usually fines, from neotraditional structures at home such as the traditional council if, for example, s/he wants to take a body home or receive one there. Social embarrassment and ostracism may also await those returning to the village without having fulfilled their home association obligations. Fear of witchcraft in the village is another potent force through which those in the diaspora can be coerced into participating (Geschiere and Nyamnjoh,

1998; Nyamnjoh, 2005). In Cameroon, such measures seem to have genuine force in getting people to pay their contributions to funds for welfare or development. It would certainly be impossible to have a high-profile death celebration without the permission of the Palace in Bali.

Still, some home association participants prefer not to pay their dues unless or until they have to, evinced by the numbers in arrears with their payments cited by association leaders. The MECA-Douala president estimates that only 500 to 800 Manyu people out of 1,800 to 2000 on the books are 'active' (that is, members in good standing) and thus entitled to bereavement and other benefits. 'Inactive members' (those who have not paid their dues for four or more consecutive months) are not entitled to benefits, but may still choose to participate in the wider life of the group, for example by attending cultural events. However, the president appreciates the financial sensitivities involved, noting that most members are women, often petty traders or housewives with little or no independent income, sometimes raising children on their own. Many male members are low-paid, too, as teachers or artisans, so he admits that asking people to come to meetings and contribute must be handled tactfully.[36] Some are even exempted from payment for reasons of income: in MECAs in Cameroon, for example, students are classified as 'non-financial members', who do not contribute money but are still entitled to MECA assistance through their family group.[37] Similar material concerns were heard in Tanzania: one retired informant in Dar es Salaam did not belong to any home association because 'pensions here are miserable. To attend meetings, even, one has to have a budget.'[38]

Many funds run by home associations are bureaucratically complex and under regular negotiation. In 2005, MECA-Yaoundé had to simplify its system and rules: previously each member contributed 100 CFA francs per month to its 'trouble fund' but there were problems of collection, so this system was changed to each family group contributing corporately, twice per year, according to the size of its membership list. For a death, each family group then pays a flat rate of 10,000 CFA francs. Even so there were disputes over the obligations of different groups in any particular death. People were told to keep a check on their own dues in the ledgers, which were open to all for scrutiny; they were effectively asked to police their own contributions.[39] It was also clear that the death of someone popular in the Manyu community would, again, bring more attendance at their funeral and therefore more voluntary contributions. While there are rules about contributions and benefits, then, in practice there is sometimes confusion even among those running home associations about what they mean.

Sanctions and the attendant problems of interpreting and enforcing rules are also found in the international diaspora. In MECA-Leicester, if someone loses a close relative each member makes a mandatory contribution of £20 or else they are out of the group.[40] In a MECA-UK group in London, a difficult situation arose when a couple with a new baby owed around £300 in dues between them. This clearly could not be deducted from the specified birth gift of £100. In the end, the constitution was interpreted for such instances to mean that a birth gift would be given in full, regardless of overdue payments, but unpaid dues would be deducted in the case of bereavement.[41] However, attendance and contributions are generally less heavily policed in home associations in the international diaspora, and the potential consequences of non-payment are generally fewer and less serious. One association leader in the UK thought that she might tackle this by developing an algorithm to calculate people's benefits precisely in relation to their contributions.[42] But overall, the sanctions do not have the same force as within Africa.

Indeed, home association leaders in the UK complained of a broader lack of commitment to their associations: people would commonly attend celebrations of key life stages, parties or other special events, but getting them to attend meetings, pay their subs and commit time was harder. In welfare terms, then, connections within international diasporic communities are looser, notwithstanding their still-impressive abilities to assist with welfare. The reasons for this may be various and complicated:

> There are constraints and not everyone can join ... If you don't have the right papers you won't want to be a member. Then people can't afford to travel to the meetings. Or they have to work – people who have to work at night or whose jobs don't really allow them the time and space to attend ... we may know these people informally, and help them informally, but they won't get formal help from the group. Many suffer from problems of stress and depression, and they have no support in this country.[43]

Perversely, then, the very reasons why people need welfare support may also prevent them from joining associations. Immigration status may be particularly important: those without secure legal status sometimes prefer to reduce their visibility by not joining a formal association and perhaps only mixing informally with trusted friends and family.[44] For most, sending remittances is the first call on their finances once their needs and those of their families in the UK have been met. Almost all members of the diaspora are subject to the time and financial constraints of studying, keeping down one or more jobs and earning enough money to support themselves in the UK, while also often under pressure from their families in Africa to send money home – pressures which can in extreme cases drive people into alcoholism and suicide.[45] As one leader of the Tanzanian Women's Association recounted:

> I've asked … why is it you don't want to join an association here? Why is it you don't want to feel part of a community? … [S]he said no, I have family whom I help and that's enough for me. You know I have brothers, sisters, cousins whom I help. I don't need to help the whole country … I have enough poor people in my little community, I don't need to go outside and create more problems for myself.[46]

Attending meetings costs money, not just in contributions and transport but also in opportunity costs for those with evening and weekend jobs who may have to take time off work. One interviewee said that he did not have time to go to any meetings 'because life is too hectic and busy here [in the UK]. So normally we meet up for kids' birthdays, Eid … In Tanzania, people have plenty of time; here, I didn't have time between studies and cooking, I was very tired, so it was a big problem to make it to a function.'[47] Despite this, some individuals maintain a commitment to multiple associations, albeit with some having a higher priority than others. As one Manyu elite in Yaoundé – a member of his village association, subdivisional association, MECA and an explicitly ethnic association – admitted, 'if I had to belong to one association, it would be [my village association] – my primary responsibility. All the others are just added pressure. I would not keep records like [my village association membership booklet] for the others.'[48]

Welfare and development

Welfare comprises most of the activity of the study home associations in Cameroon and among both the Cameroonian and Tanzanian diasporas researched in the UK. This is reflected in the fact that the majority of time in meetings is given over to discussing welfare and cultural events compared with development and other 'homeplace' matters, as the opening vignette of the book illustrates. Importantly, welfare is an intrinsic activity for home associations, structured into their normal operations and financial arrangements; specific development projects are more ad hoc and optional. Particularly in Tanzania there were examples of members with little or no material link to home: '[m]any migrants to Dar don't see themselves as migrants because they have settled here'.[49] Those with their whole family in the diaspora may see no point in contributing to development projects at home. This has a direct impact on fundraising. For example, association officials trying to raise money in Mbeya for the construction of school classrooms at Isongole in Rungwe reported: '[i]t was difficult to collect money, some people said they had money problems, some said that "all my children are here [in Mbeya], not there [in Isongole], so they won't benefit"'.[50] People may also be more prepared to put money into welfare because they can see, more or less immediately, the benefits to their fellow members and, at times, themselves. By contrast, sending money home for development projects is more open to problems of accountability, disagreements over development priorities and whether the people in the diaspora receive adequate 'recognition' for their contribution. Such concerns are understandably even more acute in the international diaspora, where they may put people off joining associations altogether, particularly when projects are perceived to have failed.

There are sometimes tensions between welfare provision, in the city or abroad, and development at home. The president of MECA-Douala was concerned that too great a focus on home development in recent times had been to the detriment of the grassroots Manyu diaspora in Douala. He claims that the group has now refocused on mutual support: '[w]e try to do the things we can for the people here now'. By contrast the patron places equal emphasis on development at home.[51] The MECA-Yaoundé committee also claimed that it spends more on projects among the Manyu diaspora in the city than at home.[52] In the international diaspora, there is some evidence that younger people are more concerned with home development than diasporic welfare. This seems to be linked with deteriorating economic circumstances, at least in Cameroon, a country viewed by its international diaspora as having regressed markedly in development terms. Criticism of socializing for its own sake could therefore fall along generational as well as along class or rural-versus-urban lines. A founding member of MECA-Leicester expressed his desire that they should be 'not just a sing-song group', while a founder of MECA-Birmingham complained that members 'eat, drink, dance and go. I say it's not just that, how useful we can be to people here and back home.'[53] Similar sentiments can be found in African cities, for example one Bali elite in Limbe complained, 'We want to see local people paying for their own development, not just relying on elites who are out to pay. They drink at cry-dies but they won't pay 100 CFA for development.'[54] This tension can be found in the homeplace itself. For example, an attempt by Manyu elites to turn their village Ekpe lodge more towards development encountered resistance from older members, who had to be bought off:

[O]lder people think that [Ekpe] is an opportunity to eat and drink, not to save for a rainy day, but in time they saw the value of the suggestion ... There are still some recalcitrants: some old people like to eat and drink. We let them do so once in a while, for example taking 20,000 out of 100,000 CFA collected to buy a carton of chicken: we indulge them, keep them happy.[55]

To some extent such problems arise because home associations evolved to fulfil one function (welfare) but are now aiming to discharge another (development). Though there may be a tension between these two goals it is not necessarily a problem. Rungwe people in Mbeya, for example, are explicitly concerned with both welfare and development. Bamasoko, an association for people from Masoko ward in Rungwe district, illustrates this: 'We wanted to promote social welfare, to uplift the standard of living of people, to solve their problems – people from Masoko here [in Mbeya]. But we also want to contribute to our homeplace, for example with schools.'[56] Equally associations that began life concerned with development at home are expanding into the field of welfare in the diaspora. The Dar es Salaam group of NDF plans to attract and register more members from lower socio-economic strata (such as carvers or petty street traders) by setting up a small loans scheme for them. This it hopes will make them more willing to contribute to development at home. As part of this strategy, NDF has established a new office in central Dar es Salaam and plans a computerized database of members in the city.[57] With income from the cess having declined sharply, NDF needs new revenue streams, and its legitimacy at home has been falling in the face of an increasingly strong and state-led self-help dynamic in the construction of new secondary schools. From that perspective, involving the wider diaspora appears to be as much about raising money as about fostering mutual support.

However, the distinction between welfare and development is an easy one to overstate. Association leaders did not always make a clear distinction between urban welfare and rural development. Rather, they saw these activities as a continuum, concerned for the welfare of people from home, wherever found. This point has a solid conceptual basis. Villagers and the diaspora are not entirely separate and distinct groups. Villagers may at various times in their lives become migrants to the town and benefit from urban welfare services; while migrants usually return home for visits or retirement and benefit from developmental goods (public or private) that they may have helped pay for. Indeed, those in the diaspora need to feel some measure of security before they are likely to contribute to a collective project or even remit money to their families. As one Tanzanian in the UK claimed, 'Others in the [association] wanted to help Tanzania first, but [I] said no, we have to help those here first, get them in a good position, before they can send help home.'[58] This is perhaps most graphically illustrated by the Manyu Women's Association in the UK where, at the end of the year, they divide up their 'trouble bank' between members, who are each given money to send back to their respective villages for Christmas.[59] Another facet of this continuum is self-interest among migrants established in town, who are prepared to finance development at home because they hope that this will alleviate demands for assistance of whatever kind from family members there. One informant stated matters in blunt terms: he was prepared to contribute to a school at home partly so that his brother's children could go there, rather than be sent to live with him in Dar es Salaam. For him, supporting development at home is partly a means 'to prevent the extended family being such a burden'.[60] Very often the distinction between welfare and development rests on a particular and narrow definition of what constitutes development and so it is a function of the ubiquity of that definition rather than a genuine difference in the eyes of many participants in home associations.

Political belonging and moral conviviality

Like any other aspect of the work of home associations it is reasonable to ask whether their welfare work fosters political belonging or moral conviviality. Does this welfare work increase bonding capital – the inward-looking and parochial aspects of belonging? Or does it increase bridging capital – the more outward-looking aspects of living together in the city? The role of the welfare dynamic in shaping and reinforcing ethnic identity has long been recognized (Little, 1965; Gugler, 2002). Language is certainly an issue: family groups and *nda kums* in Cameroon usually hold their meetings in the vernacular, although MECA necessarily has to operate in English and Pidgin English, as does BCDA-UK. In Cameroon, larger home associations are constructing community halls in the main cities. BANDECA-Douala is building a hall in Bonaberi. The Bali hall in Yaoundé was constructed in 1993–94 but is still incomplete. MECA-Yaoundé's newer hall at Essos is also incomplete but already in use. As well as providing a venue for social purposes and for special events, such structures have symbolic significance, marking the presence of the group in the city and thereby demanding its recognition.

Yet there is more evidence to support the view that home associations are not a barrier to moral conviviality. Indeed, their welfare work is again a means through which a 'progressive sense of place' might emerge because it is partly through such work that people discuss and rehearse the right way of living together in cosmopolitan cities and multi-ethnic societies, whether in Africa or the West. A number of examples show this. First, many people engage in different levels of home associations and have multiple loyalties. Spouses and friends from different home areas or, in the international diaspora, even from different African countries, may attend each others' meetings and special events such as weddings and parties, or contribute for the repatriation of a body. Those of mixed ethnic parentage may well attend both meetings, or choose the more effective one, illustrating the adaptive nature of ethnic identity.[61] For example, at a MECA-UK meeting attended, the group's response to deaths in other sections of the Anglophone Cameroonian diaspora was discussed and it was argued that inter-group solidarity would be better demonstrated if they made a collective contribution in addition to attending wake-keeping as individuals if they so wished.[62] Second, membership of home associations runs alongside membership of associations connected to old schools, mosques and churches that bring together people of different nationalities and ethnicities. The Okoyong Past Students' Association (OPSA), for example, brings together old girls of the Queen of the Rosary School in Okoyong, a renowned Catholic girls' high school near Mamfe. While OPSA focuses on providing support to the school itself, one UK-based member notes that it also brings together members in the diaspora for mutual support including condolence visits, bridal showers and born house. Football teams are particularly strong among young Tanzanian men in the UK, and those from different British towns and cities play each other. Furthermore, the numbers involved in most home associations generally seem to represent only a minority of the diasporic community in question. Third, home associations provide guidance with bureaucratic procedures in the places where they meet. Successful associations often have a good under-standing of local government bureaucracy. One Tanzanian association in the southeast of the UK that ran day trips for children managed to procure a grant from a London borough council for office equipment and activities. At a MECA-UK meeting, the chair proposed that professionals (whether inside or outside the group) be invited to talk on their areas of expertise. Suggestions included that a lawyer talk about wills, probate and the problems of dying intestate; a financial expert talk about financial markets; and a doctor talk about diet, including obesity and the risk of diabetes.[63] While not directly concerned with bridging capital, such transfers of knowledge do familiarize association members to new legal and financial systems. Finally, within Cameroon there are examples of home association branches contributing to projects not in their own place of origin but where they live. For example a BANDECA branch in Manyu gave labour as a group to the construction of the Catholic cathedral in Mamfe and supported the Voice of Manyu radio station.[64] Migrants may also be involved with other associations engaged in the improvement of their current place of residence.[65]

Conclusions

The provision of welfare to migrants remains the most important function of home associations both nationally and internationally. Moving, whether to the city or internationally, entails risk, and urban migrants are in some ways more vulnerable than those remaining at home. The importance of welfare provision also reflects the current abilities of the associations themselves: they do welfare better than they do development. Indeed, there is some evidence within the case study associations of tensions over the respective allocation of effort and resources to welfare and development. However, this may be a false dichotomy, as welfare provision can also be seen as 'developmental' in its delivery of social benefits. Urban migrants need to feel sufficiently secure in the city for them to be able to remit money home or contribute to home association development projects. By helping to increase the chance of getting a foothold in the urban context and reducing the risk of destitution and an ignominious return home, the support offered to migrants by home associations in the city can thus indirectly promote development at home. Association leaders themselves do not always see welfare and development as separate concerns but instead as forming a continuum concerned with ameliorating problems and potentially improving quality of life for people from home, wherever they are found. This continuum can be viewed temporally as well as spatially in that different forms of 'development' are being delivered to people at different stages of their migratory histories. This is actually a long-recognized dynamic in the literature: that migration is self-reinforcing, creating the infrastructure for its perpetuation and migrant reproduction in both rural and urban spaces. Welfare provision in the city should be considered as much a part of this infrastructure as, for example, a school in the village.

However, while home association welfare may provide a partial substitute for formal welfare services, the two forms are in some respects more different than may be apparent. This is demonstrated by a number of features of the former noted above: the role of personal popularity in determining death benefits; mismatches with the financial services sector; the trust evident among members; and the sanctions applied to recalcitrants who return home without having fulfilled their home association obligations in the city. These all point towards a moral economy of obligation and reciprocation under constant renegotiation. From the policy perspective, regarding welfare provision as 'developmental' in the normative sense therefore carries the same risk as that identified for the provision by home associations of public goods at home: greater formalization through engagement with the development industry risks disrupting the very socially embedded dynamics that make the system work at all.

Notes

1. Interview, Oroko diaspora (Ndian division, Cameroon) in London, July 2006.
2. Interview, Makonde diaspora in Dar es Salaam, September 2005.
3. Interview, Manyu diaspora in London, February 2006.
4. Interview, Bali diaspora in London, November 2006.
5. Interview, Tanzanian diaspora in Leicester, October 2006.
6. Interview, Manyu diaspora in London, October 2006.
7. Interview, Manyu diaspora in Luton, November 2006.
8. Interview, Manyu/Bali couple in London, November 2006.
9. Interview, Manyu diaspora in Cambridge, June 2006.
10. Bali Women's Cultural Meeting in Walton-on-Thames, November 2006.
11. Interview, Manyu diaspora in Birmingham, September 2006.
12. Interviews, MECA-Yaoundé committee in Yaoundé, April 2005, and MECA-Douala president in Douala, March 2005.
13. Interview, Manyu diaspora in London, October 2006.
14. Interview, Manyu diaspora in London, August 2006.
15. AFFORD officers speaking at African Diaspora and Development Day in London, 7 July 2007.
16. The Africa Conference in London, July 2006.
17. Interview, AFFORD officer in London, April 2006.
18. This service has roots dating back to 1962 and has been held regularly in London since 1974, moving to its current venue in 1993.
    See http://www.stanneslutheranchurch.org/swahili_congregation.htm.
19. Interview, Newala diaspora in Mtwara, September 2005.
20. Interview, Tanzanian couple in London, August 2006.
21. Interview, Tanzanian diaspora in Reading, September 2006.
22. Interview, Tanzanian diaspora in Reading, September 2006.
23. Interview, Tanzanian diaspora in London, August 2006.
24. Interview, Rungwe diaspora in Dar es Salaam, September 2005.
25. Interview, Manyu diaspora in London, August 2006; remarks by a second-generation Yoruba at AD3 in London, July 2007.

26. Interview, MECA-Douala officer in Douala, March 2005.
27. Interview, Newala diaspora in Dar es Salaam, September 2005.
28. Interview, Manyu diaspora in London, October 2006.
29. Interview, Tanzanian diaspora in Slough, July 2006.
30. Interview, Oroko diaspora (Ndian division, Cameroon) in London, July 2006.
31. Interviews, AFFORD officer in London, April 2006, and Tanzanian diasporas in London, July and August 2006; the Africa Conference in London, July 2006.
32. Speaker at AD3 in London, July 2007.
33. Interview, MECA-Douala officer in Douala, March 2005.
34. Interview, MECA-Yaoundé officers in Yaoundé, April 2005.
35. Interview, Manyu diaspora in Yaoundé, April 2005.
36. Interview, MECA-Douala president in Douala, March 2005.
37. Interview, MECA-Yaoundé committee in Yaoundé, April 2005.
38. Interview, Rungwe diaspora in Dar es Salaam, September 2005.
39. Manyu family group meetings in Yaoundé, April 2005.
40. Interview, MECA-Leicester officer in Leicester, January 2006.
41. MECA-UK meeting in London, May 2006.
42. Interview, Manyu diaspora in London, February 2006.
43. Interview, Manyu/Bali couple in London, November 2006.
44. Interview, Tanzanian diasporas in London, August 2006, and Reading, October 2006. Sommers (2001) makes a similar point about the dangers of involvement.
45. Interview, Tanzanian diaspora in Reading, November 2006.
46. Interview, Tanzanian diaspora in London, August 2006.
47. Interview, Tanzanian diaspora in Leicester, October 2006.
48. Interview, Manyu elite in Yaoundé, April 2005.
49. Interview, Rungwe diaspora in Dar es Salaam, August 2005.
50. Interview, Rungwe diaspora in Mbeya, July 2005.
51. Interviews, MECA-Douala president and patron in Douala, March 2005.
52. Interview, MECA-Yaoundé committee in Yaoundé, April 2005.
53. Interviews, MECA-Leicester officer in Leicester, January 2006, and Manyu diaspora in Birmingham, September 2006.
54. Interview, Bali diaspora in Limbe, April 2005.
55. Interview, seseku in Egbekaw, March 2005.
56. Interview, Rungwe diaspora in Mbeya, July 2005.
57. Interviews, NDF leaders, Dar es Salaam, September 2005.
58. Interview, Tanzanian diaspora in London, July 2006.
59. Interview, Manyu diaspora in London, February 2006.
60. Interview, Rungwe diaspora in Dar es Salaam, September 2005.
61. Interviews, diasporas of Banyang/Ejagham parentage in Cambridge, June 2006, and Bakweri/Bamileke parentage in London, September 2006.
62. MECA-UK meeting in London, May 2006.
63. MECA-UK meeting in London, May 2006.
64. Interview, BANDECA officer in Mamfe, March 2005.
65. Interview, Rungwe diaspora in Mbeya, July 2005.

7 MODERNIZING BURIAL AND DEATH CELEBRATIONS

Much of the work of home associations concerns a conscious process of modernizing the homeplace. The diaspora groups in this study not only break the link between place and identity by forging independent communities in cosmopolitan contexts away from the homeplace but they also constantly remake that link because of their interest in reproducing places. In practice this happens through the work that home associations do in developing home or modernizing 'culture', where culture is seen as a set of traditions and practices primarily connected with ceremony and performance. However, the idea of the reproduction of place is more useful because it emphasizes the actively constructed quality of the homeplace and gives a sense of a perpetual process of maintaining it. This process combines remaking the material landscape (the infrastructure and services people use, the appearance of the home-place) and remaking the social landscape (the rules of behaviour around rites of passage, the cultural events that make up the annual calendar, and the social mores that steer everyday lives). These two aspects of the landscape of the homeplace are interwoven in the modernizing activities of home associations.

Rites of passage around death and burial form a crucial link between the welfare activities of associations and their explicit development activities. In the diaspora, home associations provide emotional, financial and practical support for the bereaved. In the homeplace the association is actively engaged by supporting members who are repatriating corpses for burial at home. For home associations development sometimes means the improvement of a way of life at home. Improving public goods and infrastructure may enable that but are not necessarily an end in themselves. Culture is the object and medium of development; it is not a barrier to it. So development might mean better schools, roads and hospitals, but it might also mean better burials, weddings and dances; the two are very hard to separate.

This chapter looks at the story of the construction of a modern mortuary in Bali by the home association BANDECA and how this project is closely linked to the project of modernizing burial. The mortuary project provides a window both on changing patterns of migration and on the balance of influence between those living in the home area, the diaspora in Cameroon and overseas. This interest in mortuaries and transnational funerals is not unique to Cameroon (van der Geest, 2006; Mazzucato et al., 2006) but has certain distinctive elements in a political context that links funerals, ethnicity and territoriality (Jua, 2005). The chapter concludes by analysing the relationship between development and modernization in all four study areas.

Indigenizing modernity?

Over the past two decades a slew of concepts have attempted to displace the idea that a single version of 'modernity' emanates from a global Western metropole and then spreads out across the world displacing other cultures, whose traditions are as a result extinguished. The distinction between 'modernity' and 'tradition' is profoundly unhelpful as a way of understanding the social changes flowing from the accelerated integration of capitalist markets across the globe. In contrast it is argued that modernity in the Global North was built on resources (labour as well as capital and commodities) from elsewhere. Modernity is the outcome of the dialectical relationship between different locales:

> Modernity is not a western invention, but a product of the west's interaction with the rest of the world ... The debate is not between modernity and its opponents, but rather between different versions of modernity, some of which offer alternatives to what is regarded, not always very accurately, as the Western model. (Young, 2003: 98)

From the perspective of the four African case study areas the process of modernization is one in which new goods, services and ideas are often enthusiastically embraced but are incorporated into homeplaces in order to suit local needs, aspirations and ceremonies. These local value systems are not themselves unchanging, but neither are they evaporating in the face of a uniform global idea of what matters. This is not a new story. The early-twentieth-century photographic record of *Lela*, the annual dance in Bali, shows that a European foghorn was incorporated into this African occasion. The foghorn was a novelty but it served a very old end

– demonstrating the power and prestige of the Fon of Bali through a display of his possessions (Fardon, 2006b). Death celebrations (or 'cry-dies') are a particularly clear site where new opportunities and established cultural practices are combined. This is evident from what home associations and their members choose to incorporate into contemporary death celebrations and how those celebrations are organized.

In effect we are witnessing what has been called 'globalization from below' (Portes, 1997), 'local modernities' (Nyamnjoh et al., 2002: 99) or 'the indigenization of modernity' (Sahlins, 1994, 1999):

> Unified by the expansion of Western capitalism over recent centuries, the world is also being re-diversified by indigenous adaptations to the global juggernaut. In some measure, global homogeneity and local differentiation have developed together, the latter as a response to the former in the name of native cultural autonomy. (Sahlins, 1999: ix–x)

This is not a new, smooth or straightforward process, but rather it reveals the conflicting interests within and between different individuals and institutions in any place (Appadurai, 1996; Ferguson, 1999; Piot, 1999). The numerous conflicts over chieftaincy titles in Manyu, for example, are often initiated by the material success of individuals away from home. Their desire to express their new status (achieved through integration in wider economies) and receive endorsement in their homeplace is translated into the inflated importance given to chieftaincy and the consequent fierce struggles over succession to positions that in themselves are of relatively limited financial use. The notion of 'neo-traditional titles' (Fisiy and Goheen, 1998) perfectly captures this apparently paradoxical but actually logical interweaving of the outside and inside of a homeplace.

The process of indigenizing modernity is confusing because, even as there is an analytical attempt to escape from the contrast between 'tradition' and 'modernity', these are often precisely the terms used by those engaged in globalization from below. Consider, for example the following comment made by a Tanzanian in the UK talking about *utani* [pl. *watani*] or 'joking relationships' between different ethnic groups. These relationships describe a form of reciprocity in which two groups grant each other hospitality when they are away from home, but in exchange individuals from one ethnic group can demand extra food and drink and behave badly (as both a joke and a demonstration of trust) at important occasions (such as funerals) organized by the other group:

> *Watani* relationships between tribes don't apply here [in the UK]. For example, the Chagga and the Pare are *watani*, but it doesn't really apply

here; as we modernize we leave it behind. Personally I don't like those things – being offensive, even as a joke, at funerals. I don't like it but people still do it at home. Those who do it now cling to tradition. But I think it is offensive.[1]

Some (not all) members of the diaspora describe themselves as modern in contrast to those living in the homeplace, whom they describe as beholden to tradition. Similarly some with professions see themselves as modern when contrasted with farmers who are traditional, and some Christians and Muslims see their beliefs as modern in contrast to traditional belief systems. Yet these attempts to fix certain people and places as traditional and others as modern invariably break down. In the case of *watani* for example, the 'tradition' is one whose evolution from an intra-group institution to an inter-group institution is closely related to the expansion of labour migration in the colonial period (Wilson, 1957). The hospitality offered was only necessary when people started moving long distances across unfamiliar territory in search of work in mines or plantations. So *utani* is itself modern insofar as it is a product of integration into global labour markets in the early twentieth century. To give another example, the Fon of Bali, the Palace and its institutions are often talked about as emblematic of Bali Nyong'a 'tradition', yet the Fon describes himself as a 'modern Fon' and his Traditional Council is the key institution in actually enforcing the modernization of Bali advocated by BANDECA, the self-styled modernizing home association.

The process of the indigenization of modernity is more problematic for participants than Sahlins's phrase sometimes suggests. One reason is that the encounters that flow from mobility produce conflicting choices. So, people from all four homeplaces sell their labour in capitalist labour markets and generate capital, which can then be invested in 'development'. But what counts as development is not always clear. On the one hand people could use that capital to develop what they describe as their own culture; capital is reinvested in expanding what is perceived to be a 'traditional' way of life. As a result the scale of death celebrations expands, wedding ceremonies become more elaborate, demand for titles from the palace grows, and networks of obligation and patronage also expand. The logic of these investments is understood in terms of developing 'tradition' or 'culture'. On the other hand people could use that capital not to reinscribe social relations but to transform them. This might be about social mobility within the community, but might also be about reinvesting within 'productive enterprises' rather than cultural ritual and the prestige associated with patronage. In this version of development a new emphasis is placed on investing in businesses and job creation rather than in titles from the palace, on investing heavily in the education of a small number of closely related family members rather than trying to educate large numbers of relatives to a low level. The distinction between these two versions of development is deliberately overstated and the actual experience is of negotiating a path between them. Home associations provide a venue in which that process of negotiation can take place among like-minded people who share the same dilemmas because they share the same home. They are 'another example of the efficacy of ideologies of homes in ordering communal responses to modernization' (Eyoh, 1999: 291).

The 'most modern mortuary in Cameroon'

The Bali mortuary was built inside a pre-existing building in the grounds of the government hospital on the outskirts of Bali Town in 2003 by BANDECA as a 'community participation' project. Money for the project came from contributions made by different BANDECA groups across Cameroon and supplemented by further loans and donations from wealthy individuals. The total cost of the project is unclear but was probably around 19.5 million CFA francs. It is a wide, single-storey structure in good condition and comprises three sections: an office, the building containing the 'fridge', and a covered area that can be used by vehicles or people when they come to deliver or collect a corpse. Benches have been provided under this cover where people can sit and wait for corpses to be moved; the mortuary has become another site incorporated within the ritual of burial where people can gather. The mortuary is run by an attendant and a technician whose salaries are paid for by BANDECA. The 'fridge' has the capacity to store 45 corpses in fifteen chambers, making it the largest mortuary in the North West Province in 2007. The government mortuary in Bamenda, for example, has a maximum capacity of 12 corpses. For an extra payment a corpse can receive a superior level of care in the Bali mortuary: this guarantees, for example, that there will be no doubling up of corpses within the chamber. The basic supply of electricity for the mortuary comes from the government hospital but there is a back-up generator to ensure continuous electricity supply at all times. When the networked electricity supply is interrupted the mortuary generator is also used by the hospital. In normal circumstances, however, the bill for the electricity consumed by the mortuary will be sent to the government hospital. The significant profits from running the mortuary have gone to BANDECA, which has used them to subsidize their next big development project – the town water supply (Chapter 9). The basic cost of keeping a corpse in the mortuary in 2007 was 5,000 CFA francs per day. However, this is reduced to 3,000 CFA francs per day for women or 3,500 CFA francs per day for men on production of a valid BANDECA membership card. Since opening, the mortuary has been well used: over 800 corpses are registered as having been stored. The vast majority of these were individuals who died in Bali and were buried there too, but there are no restrictions on who can be stored here, and around two dozen corpses have been brought from neighbouring subdivisions before burial outside Bali, and very occasionally from overseas before burial in family compounds in Bali.

On the front wall in the centre of the building there is an immaculately engraved white plaque, which reads as follows:

> On Friday, 15 August 2003, H.E. Koumpa Issa, Governor of the North West Province, in the presence of H.M. Dr Ganyonga III, Fon of Bali, inaugurated this mortuary complex, installed by the Bali Nyong'a Development and Cultural Association (BANDECA), Dr Ndifontah B. Nyamndi being the President-General.

The plaque brings together three men representing the government, the Palace and the home association, encapsulating the sense that this is a site where a number of stories meet. The mortuary is a place where the contemporary experience of migration, remittances, and spatially diffuse families intersects with historical emotions related to loss, recognition, status and respect. It is a new site where ideas about what is sensible, hygienic and up to date intersect with ideas about the appropriate way to treat the dead. It brings together different ideas of what constitutes a proper burial (proper meaning both correct and clean) in a developing place.

Multiple explanations exist of how and why the mortuary project was selected. Many of these stories probably involve a degree of retrospective rationalization following the completion of a successful project. The mortuary was the first major development project undertaken by BANDECA after its relaunch in the late 1990s and, though the organization had existed for some years, its activities had been limited and it lacked much of a profile, particularly in the town itself. So there was a desire to have a highly visible project that would 'awaken … the people' and show members that BANDECA was 'already on the train of development'.[2] This claim is also borne out by the fact that the first round of fundraising activities among the different *nda kums* and BANDECA divisional councils in Cameroon was for development in general rather

Table 7.1 Development preferences in Bali and among the Bali domestic diaspora (percentages)

	Bali Residents	People from Bali living in Fako	People from Bali living in Douala	People from Bali in Yaoundé
Road	49	38	57	52
Water	27	46	27	35
Mortuary	13	18	8	10
Orphanage	8	0	2	0
Other	3	0	4	3
All	0	3	2	0
Number	303	96	97	60

Note: 556 people were asked 'Which is the most important development project in Bali in recent years?' Some respondents expressed more than one preference.

than the mortuary in particular. It was only later that it was decided to spend the money on the mortuary, which precipitated a further round of fundraising.

There was relatively little felt need for the mortuary among those living in Bali (Table 7.1). Whilst residents at home gave enthusiastically to the later water project, they did not donate so willingly to the mortuary project; indeed after it was announced, a mere 10,000 CFA francs were collected for the project from the home branch. By most accounts the Fon was more in line with those at home than those living away from Bali: 'he did not see why we should leave people who are living, and take care of people who are dead'.[3] Some people objected that their spirit would leave them while they were in the mortuary before they were buried. According to those outside Bali who were lobbying in favour of the mortuary this hostility to the project was indicative of the backward character of those in the 'village':

> The people in Bali were mostly against the mortuary, mostly because they are traditionalists. They still have some phobias about these things – they have a fear of death and they think that if you build a mortuary in the village it will encourage people to die.[4]

But according to most people we interviewed in the village, the opposition to the mortuary came less from this kind of concern and more from an anxiety about its relative lack of use when contrasted with the more pressing need for a functioning water supply. However, this ambivalence does show that the idea and support for a mortuary must have come from outside Bali Town.

In Cameroon it was suggested that elites in the US were the driving force behind the idea of constructing the mortuary. Some people on the BANDECA National Executive claimed 'they sent a lot of the equipment, so BANDECA implemented it and went along with it, we were drowned out because the US physically provided things'.[5] But those closer to the management of the project contradict this view arguing that little actual support for the project came from the international diaspora:

> The US were going to buy the mortuary generator but they are trying to sort themselves out as there are too many internal squabbles. The UK group wanted to know what they could do to help with the mortuary; we are still hoping they will contribute something.[6]

The assumption that those in the US were behind the project reflects the widely held view that 'if I'm in the US and my father dies, I want him to be kept [in the mortuary] so that I can come home and pay my last respects'.[7] In Bali, ideas about the ongoing relationship between the living and the dead, and particularly about the capacity of the dead to influence the well-being of the living, mean that children are expected to take care to bury their parents correctly and subsequently to continue to tend their grave. This obligation on children to pay their last respects is as true for those who live outside Bali but within Cameroon as it is for those overseas. Indeed the burden of expectation is more likely to fall on those close at hand. So there was a sense not only that the mortuary was primarily to benefit those away from home, but also that this innovation was a bulwark to established and unquestioned ideas of obligation.

Regardless of where the original idea came from, the BANDECA leadership undoubtedly had to persuade a wide cross-section of the Bali population of the merits of the mortuary project. In particular the President General is often credited for using his skills as an orator to bring people round to the idea. The leadership used two main arguments: one pragmatic and the other based on ideas of respect for the dead. The latter argument suggests that a fitting burial is important: 'that's the last moment we are seeing those who are dead, that's the best honour we can give him [sic]'.[8] The pragmatic argument was that the mortuary would make money, in particular from Bali's neighbours who would prefer to use this new mortuary rather than the one in Bamenda. This argument has proved correct: the mortuary raised about 11 million CFA francs for BANDECA in its first two years of operation, money that has been used for other projects. Indeed, the mortuary proved to be not only a means of making money out of neighbouring communities but actually a way of blurring some historical enmities:

People said the need of the village was for water. But later on people accepted the mortuary; they saw that it was a way of making Bali more developed than its neighbours. Some said that a Batibo man[9] won't want his corpse to be in the Bali mortuary but now it is OK. Now we hear over the radio that a Batibo man is in the Bali mortuary, and we like that.[10]

Having chosen the project and persuaded people of its value, there were two main strategies in further rounds of fundraising: first, a levy on all members of every *nda kum*, and, second, fundraising events at which individuals could make further donations according to their means. The following account of fundraising in Tiko (on the coast) is typical:

> Tiko gave the mortuary heavy support. Women gave 1,000 CFA and men gave 2,000 CFA in their *nda kums*. This was like the basic contribution. After that, we fixed a day for the National Executive Committee [of BANDECA] to come. We hire a public space like the Brasseries Place and all Tiko *nda kums* come for the fundraising day. The Fon comes on that day. People stand up and announce their gift … 90 per cent of the money pledged is given on that day, the rest comes later [if at all].[11]

In addition, various other organizations made donations; for example Nk'umu Fed Fed, the women's group, gave 1.5 million CFA francs to the mortuary project. Nevertheless, we were also told that the project was 'carried' by the National Executive Committee whose members had to make large personal contributions to ensure that the mortuary was completed.

Since completion the mortuary has been well used by families in Bali and nearby, primarily because of issues of cost and convenience. Formerly, if a family member died in Bali and the family wanted to use the government mortuary in Bamenda it was necessary to transport the corpse to the city and then back again for burial. Not only was this costly but if, as often happened, the Bamenda mortuary was full, then the corpse might have to be transported even further to find mortuary space. Until recently the road between Bali and Bamenda was very poor, so the corpse's last journey was potentially undignified and there was a risk that the corpse could be delayed in Bamenda while guests were awaiting the burial in Bali. However, there is also a sense of pride in Bali that this is the community's mortuary, and this too has popularized its use.

But although the mortuary has been well used, it is not used for every burial. This may be a consequence of storage costs, which can mount up. Because costs are reduced for BANDECA members some people appear to join the association after death: 'If you owe BANDECA development levy when you die, you have to pay it all before you can use the mortuary'.[12] Those families in Bali who lack the money continue with the established practice of a very quick burial soon after death. Equally those without family living away from Bali feel less need to use the mortuary: 'If you have money and children outside you go to the mortuary and wait for the children to come. But those without monies or children outside, there is no need to keep the corpse, you just bury as soon as possible.'[13] There is also a feeling, particularly among the older generation in Bali, that it is improper to store the corpse in the mortuary and that this entails spiritual risks. For example, there are discussions about whether those who committed suicide should be allowed in the mortuary because of the perceived risks to the other corpses. Also the liquid from corpses can be used in various forms of malevolent witchcraft.[14] For these reasons of propriety, the mortuary has not been used by senior Palace notables (who tend to be buried at night) or by Muslims. Several interviewees expressed the desire not to be left in the mortuary but to be buried quickly after death, even if this meant that their children did not have time to return to Bali for the burial.

Burial practices in Cameroon changed significantly over the twentieth century (Jindra, 2005) so the difference made in Bali by the mortuary is just the latest in a long line of changes. What is relatively new in this case is the introduction of novel technology that particularly suits the interests of the Bali diaspora, whether in Cameroon or further afield. The mortuary enables these individuals to have more authority over the timetable of a burial and to participate more actively in the death celebrations of those who die at home. There is an important distinction between burial – in which the corpse is interred usually to one side of a house within a family compound – and death celebrations, a series of rites designed to ensure the well-being of the deceased and the living. There are multiple death celebrations falling at different intervals after death, sometimes many years after. Historically the burial was often a hurried, low-key affair because of the inability to preserve the corpse beyond two or three days, and the larger, more important death celebrations came over subsequent months and years. Since the introduction of the mortuary, however, the burial has become a much larger-scale event because the corpse can be preserved in the mortuary (six weeks is not unusual) and buried at a time convenient to the living and combined with the death celebrations in a single event.

The manipulation of the timing of burial has enabled the domestic and international diaspora (who often foot the bill) to participate in the ceremony in person:

Formerly people died and were buried immediately. But now, because so many are out in the diaspora, we need to keep the corpse so that the family can assemble. It is expensive to carry a corpse to Bamenda and there is not always space. So that was the reason we decided to build our own mortuary – to honour our parents and relatives who die. We should give honour!'... Bali people who die in the morning used to be buried in the evening. You know we still believe our dead are living. And the living could be the dead the next day![15]

For those in employment away from Bali, practicalities must be undertaken prior to leaving for home. It is necessary to arrange leave from work and to mobilize funds to help with the expenses around death, both of which take time. Raising money, for example, may involve waiting for a meeting of the *nda kum* or of one or more *njangi*[16] in order to access savings or request a loan to pay for expenses. Such collections can be very significant with donations for significant burials exceeding a million CFA francs from a single *nda kum*. In the international diaspora it may mean making claims on formal financial products such as insurance policies.[17]

In a national context where ethnicity has become closely associated with long-term territorial belonging, burial in the family compound is becoming more important, not less. Particular emphasis is placed on the different rights and responsibilities in relation to the homeplace. Not only is it the right of an indigene to enjoy some authority over what happens in their home but it is also their responsibility to develop it: 'If you can get people motivated and attuned to the problems of the village, then that is doing something for the nation, for Cameroon.'[18] Burial is a key sign of where these rights are enjoyed most securely:

> In Limbe I am a stranger here so you must agree on certain things before you are buried. Other Cameroonians won't look after me. I must strive for the development of my village because I will end up there. You must be proud of your home. I am a stranger here. We must listen to the indigenes here. I can't take some political decisions here. I can't be buried here. If I want to be buried here I will have to go and pay some money to the council first. But in the village I don't need to consult anybody. I am a son of the soil.[19]

Since the introduction of the 1996 Constitution, identity papers in Cameroon have bureaucratically reasserted the importance of ethnicity. In addition to Cameroonian citizenship, legal identity also includes an ethnic label. This is governed not by the place where you were born but by the 'native origins' of your father (Jua, 2005: 327–8). By constructing the mortuary and facilitating burial at home, BANDECA has played an unwitting role in this process of increasing ethnic territoriality in Cameroon.

The frequency of burial at home in Bali means that it is easy to forget that this was not always common. In the past, not all families transported corpses back to the village for burial. On the plantations in the late nineteenth century and the first half of the twentieth century, for example, the repatriation of corpses was the exception rather than the rule. Both costs and poor transport made it very difficult. It was not practically possible to get corpses from the coast to Bali fast enough, and so instead people were buried in the compounds where they had lived during their working lives. For many decades this was accepted as the norm, and indeed it was considered preferable to be buried outside Bali if your children continued to live outside because this would enable them to tend your grave. Even today the costs of repatriating corpses are too high for many urban households. But increasingly individuals are worried about leaving their corpse on someone else's land because they are unsure what might happen there in the future. Data from the mortuary suggest that nearly 90 per cent of those stored there died in Bali. What this disguises is that it is common practice for the terminally ill to return to the village from elsewhere in Cameroon in the last months of their lives because it is easier and cheaper to move the ill than the dead.

Changing death celebrations

The mortuary is a physical transformation of the town's landscape that reflects (primarily) the needs of those who live away from Bali. It is a new development but it serves essentially an old purpose that reflects local values, namely the importance given to burials. Its construction has altered the timing of burial. But that is only one aspect of the debate about modernizing burial in which BANDECA is engaged. The other aspect concerns a conscious process of transforming death celebrations to be more in tune with what the Bali elite perceives to be up-to-date attitudes. This process is based on active interventions in the rules and practices associated with burials:

> We need to advance our culture. We the elites outside are the cream of Bali and we make suggestions for cultural advancements. So BANDECA has a cultural role – we make suggestions to the Fon who then consults with his traditional council … the Fon defines culture in Bali.[20]

Whilst the self-proclaimed modernizers may often be members of BANDECA living outside Bali, the new regulations are enforced through the structures of the traditional ruler and his council in the village, which endorse and encourage this process of modernization. Indeed the Fon has led the way on numerous deliberate modernizing rules, not all of which have been successful. For example, attempts to change the market cycle from an eight-day to a seven-day week proved impossible to deliver. From the perspective of the home association these attempts to transform the way of life in the village are also explicitly part of the development remit. As one elite put it, 'you cannot separate development from culture, because development must change people's behaviour and attitudes to modern life ... Culture is dance, music and the entire lifestyle of the community.'[21]

In particular the Fon of Bali, his traditional council and the elites in BANDECA have for some years sought to change some of the practices around widowhood obligations, which they see as 'inhumane'. For example it was a common practice for a widow to spend the night before the burial holding a wake over the corpse of her husband. This practice has been banned by the Fon's traditional council on the grounds that it is a health risk. Rules have also been passed to curtail the cleansing practices associated with widowhood in the months following the death of a husband. In the past, widows were expected to dress in a certain way, not to receive things from people's hands, to eat alone, to sit on the floor not chairs, and to sleep on plantain leaves. If the plantain leaves were torn in the morning (which is very easily done) it was taken as a sign that the widow was unfaithful to her husband and social sanctions were applied. Widows were expected to walk with one arm across their chest and not to touch people when they greeted them. These rules were to be followed over a period of months or even years. It has now been proposed that widowhood should be reduced to a token period of three days. This proposal was put to the traditional council, which gave its opinion to the Fon who then passed the decree that widowhood should be thus reduced. However, despite the decree, some women persist with the obligations of widowhood for much longer:

> [Widowhood] used to be a big problem for women in Bali, but now all those things are changing. Those who want to can respect tradition. When my stepfather died my stepmother said she had to do it properly, but we said no, and we had to bribe our aunts not to make any noise about it. Women are the ones subjecting themselves to it now, so we try and talk to them. They believe that something will happen to them if they don't respect tradition. But people now are trying to raise awareness and

educate about widowhood … At the family level, it used to be that your in-laws declare possession of all your things. Now that is no longer. They take something symbolically and leave the rest for the widow, while children buy things on behalf of their mothers. These old practices are dying down now, people are becoming enlightened and the old generation is fading out. But the biggest problem for women is land inheritance.[22]

The apparent refusal of widows to embrace this change fuels the elite opinion that people in the village can be unwilling to adopt modernizing measures that are intended for their own good. This opinion is indicative of the way in which most members of the diaspora talk about those in the village. Yet the same diaspora interviewee (a woman) claimed that there was little difference between women inside Bali and those outside, and explicitly described those in the village as 'civilized'; some other people also resisted the idea that those outside sought to 'modernize' those at home. Indeed sometimes the elite can be just as scathing about the general Bali population living away from home. For example, one self-described elite, while making the point that one of the Douala *nda kums* covered a wide social spectrum, said, 'every Tom and Dick is there, us and the morons all together'.[23] It would be wrong to jump to the conclusion that there is a simple cleavage in which all of those outside are seen as modernizers and all those at home are seen as the object of modernization.

Some more thoughtful members of BANDECA are aware of the need for elites to use persuasion rather than coercion when trying to modernize changes around burial practices and indeed to steer cultural change in Bali more generally:

So if you come from outside and try and tell people to change, you will be rejected. But if you come and join hands with the people, if you do it with them, you can bring change. Slowly. Elites used to just come, dictate and leave again. But now they bring changes and say 'let's do it together'. Elites must do it with the people. It is a question of approach.[24]

This process is sometimes obscured by ritual but unreflective invocations of community participation, although in some ways it has been aided by the difficulty of defining the category 'elite'. Elites can be intellectuals or professionals or those with financial resources, and whilst the general understanding is that 'elite' was contrasted with 'local', such a distinction is hard to maintain when top civil servants retire to the village or successful international migrants return to Bali to set up businesses or homes. New categories such as 'local elites' have emerged as a result. Meanwhile many living outside Bali have neither the financial capacity nor the job to claim to be an elite, nor would they want to take on the responsibilities of doing so. Furthermore it is hard for elites to dismiss those at home as 'traditionalists' when so many of those outside say that they are afraid to go home because of 'kontri fashion' (witchcraft). The fracture between villages and diasporas undoubtedly plays an important rhetorical or even ideological role but is becoming increasingly blurred. Relations between home and diaspora are given an extra dimension when the international diaspora is added. They are often portrayed by the elite in Cameroon as out of touch with the needs of those in the village: 'The Bali boys in the US want to do a library but they are elitist … the library, with computers, is not our priority.'[25] Despite increased sensitivity in the diaspora to working with people at home, the most common sentiment remains that 'people at home are quite simple and they don't understand everything'.[26] So from the perspective of elites in Cameroon the dominant idea is still that the village needs to be modernized and that they are best placed to try and co-ordinate that process.

Some individuals within BANDECA also want to modernize funerals by controlling the expenditure on death celebrations in the name of economic rationality, arguing that such expenditure is a waste of money that would be better spent in more productive ways:

> A cry-die – they should do it and forget. The person should be buried. But in the village, they bury the person, then after a month they have the next death celebrations, then after a year they come back and do it again. You know, I am a businessman; I have a business to run. It should be limited.[27]

Some burials in Bali are indeed spectacular forms of consumption, with elaborate programmes of dances, ceremonies, speeches, gun-firing, Christian services, feasting and drinking. They are also an opportunity to dress up in 'traditional regalia'. Sometimes several hundred people will be entertained, and for the burials of national politicians this figure can rise to thousands. Nowadays they can involve hiring seating, crockery, marquees, video-makers, dance groups, jujus, generators, lighting and sound systems as well as buying food and drinks. The BANDECA leadership commonly complains that, while it is hard to raise money from within the diaspora to pay for the medical costs of the living or to get a donation for infrastructure projects, it is easy to raise large sums of money to fund a death celebration. In some contexts such expenditure is portrayed as a wasteful indulgence and an unreasonable expectation that is placed on those living outside.

But death celebrations are used to flaunt the economic success of the living while officially lauding the dead. It is the very success of migrants (whether nationally or internationally) that fuels these expanded death celebrations. It is the choice of those outside to invest their money in this way: this is development of the culture within the terms of the culture, the logic is indigenous and concerns the expansion of the social life of the home. Bali is near enough to the main centres of the diaspora (Douala and Yaoundé) to make a weekend visit practicable and large groups of friends and colleagues can be transported to Bali for the occasion. Death celebrations are the main opportunity for conspicuous consumption in the village setting, and status is an immensely powerful lever when it comes to influencing how people opt to spend their money. There is a contradiction here between the elites' own desire to show off and their simultaneous ability to blame people in the village for this extravagance. Some are conscious of this antinomy: 'When there is a death, the more people attend your death celebration – this is very important for us. We elites condemn spending so much money on cry-dies but when it is our turn, we all do it!'[28] What is much less clear is how the ordinary people of Bali Nyong'a feel about the pressure to restrict death celebrations. Logically such a change would produce resentment not only because these are enjoyable social occasions but also because they are important in the local economy, driving demand for palm wine and food supplied by local producers and retailers.

One practical response to reduce expenditure has been to relocate the death celebrations (not the burials) away from Bali to the main centres of the diaspora population in the plantations and cities. This has the advantage of reducing transport costs for those attending and also means that the occasions have a more clearly defined start and finish because the families involved have to hire a venue rather than use the family compound. It also rather starkly reveals to be disingenuous the claim that the inflation of death celebrations is driven by the desires of those living in Bali. Another rationalizing response is for different families in the diaspora to club together and have one big death celebration simultaneously for several people. Combining occasions in this way maximizes the event's size and achieves economy of scale because they only have to hire equipment once. For some groups such as those in Douala and Limbe this process has been formalized so that all the death celebrations from within the *nda kum* are combined on one day every year. As the head of the Bali people in Douala argues, 'it is cheaper and more efficient this way'.[29]

This transfer of 'traditional' activity from the homeplace out to the diaspora is symptomatic of a wider trend in which some Bali diaspora members in Cameroon are seen by those in BANDECA as in need of cultural education: 'We need to find new ways to promote culture, and

BANDECA is coming up with a programme of action.'[30] Some *nda kums* on the coast, for example, have paid for xylophone players and other musicians to come and teach them how to sing and dance: 'The *nda kums* are about teaching our culture to the younger ones.'[31] This is necessary because many of the members of the *nda kum*s are the children or grandchildren of migrants who came to work in the plantations. Their knowledge of both esoteric and public aspects of Bali culture and language is, as a result, limited and so it is sometimes hard for them to participate in Bali occasions: 'They have become great men, but they were not very integrated with the culture. So once in a while when we meet we try to bring out certain salient cultural values that we discovered are disappearing.'[32] There is a sense of consciously re-educating people about their ethnic identity, both as a response to the increased political importance placed on belonging to a home and as a means of mobilizing diaspora resources for home development.

To conclude, then, this example illustrates how ideas of modernization are often central to the language used by home associations to explain their development activities. However, to think of modernization as the erasure of local cultures is misleading. Rather, what the mortuary and other changes to practices associated with burials and death celebrations show is that this process is better understood as the indigenization of modernity. The home association seeks to steer a communal response to the process of engaging with national and global labour markets, a response that is primarily of benefit to its members in Cameroon and justified by a logic of indigeneity. By changing the mechanics, rules and scale of death celebrations those outside not only fulfil their obligations to their kin but also gain status through the expansion of social life. The aim of joining the diaspora is to acquire wealth, but having acquired it members of the diaspora sometimes cash it in in traditional ways, whether in the homeplace itself or in the diaspora. It is hard, also, to resist the sense that part of this appropriation of modernity is motivated by the desire for a secure base in a rapidly changing world:

> Your origin is your tradition and you are dependent upon it. Tradition is just identity. You need to identify with a globalizing world within your limits, you cannot be anyone if you don't identify. If you leave your house you need to come back to your 'house' and to feel free. You need a base and a sense of belonging. It's about the maintenance and guarding of tradition. A feeling of being at home, out of home.[33]

But at the same time there is an alternative tendency at work that answers to a quite different logic – the logic of a different kind of development, best understood in terms of business, productive investment, capital mobility and accumulation. In this context the home association, again primarily representing the interests of the elite, attempts to place limits on the expansion of funerals and find ways in which the maximum cultural benefit can be achieved at the least cost, since they are the ones bearing that cost. Transferring death celebrations away from the homeplace and into the diaspora is one example. So, too, the association used a business logic to justify the construction of what was initially an unwanted development object – the mortuary. Since the mortuary makes money it has become popular and is considered a success, and enables the work of the association to continue in other fields.

Negotiating a path between development as investment in social life and development as investment in productive enterprises may appear difficult. Certainly there are contradictions that are difficult to reconcile such as the claim that the inflation of death celebrations is driven by those at home. However, there are also ways in which these two different logics of development articulate. The language of indigeneity and culture can also be effectively incorporated into a process of capital accumulation, as the following example from Bali shows:

> we are trying to negotiate with the people who live around the Squares [the centre of Bali Town], those who don't have money to invest, to lease out their properties to those outside. We want Bali to develop while retaining our culture, so we should lease these properties out to indigenes of the place. We would rather Bali indigenes do it.[34]

Indigenizing modernity is not a straightforward process but somehow it seems to work.

Culture, development and modernization in the other homeplaces

Similar processes are at work in the other Cameroon home areas. In Manyu further aspects of home culture (female circumcision, naked dancing) are seen by representatives of MECA to be in need of modernization, in addition to widowhood. As with Bali there is a deliberate policy of cultural revival within the diaspora, using family meetings to teach dance and music for example. The commitment to investing in culture is illustrated through the increased interest in initiation to ever-higher levels of membership societies such as Ekpe. This investment in culture is a vital means for those who live outside 'to become one with the village',[35] and it is once again seen as key to ensuring a secure base in a globalizing world. Only those confident of their economic autonomy are likely, for example, to invite a diaspora meeting's mockery by refusing to call the established libations for ancestors on the grounds that they run counter to Christian belief.[36]

There are also some clear affinities between the example from Bali and the work of DDTs in Tanzania. Sometimes these similarities are literal; for example the lack of a mortuary in Newala was seen as a barrier to diaspora participation in burials at home: 'lots of relatives in Dar would like to come for the burial but it has to be done the same day. Most Christians take their dead home if they can afford to do so, but very few Muslims do.'[37] Sometimes there are similar anxieties, for example fear of witchcraft in rural areas is used to explain why some people will not invest in houses or return home. In response the home association sets out to 'modernize cultural activities' by trying to educate people at home and in the diaspora and by leading the way in investing at home and going home for burials. In Rungwe there are comparable stories about the way that widowhood rites have been modernized by reducing the duration of mourning to a few days and how the extent of feasting during death celebrations has been curtailed for economic reasons: 'people were running away' because they couldn't afford to slaughter a cow when somebody died. Furthermore those running home associations were worried about the decline of culture in the diaspora and called for a renaissance:

> If there is a birth the clan comes. They used to bring a cock for a boy and a hen for a girl, but now this practice is dying out and they just send an SMS [mobile phone text message]. These are the cultures we want to maintain. It is important to preserve Nyakyusa culture because that's our identity. If you don't have your culture it is like being naked.[38]

The main difference between the Cameroonian and Tanzanian case studies in this discussion concerns the relationship between the state and the home association in relation to modernizing culture. Whereas the political climate produced by government policy in Cameroon endorses, compounds and amplifies the diaspora's desire to modernize home, that in Tanzania is more limited, circumspect and inhibiting. The efforts made by the Village Museum in Dar es Salaam to organize ethnically defined 'cultural weeks' are indicative of this context. This open-air museum, established in 1967 as the ethnographic department of the national museum, represents the Tanzanian nation by bringing together examples of vernacular domestic architecture from all around the country and displaying them side-by-side. Government cultural officers identified people in the countryside to come to Dar es Salaam and put up authentic houses. The museum's technical department worked with these different groups of builders to learn how to maintain the houses. This is an effective symbol of the way that the Tanzanian nation has successfully ordered the representation of diverse ethnicities as subordinate, equal and under state control.

Since 1994 the Village Museum has sought to enliven and renovate its displays and introduce other elements (such as performances of music and dance) to its programme. The principal strategy has been to focus on individual ethnic groups and to bring people from home and the diaspora together at the museum for three days to work on renovating 'their' house, to dance, prepare food, tell stories, perform oral histories and learn about their culture. In seminars people discuss history, burials, initiation and marriage rites, and how they bring up their children and they produce a written document as well as video and audio recordings. Such a policy produced a sceptical response from Tanzanian journalists who felt it might foster ethnic competition. The museum's curator defended the policy in terms of the relationship between globalization, culture and identity. He claimed there was a need for local media to help prevent Tanzanians from losing their identity as a result of the rising influence of the BBC and CNN:

> We told them it was nothing to do with tribalism, that we are trying to preserve our cultures. If we lose these, it will be our cultural loss and there will be no way to recover our cultural heritage once it is completely lost. This is our heritage, our roots, our identity. We should enter the global village with our identities! We can go to the global village as Tanzanians. But we don't have a Tanzanian culture, we have small cultures: the Bena, the Chagga … We can combine them to make something bigger that is Tanzanian culture.[39]

His view is that the museum is building on the success of Tanzanian nation-building, and that participants in these ethnic days are politically mature enough to celebrate cultures without looking down on other ethnic groups or harming the nation: 'We are far away from there. Some say, now you are bringing tribalism back in. We say, that is gone, that is history.'[40] In this respect a Tanzanian government institution is not only taking on the role of leading a cultural renaissance that in Cameroon is undertaken by the home associations, but is actually active in bringing home associations into existence. The museum's director explains how they organize the cultural weeks. After contacting prominent individuals from the group they want to work with:

we put a general invitation in the paper and on the radio, saying that we would like, for example, Haya people to work with the museum to act like hosts ... Some ethnic groups have their association, they are better organized, they are claiming to help development in their home areas. Those which didn't have such associations we encouraged them to establish them and they did ... For example the Makua had no organization when it was their week, so they formed one, and it was then registered with the Registrar of Societies. We united them.[41]

The Makua association in Dar es Salaam was formed jointly with the Yao because they had organized a shared cultural week in the museum and they both direct their development work towards Masasi and Tunduma districts. The museum initially provided them with administrative support such as phones and secretarial support.

These associations then help to plan the programme of events. They raise funds, and costs are shared between the association and the museum. The museum organizes a guest of honour (often a government minister from a different ethnic group) to open the event, arranges for publicity and suspends the usual entrance fee to encourage high attendance. At the end of the event the museum asks those who have attended to organize a meeting with government officials to discuss development in their homeplace. There were 12 such events involving 19 ethnic groups between 1994 and 2005, and now other groups are volunteering. Clearly this is a relatively limited initiative, but it is a very telling one in the light it sheds on both the public perception of ethnicity in Tanzania (Jerman, 1997) and the changing attitude towards ethnicity within the state: 'there are no government restrictions anymore, in fact they are helping us ... Ethnicity is the basis of our identity, but politicians tell us the basis of our identity should be Tanzanian. It sounds more modern.'[42] Whilst the first reflex in Tanzania is still to question association along ethnic lines, the government has recognized the developmental benefit of linking home and diaspora, resulting in a renewed interest in local cultures.

Notes

1. Tanzanian diaspora, Reading, UK, September 2006.
2. Bali diaspora, Buea, February 2005.
3. Bali diaspora, Bamenda, March 2005.
4. Bali diaspora, Buea, February 2005.
5. Bali diaspora, Limbe, February 2005.
6. President General BANDECA, Bali, April 2005.

7. Bali diaspora, Buea, February 2005.
8. Bali diaspora, Bamenda, March 2005.
9. Batibo is a subdivision neighbouring Bali.
10. Bali diaspora, Tiko, April 2005.
11. Bali diaspora, Mutengene, February 2005.
12. District Medical Officer, Bali, February 2005.
13. Bali, March 2005.
14. Traditional healer, Bali, March 2005.
15. Bali diaspora, Limbe, February 2005.
16. *Njangi* are rotating savings and credit associations (Ardener and Burman, 1996).
17. The Bali Cultural Association in the USA decided 'to negotiate a good life insurance policy for its members to respond to our cultural need of burying the dead at home.' (Jua, 2005: 330).
18. Bali diaspora, Douala, April 2005.
19. Bali diaspora, Limbe, April 2005.
20. Bali diaspora, Bamenda, March 2005.
21. Bali, February 2005.
22. Bali diaspora, Bamenda, April 2005.
23. Bali diaspora, Limbe, February 2005.
24. Bali diaspora, Bali, March 2005.
25. Bali diaspora, Bali, March 2005.
26. Bali diaspora, Douala, April 2005.
27. Bali diaspora, Mutengene, February 2005.
28. Bali, March 2005.
29. Bali diaspora, Douala, March 2005.
30. Bali diaspora, Bamenda, March 2005.
31. Bali diaspora, Yaoundé, April 2005.
32. Bali, February 2005.
33. Bali diaspora, Douala, April 2005.
34. Bali, February 2005.
35. Ajayukndip village, Manyu, February 2005.
36. Jokes made at the installation of the new Manyu Minister as Patron of MECA-Yaoundé, March 2005, in reference to a Manyu (Pentecostalist) chief's refusal to perform libations.
37. Newala diaspora, Dar es Salaam, September 2005.
38. Rungwe diaspora, Dar es Salaam, July 2005.
39. Village Museum Curator, Dar es Salaam, August 2005.
40. Ibid.
41. Ibid.
42. Ibid.

8 EDUCATION AND INEQUALITY

Diaspora associations' investments in education and health are central to the production and reproduction of homeplaces. Yet as chapters 4 and 5 made clear, home associations differ in structure and character, and their capacity to do development work is variable. A survey of the education and health projects that the home associations in the four study areas have undertaken reveals important differences in their capacities, and is outlined below. First, the associations in Cameroon and Tanzania differ in their international connections: the international diaspora (in Europe and the US) is far more active in Bali and Manyu than in Newala and Rungwe. Second, there are significant inequalities between the Newala and Rungwe domestic diasporas in terms of their relative size and capacity. These inequalities have repercussions for the provision of secondary education, which has been the priority for the Tanzanian associations and is analysed in detail below. What emerges from all four home areas, however, is that the domestic diaspora has a key role to play in the provision of social services at home, and particularly in the continued leveraging of support and resources for projects at home. Key individuals in the diaspora are relied upon to broker support from other sources such as governments and donors.

This chapter pays particular attention to education since it is central not only to the work that diaspora associations do, but also to the geography and character of the diasporas themselves. In all of the associations the leaders and committee members were an educated elite, often with postgraduate or professional qualifications (some earned abroad) and with established careers in government, the private sector, health or education. But the relative position and number of elites varied among the four homeplaces, as did their transnational connections. In particular the uneven provision of formal education to rural populations, which began in the colonial period, has meant that some diasporas are now better placed to support the development of home than others. This argument is developed in the second part of this chapter through a comparison of the Newala and Rungwe home associations' investments in secondary schools.

Diaspora provision of social services

Bali

In terms of social service provision BANDECA's two largest projects have been the mortuary (Chapter 7) and the water supply (Chapter 9). However, health and education have also been key concerns for the Bali diaspora. Indeed education is inscribed in BANDECA's constitution, which states a commitment 'To contribute on a philanthropic basis to the educational and cultural advancement of the Bali Nyong'a people'.[1] The international diaspora has undertaken various projects, sending both things (donations of books, computers and health equipment; provision of scholarships) and people (doctors to conduct health fairs). For example BCDA-UK sent 2.5 million CFA francs for primary school text-books as its annual development project in 2006, while BCA-USA sent 400,000 CFA francs for construction work at Government School Kutadntsi and made small awards for good Bali pupils,[2] as well as donating computers to some primary schools. As a member of the US diaspora argued, 'there is no electricity in the primary schools ... [but] at least by the time they get to secondary school they have seen one'.[3] At secondary level, the US diaspora has provided 12 scholarships equivalent to 70,000 CFA francs each.

The US diaspora has also actively supported health in Bali, sending three containers of medical and other equipment to Bali hospital via Douala port. However, as in Manyu, some of this remains in storage because the hospital lacks the skills and staff to use it. In recent years Bali in the US have organized health fairs, where doctors from the diaspora return home to give free consultations and dispense medicines donated by pharmaceutical companies. This was controversial, however: although the beneficiaries appreciated the fairs, the District Medical Officer complained that the doctors involved did not always dispense the correct medication or dosages, and that the medicines were sometimes out of date. There was no follow-up for patients; some would not even go to hospital with problems, preferring instead to wait for the next free health fair.[4]

The Bali diaspora in the USA is now planning a multi-function complex with the Bali Rural Council (rather than BANDECA), including a museum, computer training centre and public library. Some 10,000 books have already been shipped with another 10,000 to follow. Again, however, some elites in the Bali domestic diaspora and in Bali itself have challenged the appropriateness of such projects. BANDECA leaders complained that the US diaspora was not meeting the most urgent needs of those at home:

> The diaspora has been away so long, they are not in touch with the realities on the ground. They want to import development models from where they are … Bali [people] in the US take the basic necessities for granted. They can't understand the water supply problem, they don't feel the problems as we do here. The US priority project is a library. But here that is not a priority. The local population wouldn't know what to do with it.[5]

The domestic diaspora has supported schools and health facilities in Bali on a smaller scale than the international diaspora, although the lack of any specific BANDECA project has meant that support has come through other channels. Nk'umu Fed Fed, the Bali women's home association, has renovated health centres at Gungong and Wosing at a cost of 800,000 CFA francs, and has worked on a number of small educational projects across the subdivision. It has paid for the construction and roofing of classrooms and administrative structures in primary schools, sometimes working in conjunction with other bodies including the British Council and Catholic Mission Bali. It also funds scholarships for girls who do well in science, every year contributing 100,000 CFA francs, which is shared between the five secondary schools in Bali. Other investors include a group called Bon Ba Nyong'a (Children of Bali Nyong'a), comprising a dozen or so young businessmen in Bamenda, who invested 4.4 million CFA francs to build the private Star Bilingual nursery and primary school in Bali.

In terms of health and education facilities, then, Bali's international diaspora is more active than the domestic diaspora. This needs to be balanced by the fact that BANDECA's two main development projects (the mortuary and water supply) relied mostly on domestic, rather than international support.

Manyu

MECAs in both the international and domestic diaspora have been particularly active in contributing to public goods in the division, particularly in health and education. In contrast to the village development associations – the village-level home associations, which through their city branches in Cameroon form MECA's membership base – MECA has concentrated on Mamfe town on the grounds that doing so strengthens services centrally and sidesteps the risk of MECA leaders favouring their home villages or being accused of so doing. Mamfe General Hospital has been the beneficiary of various MECA projects for rehabilitation and equipment, with various MECAs giving cash (MECA-Yaoundé gave 2 million CFA francs) and support in kind. The international diaspora has also been very active. MECA-USA gave second-hand medical equipment including ECG and X-ray machines, while MECA-UK gave an incubator, hospital beds and a lawnmower. Subsequently, from 1996 to 2004, MECA-UK supported the rehabilitation and running of the children's ward at Mamfe hospital, sending equipment and books and paying for the salary of the ward matron. A local women's group claims to have undertaken rehabilitation work on behalf of MECA-UK, which sent a total of 2.4 million CFA francs for the project. MECA-Germany has also sent mattresses and medicines.

More recent MECA health projects have included the provision by E-Meditech, an American Christian NGO, of medicines to Mamfe hospital in conjunction with MECA-USA. MECA-Yaoundé has sent medical teams to give free consultations and medicines. At the time of fieldwork, MECA-Switzerland was planning to send further second-hand medical equipment to Mamfe hospital and sponsor its chief medical officer to go there.

Despite these considerable efforts the suitability and sustainability of donations were sometimes challenged in Mamfe. Medical equipment could be rendered useless because it came without instructions and because the necessary expertise to use it was lacking; there were allegedly also voltage incompatibilities.[6] Other equipment donated by the diaspora may be taken by doctors when they move on, and some pilfering of donated medicines has been witnessed as they were being delivered to the hospital.[7] Subsequent renovation has obliterated MECA's rehabilitation work there. MECA-USA's 'multipurpose centre' in the hospital grounds is supposed to include a dispensary as well as a mortuary, but this part of the building remains as empty as the rest. Such experiences make NOMA's plans to conduct 'telemedicine', at a Mamfe clinic that they hope to link to a doctor in the US, seem a distant prospect.

The village development associations have built and equipped health centres in their own villages in Manyu. Elites from the enclaved village of Eschobi, for example, persuaded SNV (the Netherlands development organization) to build a health centre there in around 2001. SNV employed its own technicians for the work but used local materials and labour. A local first-aider was trained but was not a permanent resident and so was available only for emergencies, which was problematic given the lack of a mobile phone network in the village. The village applied to Mamfe Rural Council for a nurse, who was promised but never seen, and the dispensary had no drugs. Constructing basic infrastructure may be relatively straightforward; getting the necessary equipment and skilled personnel and sustaining their use is quite another matter.

In terms of education Manyu is characterized by historically poor and geographically uneven provision, and the diaspora has provided valuable support since the early efforts of those working in the plantations. Paying school fees was a major reason and focus for the credit unions, *njangi* and other similar financial services organized by plantation workers. However, secondary education provision across Manyu remains poor. In 2003/04 the division had only 11 functioning state secondary schools (of which 5 were high schools), with another 2 going operational the following year, plus 3 faith-based high schools. The 11 state schools had a combined enrolment of 5,825 pupils but only 204 teachers across all subjects.[8] These schools are predictably concentrated in the central area of the division and along the middle and upper reaches of the Manyu River Valley, which are more densely populated and relatively accessible. This leaves children in the more sparsely populated and enclaved parts of Eyumojock and particularly Akwaya facing greater difficulties in accessing secondary education. This is compounded by poor primary school provision, which faces similar problems: many primary schools exist and function without sufficient permanent structures, sometimes without any. Again, they are severely understaffed: a report from 2004/05 records a shortfall of 575 primary and nursery school teachers, more than half the total needed.[9] Even where teachers are nominally appointed, many are 'ECI' (*en cours d'intégration*, that is, graduate teachers newly in post) and have not been paid for up to two years, causing widespread absence from duty. Missionary engagement in the Mamfe area is reflected in some school provision, for example the Presbyterian high school in Besongabang, on the site of the original Presbyterian mission there. This formed part of a wider pattern of colonial engagement which relatively favoured the Banyang, both educationally and politically.

Most diasporic support for education comes via the village development associations, which commonly engage in the construction, roofing or rehabilitation of village primary and/or secondary schools in conjunction with the community and sometimes other civil society actors such as parent–teacher associations. As well as infrastructure projects, village development associations sometimes contribute to scholarships or prizes for deserving students. At a meeting of Ntai Egbe Areng (the development association for the village of Bachuo Ntai) in Yaoundé, for example, the head teacher of the government secondary school in the village was canvassing for contributions for the end-of-year prize award ceremony, which rewarded academic performance, discipline, punctuality, sporting prowess, cleanliness, and duties such as manual work and prefecture; a teacher's prize was also available.[10] The Upper Banyang Cultural and Development Association in Kendem, one of the newer, subdivisional-level development associations, mobilized funding from the domestic diaspora and Tinto Rural Council to replace the roof of the village school during the 2005 Upper Banyang cultural week.

In education, then, the contributions of the village development associations exceeded those of MECAs, which are generally more focused on health and have attracted the most support from the international diaspora. The domestic diaspora thus predominated in material contributions (cash or in kind) to educational projects, made through the village development association city branches, while villagers usually provided labour for construction. The direct input of the international diaspora into education was much smaller and patchier by comparison: Ossing village had received funding for construction at the government secondary school from the Ossing Elements Cultural Association-UK;[11] the US Manyu diaspora raised funds for scholarships for Manyu students in Cameroon; and NOMA sent books for a library in the NOMA centre in Mamfe but, at the time of fieldwork, these were in jumbled piles in a back room.[12]

Newala

In Newala all diaspora support for development in the district has been channelled to education provision through the DDT the Newala Development Foundation (NDF). From 1989 NDF used their share of local crop cess, local labour and support from the Dar es Salaam diaspora to construct seven secondary schools, which took students to Form Four. As with other DDTs in Tanzania, NDF collaborated with Newala District Council in secondary education provision. The council collected the cess that funded NDF, set at Tsh10 per kilogram of farm produce sold by farmers in Newala to the Mtwara Regional Cooperative Union. Of this, Tsh5 was allocated to education, Tsh2 to buying desks, and Tsh3 to the 'Mtwara stadium fund', a project which never came to fruition. In

1993 the development levy was also transferred from the council to the foundation. NDF contributed 14,000 desks and invested in five minibuses to provide transport to the public and for pupils (Kiondo, 1995).

Newala District had no secondary schools until NDF upgraded St Peter's Middle School to Newala Day Secondary School in 1989. NDF then upgraded six more existing primary schools, including Tandahimba (1990), Mnyambe (1992), Mahuta (1996), Luagala (1996) and Kitangari (1996); Nangwanda Girls (1994) took over buildings that were formerly a military academy for Tanzanian militia and before that had been used by FRELIMO. In 1996 a new district, Tandahimba, was carved out of the east of Newala District. A new DDT (Tandahimba District Trust Fund) was subsequently established, splitting off from NDF and assuming responsibility for the three schools that now fell under its jurisdiction. All the schools constructed by NDF were handed over to government management except for Kitangari Secondary School, which has been run privately by NDF since it opened. We return to the case of Kitangari in more detail below.

Since NDF has no connections to international 'branches' of the Newala diaspora it relies entirely on its Foreign Relations committee in Dar es Salaam to access external support. This committee comprises the Newala elite in the city and has been particularly successful in attracting external resources for NDF schools, mainly Kitangari. These resources have included support for construction of school buildings, donations of equipment, and volunteer teachers, coming from donor governments or INGOs in South Africa, Canada, Japan, China, the US and the UK. Members of the domestic diaspora have also made personal donations: one gave a computer to the NDF office and textbooks to Newala Day; another gave a tractor.

Rungwe

As in Newala, the Rungwe diaspora is mosly concerned with expanding access to education at home and has also had to rely on its domestic rather than international connections. The earliest efforts in school building were organized in the 1980s through the district education trust, RUDET, but more recently a plethora of diaspora associations have sprung up to channel support to smaller geographical areas within the district.

In the 1980s support for education at home among Rungwe migrants in Dar es Salaam was organized on an ad hoc basis by the parliamentarian for Rungwe under the auspices of the Rungwe District Technical

Schools Fund (RDTSF). Though established in 1981 it was later registered (in 1988) as RUDET and was led by Rungwe elites including the Minister for Education, the parliamentarian, and the Rungwe District Commissioner. An impromptu Rungwe Association with approximately 20 regular attendees met every one or two months at the home of the Chair (the Minister for Education) or the Secretary (the director of the Dar es Salaam Business College). Contributions of Tsh10,000 per person per meeting were paid into a bank account in Rungwe, and by 1987 five schools had been opened through a combination of diaspora and local contributions and local labour. Once RUDET gained registration as a DDT it was integrated into the Rungwe District Council structure, with the RUDET board including four ward councillors, the District Executive Director and the District Education Officer. Nine per cent of the district development levy and varying proportions of crop cess income (on coffee, tea, cocoa and other commodities) went direct to RUDET's budget via the District Council. Between 1982 and 2005 RUDET supported the construction of 31 schools across Rungwe, although the trust's role in construction declined significantly after 1997.

The reasons for RUDET's decline are returned to below, but part of the explanation lies in the emergence from the mid-1990s of smaller home associations supporting school construction and other projects in more geographically specific areas of Rungwe (see Chapter 5). For example Rungwe East Development Foundation (RUEDEFO, covering Rungwe East constituency) collected Tsh1.7 million for the construction of Forms Five and Six at Lufilyo Girls' School, while the Selya Development Foundation (SEDEFO, covering four wards) contributed about Tsh6 million towards schools in Selya between 1998 and 2005.

The domestic diaspora and education provision in Tanzania

The preoccupation with secondary education among home associations in Tanzania reflects the fact that access to secondary education has historically been low in Tanzania (URT, 2000). Recent government plans stipulating that every ward in the country should have at least one secondary school have also oriented many civil society organizations towards education. Following earlier poverty reduction plans, which focused on the provision of free quality primary education, the Tanzanian government launched the Mpango wa Maendeleo ya Elimu ya Sekondari (MMES: Secondary Education Development Plan, 2004–9) to improve access to and the quality of secondary education. Ward schools

Table 8.1 Educational provision at secondary level in the Cameroon and Tanzanian home areas

	Population	No. of secondary schools	Population per school
Manyu	218,000	16	13,625
Bali	63,809	6	10,635
Newala	183,344	12	15,279
Rungwe	306,380	45	6,808

Sources: fieldwork 2005.

are to be constructed by 'communities', who are to contribute 25 per cent of the construction cost, with the rest made up from public money (URT, 2004). In practice 'communities' contribute cash and labour under the direction of the Ward Development Committee and are assisted by district engineers. The school is then handed over to government management, which covers the cost of teachers' salaries and teaching materials. In 2005, regular exhortations to 'communities' that they should 'participate' in the construction of their secondary school came from the President and the Minister for Education, and were echoed at the local level by parliamentarians and district, divisional, ward and village officials. Commonly schools are opened when they have up to four classrooms for two streams each of forms One and Two, an administrative block, one or two teachers' houses, and toilets. The government estimates the construction cost of a new, fully equipped school at Tsh7 million for every school year. For a school going up to Form Four this figure would need to be multiplied by five (URT, 2004: 41). The schools are therefore large financial undertakings and 'communities' across Tanzania are unequally positioned to raise such sums. This point is demonstrated by the comparison of Newala and Rungwe. In mid-2005, Rungwe had 31 schools with a further 14 under construction, whereas in Newala there were only 8 schools with a further 4 being constructed. Despite the stated MMES commitment to prioritize 'underserved areas', the differences are still huge (Table 8.1). In what follows we look at secondary provision in Rungwe and Newala in more detail in order to draw out the different roles that domestic diasporas play in developing their homeplaces. This is done by focusing on three schools: Isongole and Mwatisi in Rungwe, and Kitangari in Newala.

Constructing community schools in Rungwe District

Rungwe, unlike Newala, has had a secondary school since 1961, when the Moravian mission opened a school for boarders in Rungwe village. It was handed over to the government in 1970. This was the only secondary school in the district until the early 1980s, when RUDET and the community began to construct schools. Between 1982 and 1997 11 schools were built, and managed by either government, the church, or Wazazi (the national parents' association). Following a brief hiatus between 1997 and 1999, efforts were renewed and 19 schools had been built and one renovated by 2005, with a further 14 schools at various stages of construction. Although MMES aimed to have one school in every ward, Rungwe had surpassed this expectation with 45 schools for 30 wards. The newly appointed District Education Officer remarked that he had not witnessed this level of community effort in other districts in Mbeya Region.[13] This impressive record was achieved through a combination of contributions and communal labour by local people who paid discrete levies for schools, collected stones, sand and gravel, made bricks, and helped construct the buildings; support from local government, parliamentarians and various government and party officials; and a shifting cast of individuals and associations in the diaspora who contributed in cash and kind.

RUDET was the most important home association in the district until the mid-1990s, but after 2000 it was able only to 'encourage' the construction of many of the new schools.[14] In 2004 the trust supported the construction of 25 schools across the district: 15 were awarded sums of under Tsh200,000, and only 3 were granted over Tsh800,000.[15]

RUDET's role changed for two reasons. First, it elected to support all schools in some way rather than concentrate funds on a selected few. This enabled RUDET to respond to the specific needs of schools close to completion. Many schools were not complete when they began to accept the first streams into Form One because of financial constraints and the pressure to open. The intention in most schools was to have the absolute necessities in place and to improve and expand on these year on year as students progressed through Forms One to Four, thus spreading the cost to the community over time. Second, RUDET's main income streams suffered a major blow when the Tanzanian government abolished the development levy and placed a 5 per cent cap on crop cess in June 2003. The acting District Executive Director estimated that the council's income from local taxation had since declined by almost 50 per cent.[16] RUDET's council grant had been stalled; RUDET claimed that the

Table 8.2 RUDET accounts in Tanzanian shillings

	2004	2003
Income		
Crop levy	23,109,130	19,219,267
Other	148,268	4,720,940
Donations/gift	1,927,200	9,900,000
Total	25,184,598	33,840,207
Expenditure		
Personnel	8,845,680	8,455,905
Schools	10,936,250	13,288,590

Source: RUDET accounts, 2004, Tukuyu.

Table 8.3 RUDET income from crop cess in Tanzanian shillings

	2004	2003
Coffee cess	2,395,806	2,039,281
Cocoa cess	7,299,600	10,057,653
Tea cess	13,413,724	7,122,333

Source: RUDET accounts, 2004, Tukuyu.

council still 'owed' them Tsh10 million.[17] At the same time, prices of inputs and commodities fluctuated in a liberalized agricultural sector (Mwamfupe, 1998), affecting the two major cash crops in the district (coffee and tea). Since sales could now be conducted through private channels as well as the primary societies, collection of the crop cess became more difficult. Nevertheless the cess was the most significant income stream for RUDET in 2003 and 2004, with the recent expansion into tea production providing a much-needed boost in 2004 (tables 8.2 and 8.3).

However, even with RUDET's finances under strain, community schools continued to be constructed across the district. They were supported in novel ways by new home associations in Dar es Salaam and Mbeya, which identified with smaller parts of the district. Below we briefly consider two cases that give some insight into the relative roles of the domestic diaspora, local communities, and government and party officials.

Isongole Secondary School

Isongole ward lies in the north of Rungwe District on the border with Mbeya Rural District. It is already served by one of the secondary schools built during RUDET's early days, now run by Wazazi, but villagers wanted a new government school because the fees would be lower. The Wazazi school charges annual fees of Tsh150,000 for day students, which must be paid up-front, while government secondary school fees have been set at Tsh40,000, are further subsidized by 50 per cent, and can be paid in instalments. Isongole Secondary School is in Mbeya One village, close to the ward offices and adjacent to the main tarmac road that runs through Rungwe. The community, organized by the Ward Development Committee, began construction of the school in 2003 and it opened in 2004. By mid-2005 it had four classrooms for two streams in forms One and Two, with a further three under construction to accommodate forms Three and Four. Having been told to expand further to four streams for each year, the community has made plans to build two classrooms every year for the next four years.[18] Funding for the existing buildings came from a range of sources.[19] Locally, the District Council contributed Tsh1 million, ward levies were collected (Tsh10,000 per person) and RUDET gave Tsh100,000. Isongole ward comprises eight villages, each of which was charged with the construction of a particular building in the school, as directed by the Ward Development Committee. More expensive buildings were given to more prosperous villages: for example Ntokela (population 3,000) was building two classrooms, while Ndwati (population 800) was building one staff house. The village of Ngumbulu, which was also expected to build a staff house, was making slow progress because it was located 19 km away from the school. Government had provided funding for the construction of one staff house, teaching materials and the payment of full-time teachers (although in 2005 the school had no biology, chemistry or Swahili teachers and needed another maths and physics teacher, and was itself paying five part-time teachers). Government was also sponsoring some of the poorest students (six in Form One). However, government subsidies for fees (Tsh20,000 per student) had only arrived for those in Form Two by mid-2005, and a further grant to the school of Tsh10,000 per student earmarked from MMES funds had also not arrived. Parents' fees had all been paid.

The Isongole diaspora in Mbeya and Dar es Salaam, most of whom conduct business, also got organized to contribute to the construction of the school. They began building a two-classroom block but the death of their chairman and the subsequent disappearance of the money collected set back progress. Under new leadership the diaspora's classrooms were being roofed. Contributions, generally ranging between Tsh50,000 and Tsh100,000, were solicited on an individual basis by key people who were then expected to raise money among their communities and personal networks. In Mbeya, two representatives sought out those from the different ethnic groups resident in Isongole: one concentrated on collections among Safwa and Nyakyusa, the other among Kinga. The majority of contributions were collected from the Safwa diaspora, reflecting their domination of the ward. However, this fundraising also reveals how diasporas reproduce ethnic difference, since the collectors complained that the Nyakyusa were unwilling to contribute to what they considered to be a 'Safwa school'. Such antipathy has historical roots: strained relations between the Nyakyusa and the Safwa go back to the colonial period, if not before (Wilson, 1959; Charsley, 1969). Monica Wilson refers to Nyakyusa crossing the Poroto Mountains to settle in 'Safwa country' in the 1940s (1951: 4) and suggests the Safwa would have been 'conquered and absorbed' were it not for the 'vigilance of the British Administration' (1959: 19). Today political belonging, while discouraged in political discourse in Tanzania, can nevertheless be discerned in particular circumstances such as in local competition for representation and resources, and in diaspora support for the construction of a community secondary school.

Mwatisi Secondary School

Mwatisi is a school in the town of Mwakaleli in Kandete ward of Rungwe District. Mwakaleli was historically an important centre in Rungwe because of the Lutheran mission located there at the end of the nineteenth century. It is also the location of Mwakaleli Secondary School which, in 1982, was one of the first schools to be opened with assistance from RDTSF. As in Isongole, Mwatisi Secondary School is a community school, with individual villages each given the task of constructing a different building. However, although the school opened in 2004, classrooms have so far been completed only up to Form Two. Two classrooms were thus serving all 4 classes of about 45 students in mid-2005. The school has four teachers and lacks staff in several subjects. The first round of community contributions for school construction had been set at Tsh1,500 per household, plus labour, and a second round was under way in mid-2005. Contributions were collected by the village chairman and overseen by the Ward Executive Officer, who pointed out that 'the District Executive Director [DED] ordered that every ward should have its own secondary school, so opposing that [that is, by not paying] is to oppose an order from the DED'.[20] At least 20 people were called to appear before a ward tribunal because they failed to pay the first contribution.

Further contributions for the school were solicited through fundraising events organized by the parliamentarian for Rungwe East and local government officials. The *harambee* (a community fundraiser) is held annually in a different ward in Rungwe East, which secures further contributions from local people, the domestic diaspora and invited guests such as national and regional government officials who either have a link with Rungwe or who are personal friends. In 2002 the *harambee* was held in Kandete, with the Regional Commissioner for Kilimanjaro (who comes from Kandete) officiating as guest of honour. A total of Tsh26 million was raised for the school, Luteba dispensary and a water project to cover the four wards of Mwakaleli. The parliamentarian was also able to secure a contribution of Tsh1 million towards the school from a Kenyan minister with whom he had studied in the UK. A plaque on the wall of the school's administration block commemorates the laying of the foundation stone by the Kenyan minister. Other contributions came from the parliamentarian himself, RUDET, the DED's office, the District Commissioner's office, the Rungwe Small Tea Growers Association, and the Rungwe East diaspora in Mbeya and Dar es Salaam. Prior to the 2002 *harambee*, prominent members of the Kandete diaspora were personally contacted by the parliamentarian to solicit funds. Some gave individually and some through one of the diaspora associations that have recently mobilized to support development in different parts of the district. These include associations such as Rungwe East Development Foundation (RUEDEFO), which is concerned with development in the constituency; Shirika la Maendeleo ya Busokelo (SHIMABU), which supports Busokelo Division within Rungwe District (and is coterminous with Rungwe East constituency); Selya Development Foundation (SEDEFO), which supports four wards in the constituency to the south of Mwakaleli, but which nevertheless contributed Tsh300,000 during the 2002 *harambee* for Kandete; and *Wazaliwa wa Kandete waishio Dar es Salaam* ('Those born in Kandete who are living in Dar es Salaam'), which supports the ward. It is worth quoting at length the chairman of the Kandete diaspora association on how money was raised in Dar es Salaam:

> In 2003 the ward councillor for Kandete and the Pastor from Ndola came to Dar es Salaam to meet with the residents of Kandete ward here. They asked for support in their development endeavours and they wanted help with the construction of Mwatisi Secondary School ... We formed a committee here to help the Ward Development Committee (WDC) at home. I am Chair, I mobilize all of those from Kandete ... there are 257

people from Kandete here in Dar es Salaam. Every person contributes Tsh5,000 a month. Between November 2003 and January 2004 they wanted to collect a lot of money – Tsh3.5 million – to enable them to open the school. Ten of us from this sub-branch [the Dar es Salaam branch] of the WDC agreed that committee members should raise this money through our friends. Most of the others are low-income earners. We raised Tsh3.4 million and sent it home for the school with a member of the committee to see that the money was properly used. We continued to collect money and we have now contributed in total Tsh5,752,000 … they have sent us requests for more help, at the moment they have a problem of desks, and every desk is Tsh13,000. They need 80 desks for two classrooms. We will send the money this month, as some of our colleagues who are well off have said that they will make sure that the school will get desks … they know how to raise money'.[21]

Although the Kandete diaspora is well organized with regular contributions being collected, the extra funding required for the school relied on a few well-placed individuals who used their own contacts, often through work or political party connections, to raise the required amounts. Similar accounts of fundraising among the domestic diaspora and 'key resource persons' who, importantly, were often not members of the diaspora in question, came from schools all over Rungwe East. In contrast to Isongole, then, the Kandete contributions did not reflect ethnic or regional affiliations. Rather, fundraising was done among colleagues in the knowledge that reciprocation would be expected at some point in the future.

NDF and community schools in Newala

NDF, the only home association for Newala district, was at the forefront of secondary school construction from the mid-1980s to the mid-1990s and continues to manage Kitangari Secondary School. Yet as with RUDET, NDF's income has declined in recent years, severely constraining its ability to respond to the government's drive to put a secondary school in every ward. NDF's position has been further undermined by the creation of Tandahimba District in the east (carving a new district trust out of NDF), and by the instability of the cashew crop. The crop cess, which mostly comes from cashew, has until recently underwritten NDF's recurrent expenditure (Table 8.4). Cashew production was relatively good until 2000, but thereafter production declined and world market prices fell (Tadreg, 2007). The accounts also show the meagre returns on NDF's short-lived attempt to diversify its activities into the domain of agriculture, when it tried to help cashew farmers increase their production by selling them sulphur dust as a fungicide. NDF officers claim that farmers did not always pay and the sulphur project was clearly not financially viable, returning a profit of little over 4 per cent.

The abolition of the development levy and the cap on the crop cess in 2003 further compounded NDF's poor financial position. The District Council now collected less, and divided the money earmarked for education between NDF and the council. NDF board members have loaned money to NDF in order to cover its running costs, including the management of Kitangari Secondary School and the maintenance of a ten-person secretariat in Newala Town. In 2005 NDF took out a Tsh16 million bank loan (at a 19 per cent interest rate) using its buildings and vehicles as collateral. Even allowing for inflation, such a sum equates to a sizeable proportion of the income that it previously gained from the cess (Table 8.4). On the other hand, NDF has shown considerable entrepreneurial skill in obtaining significant grants from international donors for construction and refurbishment at Kitangari. The fact that two current NDF leaders have useful government and diplomatic contacts has been key to securing these donations. But while such capital works undoubtedly improve the infrastructure and living conditions at the school, they do nothing to improve NDF's underlying lack of a steady and sufficient income stream.

Table 8.4 NDF income and expenditure account (Tanzanian shillings), 2000.

	2000	1999
Income		
Crop cess	87,556,845	64,145,974
Donations/grants	20,537,410	329,500
School fees/other	5,889,716	16,085,080
Profit from sulphur project	258,000	—
Total	114,251,971	80,560,554
Expenditure		
Personnel	21,883,495	17,967,720
School/admin/business	49,860,451	34,126,192
Total	71,743,946	52,093,912
Surplus	42,508,025	28,466,642

Source: NDF balance sheet and accounts as at 30 September 2000. Dodoma: Co-operative Audit and Supervision Corporation.

In this context, the building of new schools in Newala has been undertaken by communities without input from NDF. In mid-2005, four community schools had been opened and a further four were under construction. The new community secondary school being built in Kitangari, for example, relied on contributions from residents, set by the divisional and ward officials at Tsh200 per household; a sliding scale of Tsh500–5,000 for local businesses; Tsh10,000 from each primary school; Tsh5,000 from the head of each government department; and Tsh2,000 from all other government employees.[22] The relatively low household contribution, compared with those levied for schools in Rungwe, reflects differences in household income between the two districts. The community also contributed labour by collecting sand and water and making bricks. Other contributions came from local businessmen, such as a wholesaler and guesthouse owner who gave bags of cement and offered transport. Newala District Council gave 90 bags of cement and 4 lorryloads of large quartz boulders for the foundations. Support also came from the Rural Integrated Project Support Programme, a FINNIDA-funded project covering Lindi and Mtwara regions, which had begun in 1988 and was soon to end. But there were no contributions from the domestic diaspora, nor from NDF.

The intersection of history, politics and identity in Tanzania

The domestic diaspora has played an important role in the provision of secondary education in Newala and Rungwe. Across Tanzania, informal support to community schools in the early 1980s became formalized by the end of the decade as District Development Trusts channelled local and diaspora contributions to schools in collaboration with district councils. Kiondo refers to this as a kind of 'privatization of development' (1995: 163) whereby public goods are provided via a combination of external donations and local taxation but the institution delivering them is not held to account through universal franchise, even if the trust leaders hold elected posts. Kiondo suggested that the local state in Tanzania had become 'politically and economically marginalized in the period prior to the creation of the [trust] funds' (1995: 164). However, continued local government reform in Tanzania has changed this picture. In Newala, NDF continues to channel the support of a small elite in Dar es Salaam and Newala Town to the management of Kitangari Secondary School, but has been unable to contribute to the construction of new schools. Yet NDF remains the central mechanism through which elites in the domestic diaspora engage with home. In Rungwe, by contrast, the domestic diaspora has continued to support new schools, albeit not through RUDET. Rather, RUDET has been bypassed as a number of smaller home associations tied to villages, wards, divisions, and constituencies have emerged to better suit the political strategies and developmental obligations of Rungwe's diasporic elite. The district trusts have been marginalized but the outcomes in Newala and Rungwe have been very different, revealing both the material effects of the interweaving of history, politics and identity in the different places, and the consequent capacity of the diaspora to undertake development at home.

The comparison of Newala with Rungwe reveals that the history of access to education has been critical in shaping the diasporas from each place and their capacities to invest further in education at home. Newala is objectively the poorest of all four homeplaces[23] and continues to be under-served in terms of secondary education (URT, 2000).[24] It also has the smallest diaspora active in the development of home, both in Tanzania and in the UK. In fact, the four secondary schools that had recently been opened and the four under construction in Newala were largely achieved by local communities with little diaspora investment through NDF or any other association. But in Rungwe, by contrast, diaspora involvement had helped local communities to open 19 new schools, renovate 1, and start construction on a further 14.

The structure and character of Newala's diaspora reveals the problems that the historical lack of educational facilities has posed for recent community development efforts led by a small elite. Although the rate of out-migration from Newala is high (Tadreg, 2007) and the diaspora in Dar es Salaam has plenty of associations that organize the burial of kin and neighbours, the capacity of this diaspora to make contributions to an association such as NDF is severely limited because its members have generally not reached the middle or higher echelons of government service or of the private sector. The so-called *wamachinga* leave the south citing a lack of opportunity and arrive in Dar es Salaam with little more than their entrepreneurialism to help them manage life in 'Bongo'.[25] In another example of the ways in which diasporas consider the well-being of those at home and in the diaspora as part of the same social field, the NDF branch in Dar es Salaam aims to engage the *wamachinga* through small loans, arguing that it needs to increase the economic footing of the diaspora before expecting contributions to home. As noted in Chapter 5, NDF has no international 'branches' and in the UK the Newala diaspora is very small.[26] Those from Newala in the UK had all been to secondary school and had either already obtained, or were pursuing, graduate or postgraduate qualifications in the UK with government, private or self-sponsorship. In a national context where, until recently, a minority completed Form Six,[27] such observations underline the relationship between education and individual mobility.

The underprovision of formal education in Newala goes back to the colonial period. The Arab traders who passed through the Makonde Plateau during the eighteenth and nineteenth centuries brought Islam and Koranic schools, so that 'by 1910, every village on the Makonde and Mwera Plateaux was said to have a *mwalimu* [teacher]' (Iliffe, 1979: 213). Students at Koranic schools learned to recite the Koran but were rarely literate (Iliffe, 1979). Instead the provision of formal education went hand in hand with evangelization, and by the end of the nineteenth century Christian missionaries, in particular the Anglicans and Benedictines, were also in the business of winning souls in the area (Clayton, 1993). In 1876 the High Anglican Universities' Mission to Central Africa (UMCA) founded a mission at neighbouring Masasi, only establishing many 'bush schools' (rural kindergartens) on the Makonde Plateau from the 1920s onwards, while the Benedictines also founded missions in the lowlands. Neither the UMCA nor the Benedictines established secondary schools on the plateau, instead focusing their efforts on their lowland missions at Chidya and Ndanda respectively. It was a Christian minority who attended the mission schools: indeed, the colonial administration's support of mission schools over the longer-established Koranic schools aroused suspicion among the Islamized Makonde (Liebenow, 1971). In Newala in the 1950s, many locally appointed administrators had attended Koranic schools but had not completed secondary school (Liebenow, 1971). By 1955, Newala had primary schools (25 UMCA, 16 Roman Catholic and 4 government), middle schools (3 UMCA, 1 Roman Catholic and 1 government), but no secondary school (Liebenow, 1971). This remained the case until 1989 when NDF opened Newala Day Secondary School.

In Rungwe, by contrast, four Lutheran and Moravian missions were established in the early 1890s (the Lutherans in the west at Manow, now Selya, and at Mwakaleli; and the Moravians in the east at Tukuyu and Rutenganio). They also established 'bush schools', which were later replaced by primary schools providing vernacular instruction. Primary schooling was also greatly expanded during the last ten years of German rule in the areas where German missionaries worked (Iliffe, 1979). The provision of primary and middle schools was particularly important given the quality of the more common 'bush schools', where many students did not learn to read or write (Wilson, 1951). By the 1930s the missions had schools that took children up to Primary Standard IV, and at Rungwe there was a mission boarding school (Wilson, 1959); however, the English class was closed down in keeping with the colonial state's preference for the 'adaptive', rather than 'literary' education model (Iliffe, 1979). The colonial state also made limited provision for the education of a select few through Native Authority and Administration primary and middle schools, which in Rungwe were characterized by a district officer as 'aristocratic schools' (Iliffe, 1979; 328). Nevertheless, the missionaries' educational work brought advantages to those groups among whom they worked, which were to reverberate through the postcolonial era. The Nyakyusa of Rungwe, for example, were one of the over-represented groups among the Tanganyikan students at Makerere in the 1930s (Iliffe, 1979). And in 1961, the government upgraded the Rungwe mission boarding school to a secondary school.

Inequality in access to education continued into the postcolonial era. At independence, despite the lack of post-primary facilities, Newala was considered to have a surfeit of primary schools relative to other parts of the country (Liebenow, 1971). Literacy rates in the south reportedly ranged from 85 per cent in Masasi, where the missions were located, to 45 per cent in Newala, to under 20 per cent in the coastal districts (Wembah-Rashid, 1998). The government's prioritization of primary schooling meant that in Newala, all bush schools and some primary schools were closed down and their teachers were transferred (Wembah-Rashid, 1998). This had severe repercussions at the local level. Based on his research in the 1960s, Liebenow (1971) considered the Makonde to be among the most poorly educated groups in Tanzania. By the late 1980s, the regions of southern Tanzania (Mtwara, Lindi, Ruvuma) were faring reasonably well in primary education, but less so in secondary education, with Mtwara's and Lindi's share of secondary school pupils (including private schools) nationally being less than two per cent (Seppälä, 1998a).

Following political liberalization from the early 1990s the role of DDTs in providing education became closely interwoven with local and national politics. At the local level DDTs are bound up with district politics and the rewards associated with leaders' abilities to 'bring development' to a given locality. In Newala, all three NDF Chairs either had been or became parliamentarians, two of them during their time as NDF Chair. As an elite in Dar es Salaam put it, 'if you are contesting the Newala constituency and you're not with NDF you're wasting your time'.[28] The incumbent NDF Chair was duly elected parliamentarian for Newala during the 2005 elections. He campaigned on his record in education, reminding people that the district's first secondary schools had been built under his watch as both Newala District Commissioner and part of the NDF leadership. He was also aided in this endeavour by a grant of Tsh5.6 million from the Foundation for Civil Society[29] for 'good governance' seminars in the district, to which participants from many villages were invited with laid-on transport and attendant *per diems*. The seminars included sessions on the history and future of NDF, and strategies for resource mobilization. In contrast to NDF, RUDET's political utility was undermined in 1995 when Rungwe was split into two constituencies, Rungwe East and Rungwe West. RUDET had been chaired by the parliamentarian for Rungwe District between 1988 and 1994, but following the division efforts were diverted to the new constituencies, and new funds were set up in Dar es Salaam (RUEDEFO and RUWEDEFO) through which the two parliamentarians sought resources for their constituencies/home areas, bypassing RUDET in the process.

In Newala, however, although NDF is financially constrained, it is still an important player in district politics, not least because it is the only home association through which the domestic diaspora can have any leverage at home. This has brought it into conflict with the District Council,[30] most recently over Kitangari Secondary School, managed by NDF since its construction in 1996. It is NDF's most significant development project in the district and has attracted much external donor support. But the council complains that NDF management of just one secondary school is an inefficient use of the local crop cess when government is responsible for all other schools in the district, including building new ones. The council also questions the quality of the built environment and the standard of education offered at Kitangari. As the District Planning Officer put it, 'what NDF is doing is like standing on a moving train carrying luggage on their head'.[31] The council would therefore prefer to manage the school itself. However, such a decision would need to be taken by the full council, and since many of the district councillors[32] are also members of the NDF board, this has yet to happen. Presumably NDF would cease to receive a share of local crop cess if the school passed to government management.

Such disputes are not new in Newala. In the early 1990s a series of disagreements erupted between NDF and local and regional government over NDF's use of the crop cess to buy primary school desks. When the Mtwara Regional Development Committee (RDC) directed that the desk funds should go to Newala District Council instead of NDF, citing misuse of the money, NDF refused. The Mtwara RDC then ordered Mtwara Regional Cooperative Union, which collected the cess, to forward the funds directly to the council, which it duly did. The following year NDF made a complaint to the Minister of Home Affairs and the Deputy Prime Minister, this time accusing the council of misusing the funds. In Newala, NDF boycotted the District Development Committee (Kiondo, 1995).

Underlying these tussles over local taxes is a tension over who should be responsible for development in Newala. NDF has resisted the council's claims on Kitangari on the basis that only NDF can be trusted to expand the school to provide forms Five and Six. Such fears are not unfounded given the persistent underinvestment in the region (Wembah-Rashid, 1998). There are still only two other schools in Mtwara Region offering forms Five and Six, neither of which are on the Makonde Plateau. If the school does come under government management NDF will suffer a severe blow to its credibility among those at home and among donors; it will also lose its leverage with voters and local government.

In Tanzania, popular explanations for regional inequalities in education have tended to invoke cultural differences between ethnic groups. Although public discourse on ethnic difference is politically sensitive, nevertheless particular ethnic groups are widely held to be more 'development-minded' because of their relatively early access to formal education. The Chagga, Haya and Nyakyusa, among others, are claimed to have reaped the rewards of education and used their positions (public and private) to reinvest, often in education, at home. These ethnic groups have thus developed a 'culture' of mutual support and investment at home, which is shared among a large pool of educated people in the domestic diaspora. In contrast other groups, including the Makonde, are identified as 'less developed', either because missionary education did not reach them or because they did not take advantage of it in the manner of their highland compatriots. In such areas, the consequent lack of development has become associated with the 'culture' of particular ethnic groups.

In Newala such attitudes are common among outsiders, for example among local government employees in reference to local populations (Seppälä, 1998a; also Marsland, 2006), but they are also discernible in elite diaspora discourses about home and the work that they do there. The provision of schools is the mechanism through which elites assume responsibility for 'educating' people in the village to become 'more developed', echoing the attempts to modernize home discussed in Chapter 7. For NDF officials, for example, investing in schools in Newala is ultimately about making the local population more modern. Education was seen by elites as central to development and would lead to various improvements such as economic advancement (such as the 'correct' use of agricultural inputs, doing tax returns), political engagement (such as registering to vote) and social development (such as family planning). Cashew farmers in the district were accused of squandering their income on conspicuous consumption at home or in Dar es Salaam, on marrying extra wives, buying witchcraft in Mozambique, or *ngoma*. In this context, NDF officials claimed, education would encourage people to invest in housing improvements or business activities instead.

Yet home association leaders in Dar es Salaam, faced with the constant challenge of mobilizing support among their folk in the diaspora, often despaired of what they described as the 'culture' of their people in the diaspora as well as at home. Those in the diaspora, it was argued, needed to be educated about the value of self-help and investing at home, otherwise their home areas would be left behind and the benefits of rural investment would be reaped by others. The Nyakyusa from Rungwe felt they had recently 'fallen behind' other groups and that they needed to re-discover their zeal for development. In this sense 'culture' is not static or innate, but dynamic and acquisitive. Many diaspora leaders claimed that they needed to follow the example of those ethnic groups whose 'culture' oriented them towards supporting development at home. As one elite in Dar es Salaam put it, 'the Chaggas are more home-loving than we are … but if we can learn from them …'

But the problem of mobilization is not simply one of rediscovering or developing a more 'home-loving' culture. Rather, the efficacy of diaspora mobilization is bound up with the intersection of history, politics and identity, and can work out differently in different places, as the comparison of Rungwe and Newala reveals. In Rungwe the decline of RUDET, for example, was driven not only by the new parliamentarians' political aspirations but also by those in the urban diaspora who want to ensure that their collective development efforts are acknowledged by their own rural kin. Associations based on administrative areas such as villages, wards and divisions, or on historical areas such as chiefdoms or the territories of *abanyafyale*, rather than a (large) district, more easily connect the diaspora to the homeplace that expects their contribution. Leaders of urban associations complained that collections for public goods located in the district, but not necessarily in the homeplace, were often met with the response, 'Why should I give if my family will not benefit?' In Newala, however, the intersection of history, politics and identity has produced a differently organized diaspora. While the Rungwe diaspora is more fragmented, Newala's historical acephalous social and political organization, coupled with the neglect of colonial and postcolonial governments, has bound the relatively small elite together in a common concern for the position of the district within the nation-state. There is a widely felt need in the domestic diaspora for indigenes of Newala to counter long-term state neglect. NDF provides the only vehicle through which they can attract external resources from donors that cannot be controlled by local or central government.

Conclusions

The contributions that home associations make to social services at home may in some instances be relatively small, but in contexts where substantial investments in those services rely on prioritization by governments or donors, they are by no means insignificant. The kinds of projects taken on by diaspora associations are those often overlooked in grander schemes: they are small-scale, locally specific, and responsive to local needs. Diaspora associations do make a difference in the health and education sectors in their communities of origin.

However, there is an uneven geography of diasporic engagement with development at home. The Cameroonian international diaspora has made far more contributions to development projects in their homeplaces than the Tanzanian international diaspora. It does not necessarily follow, however, that an organized international diaspora contributes more than the domestic diaspora. For example, the domestic diaspora has predominated in investments in education in Manyu, and in both Cameroon and Tanzania the domestic diaspora plays a key role in brokering support from external sources such as governments and donors.

The closer consideration of the Tanzanian case presented here further reveals the inequalities inherent in devolving social service provision to communities. Diasporas may contribute to the improvement of the quality of life at home, but clearly those at home are taking on the greatest burden in education improvement by paying crop cess and by contributing household levies and labour. Furthermore, the comparison of Newala and Rungwe shows how history, politics and identity intertwine to produce differently organized diasporas with different capacities for development at home. The underprovision of secondary schools in Newala is partly explained by the burden placed on a small educated elite, but it is also a reflection of the capacity of local communities to provide their own social services. The Tanzanian case reminds us of the need to pay attention to the unevenness of diasporic engagement with home: which diasporas are helping to reproduce which places? The evidence presented here suggests that, while diasporas can make a contribution to improving the quality of life at home, some homes are likely to get more help than others.

Notes

1. BANDECA constitution, 1999, p.2.
2. Interview, Subdivisional Inspector of Primary and Nursery Education, Bali, January 2005.
3. Interview, Bali, February 2005.
4. Interviews, District Medical Officer, Bali, February 2005; member of US diaspora, Bali, February 2005.
5. BANDECA official, Bali, April 2005.
6. Interviews, Chief Medical Officer, Mamfe General Hospital, February 2005; electrician, Mamfe, February 2005.
7. Interviews, MECA officer, Douala, March 2005; electrician, Mamfe, February 2005.
8. *End of Year Report 2003/04*, Divisional Delegation of National Education for Manyu. These numbers have apparently increased since 2005 with certain schools being upgraded to high school status and one or more new secondary schools established (interview with member of Manyu diaspora, London, October 2006; pers. comm. with Manyu research assistant, December 2007).
9. *The placing of teachers in primary/nursery education in Manyu 2004/2005*, Divisional Delegation of Education for Manyu.
10. Circular from the Principal, GSS Bachuo Ntai, re prize award ceremony, April 2005; presented to a meeting of Ntai Egbe Areng, Yaoundé, April 2005.
11. Interview, member of Ossing diaspora, London, October 2006.
12. Interview, Subdivisional Inspector of Nursery and Primary Education, Mamfe, February 2005; minutes of MECA-USA leadership, 4 November 2006, http://www.mecausa.org/minutes.html.
13. Interview, District Education Officer, Tukuyu, July 2005.
14. Interview, RUDET executive committee, Tukuyu, July 2005.
15. RUDET accounts, 30 June 2004.
16. Interview, Acting DED Rungwe, Tukuyu, July 2005.
17. Interview, RUDET executive committee, Tukuyu, July 2005, and RUDET accounts, 30 June 2004.
18. Interview, Headmaster, Isongole Secondary School, Mbeya One, July 2005.
19. Ibid.
20. Interview, ward executive officer, Kandete, July 2005.
21. Interview, Kandete diaspora, Dar es Salaam, September 2005.
22. Interview, Division Officer and Ward Education Coordinator, Kitangari, August 2005.
23. To take a crude measure, 43 per cent of the population of Newala live below the Tanzanian daily poverty line, and 32 per cent in Rungwe (URT, 2005). Comparative data for Cameroon is not available.
24. In 1999 Newala had a total of just four secondary schools, while Rungwe had twelve (URT, 2000: 51).

25. Meaning 'brains' but referring to Dar es Salaam: the implication being that to survive in the city you need to be sharp.
26. During the course of this research we were able to trace three people from Newala in the UK. Ours was not an exhaustive search but the difficulty of finding them compared with the relative ease of finding those from other parts of the country is instructive.
27. In 2006 the Gross Enrolment Rate in forms Five to Six was 3.2 per cent, having risen from 1.8 per cent in 2002 (Hakielimu, 2007: 5).
28. Interview, July 2005.
29. Established by DFID when it outsourced its Civil Society Programme to CARE in Tanzania, the FCS is now an independent grant-making body funded by donors.
30. 'District administration' refers to all government-appointed departments including the DED; not elected representatives.
31. Interview, Newala, August 2005.
32. Councillors represent wards and thus hold an elected position.

9 INFRASTRUCTURE AND ACCOUNTABILITY

What happens when a home association attempts to undertake a large infrastructural development project? This chapter looks at the strengths and weaknesses of home associations as agents of development through the lens of BANDECA's water-by-gravity project in Bali. That the water project was funded and executed reveals the capacities of diaspora associations to raise money among themselves and also to extract resources from governments. However, the fact that most of the money for the water project was raised from the domestic diaspora raises questions about the assumed connection between transnational migration and development. Furthermore, the problems encountered by the project offer a window on the tensions within home associations, and between associations and local, national and international politics. Whilst at the time of the research the story of the Bali water project was one of frustration and failure, the subsequent efforts to rectify the technical problems and the determination to see the project through to completion also illustrate the extent to which home associations persist where other development actors might withdraw after initial failures.

Piped water in Bali

From at least as early as 1948 the Fon of Bali was lobbying British colonial officials to provide the town with a piped water supply.[1] In 1949 and 1951, plans and a budget of £3,000 were set and the original hope was to fund the project from the Community Welfare and Development Scheme.[2] However, the next budget for the project put the costs at £13,500, which far exceeded the total available in the Community Development and Welfare Scheme for the whole province.[3] In 1952, Bali was attacked by a combined force of a number of their neighbours seeking to reclaim land. This Bali-versus-Widikum war was finally controlled by Nigerian troops, and in the subsequent inquiry the colonial government found in favour of Bali and forced their opponents to pay them compensation of £9,000. In 1955 the community and colonial officials agreed that this money would be put towards the construction of the water supply. But by this time the cost of the project (which involved importing hydrams and steel pipes from Glasgow) had risen to £19,500 and the balance was drawn from government funds.[4] A year later the engineer running the project, William Priestner, reported that a further £4,000 would be required to complete the work. This was loaned by the colonial government to the Bali Native Authority, which was expected to repay it from water rates.[5] The new water supply was opened in 1957 and the Bali Native Authority was made responsible for operating it.[6] This first episode in the history of Bali's water supply is a good place to start this chapter for two reasons. First, it illustrates the way that costs spiral on this kind of project. Second, it illustrates the tension between government involvement and community participation. On the one hand the financial contribution made by the Bali community was unprecedented in colonial Cameroon, but on the other hand they still depended on government for a considerable proportion of the capital costs and the salary of the engineer and the workforce. On completion the water supply was run by an organ of government (the Native Authority) and consumers paid standard rates levied on all consumers of government supplies across Cameroon (Page, 2000). Yet the first water supply is frequently remembered as entirely a product of Bali resources (Gwanmesia, 2003). As people in Bali claimed, 'we were the first community to install a water system in North West Province with our own resources'.[7] The point is not to say that this was really a government water supply all along, but that it has always been the product of both local and government resources.

In 1980 the Ministry of Mines, Water and Power contracted a Belgian company to disconnect the hydrams and construct a new water intake from the river and a water treatment works at Gola, which supplied water to the existing reservoir tank at Jamjam and thence to the pipe network in town. The new system required considerable electrical pumping and chemical inputs for treatment. The cost of this construction work was met by the Government of Cameroon using World Bank loans. In 1984 it was handed over to the Société National des Eaux du Cameroun (SNEC), a relatively new government-owned but corporately structured company, which ran water supplies across the country. The people of Bali resented SNEC because they felt they should be compensated for the appropriation of 'their' pipes and reservoir tank, the price of water rose, and public taps were closed down in an attempt to coerce more people into paying for house connections. Bali Rural Council (BRC) fell into debt with SNEC because of its failure to pay the bills for the remaining public taps. In January 1994, public demonstrations against SNEC were used to force the SNEC engineers out of town or, as people in Bali put it, SNEC was 'peacefully' 'chased' from town (Page, 2000). At a meeting held in the Fon's yard in the Palace the following month, a community water committee was elected to manage the water. Bali Community Water Supply (BACOWAS) managed Bali's water from 1994 to 2000 when it was absorbed into the recently revived BANDECA, becoming the Water Department of the Utility Committee. The community took control of the town's water supply.

During this period water was not free. Under BANDECA, fixed annual dues of 100 CFA francs per month per person were levied and connections to households were metered. In 2003 the connection fee was 15,000 CFA francs (plus pipes) and the water rate was 200 CFA francs per cubic metre (compared with a SNEC rate of 337 CFA francs per cubic metre plus bill charges and meter rents). A special levy was also placed on 'Bali elements' living away from the town. Under community management, between 1994 and 2002 the number of households subscribing to piped water rose from 491 to 1,179. Income from water bills paid for personnel, chemical treatment, maintenance, electricity bills and network extensions (Gwanmesia, 2003).

However, the community water supply was under considerable financial strain, particularly because of the cost of the electricity needed to pump water up from the river to the treatment works. The Bali Water Committee sought help from external donors and the diaspora to enable it to continue. Within Cameroon and from further afield money was remitted both privately and collectively to cover the costs of water supply. For example in 1996 BCDA-UK sent a collective contribution of 500,000 CFA francs for water in Bali. When the pump broke down, a member of the Bali diaspora in Germany donated a replacement pump worth 3 million CFA francs, although the pump proved not to work. In 1996 BCA-USA formed a Water Committee, which liaised with BACOWAS. The Water Committee collected US$10 contributions towards the purchase of water-purifying chemicals and to support the Gola pumping system. They also established a Block Payment Plan, which allowed those resident in the USA to pay the annual water bill for a private compound in Bali. The money was collected and sent via the BCA-USA Water Committee, using their website to publish estimated annual compound bills and to appeal to members to send cheques. By 2001 about 20 people in the USA were participating in the plan. The diaspora in America was encouraged to connect homes in Bali to the water supply to reduce the number of public taps and the attendant problems of collecting money.

But both the water supply and the payment system were essentially unsustainable. Electricity bills were approximately 5 million CFA francs per year (44 per cent of income in 2001/02; Gwanmesia, 2003) and the chemicals for treatment cost 3.5 million CFA francs per year. The electricity supplier was pushing for payment of past debts from SNEC days. Non-payment of water bills in Bali was a huge problem for BACOWAS. In April 2000, 9.1 million CFA francs were unpaid (of which 3.5 million were owed by government offices in Bali). Public taps were closed because of the difficulty of collecting money.

'A most pressing emergency':[8] the water-by-gravity project

Water supply was the priority project for many people living in Bali following BANDECA's revival in 1999, but in the end it was the mortuary project that was undertaken first. Once the mortuary was completed BANDECA turned its attention back to water. The water supply was in constant danger of failure and the system was only able to supply a minority of the population living in the centre of the subdivision. An affordable and sustainable solution had to be found.

Technical studies and a plan for a water-by-gravity supply system to replace the ailing electric pump system had already been commissioned by BANDECA in 2000. The project would be a huge undertaking and required investment of up to 100 million CFA francs, well beyond the capacity of the Bali community. External support would be required. The Ministry of Mines, Water and Power was lobbied by key Bali elites who were well placed either in the CPDM or in government administration. The Minister of Mines, Water and Power was said to be 'well-disposed' towards Bali since his mother came from the town; he was personally acquainted with several Bali elites; and he had previously been given a traditional title by the Fon of Bali on his appointment as Assistant Secretary General of the Presidency. The elites' lobbying was successful, and in 2004 the government granted 82.9 million CFA francs (before tax) for the Bali water project from funds received from the Heavily Indebted Poor Countries (HIPC) initiative of the World Bank.[9] A tender was subsequently released for the construction of a system that would capture the water from three springs in the hills above Bali Town and for the pipe that would carry the water to the reservoir tank. This system would use gravity as the motive force and so would disconnect the system from its dependence on the electricity network. It would also use spring water rather than river water, and so would obviate the need for chemical water treatment. The contract was awarded to a Bali businessman based in Bamenda.

The original technical studies were designed to supply water to just 6,000 people in Bali Town. In order to increase the overall capacity of the system, during a site visit with the Governor of North West Province, the Fon of Bali and the President General of BANDECA in March 2004, the contractor suggested that a further two spring sources could be linked to the catchment network. It was decided that BANDECA would sponsor the construction and connection of the two further spring sources, at an estimated cost of twelve million CFA francs.[10] The five catchments would then provide water to 8,000–10,000 people.[11]

Later that year BANDECA undertook a countrywide fundraising campaign, beginning with a payment to the contractor of two million CFA francs from the profits of the mortuary.[12] The President General of BANDECA wrote to all of BANDECA's divisional councils in Cameroon asking them to raise money for the project. Each divisional council made their own plans; for example the Yaoundé Divisional Council levied all four hundred members (elders 4,000 CFA francs, youth 2,000 CFA francs, women 2,500 CFA francs)[13] prior to the fundraising event itself, raising a total of 3.4 million CFA francs. The President General personally toured all of the BANDECA divisional councils in Cameroon, attending fundraising events for the water project in each place. In Bamenda, Yaoundé, Limbe, Tiko, Douala and Buea over a million CFA francs were raised at each event; contributions were received from a total of 15 divisional councils from across the country; and donations were sought from non-Bali people through personal ties of well-placed elites.[14] In just three months BANDECA raised a total of 22,526,950 CFA francs, enabling it to contribute 13 million CFA francs for the two additional catchments. Part of the remaining 9 million was used to pay the electricity bill to ensure supply via the electric pumping system in the interim.[15] In Bali, communal labour was organized by quarters to dig the necessary pipelines from the new catchments to the storage tank at Jamjam. Seven and a half kilometres of trench were dug in one day.[16] The President of the Bali Divisional Council of BANDECA (the home branch) estimated the local labour input to be worth 3.75 million CFA francs.[17] BRC also contributed 3.5 million CFA francs to the construction of the access road to the new catchment area.

Table 9.1 Sources of funding for the Bali Town water-by-gravity supply[18]

Source	Funding (CFA francs)	Contribution
Ministry of Mines, Water and Power	82.9 million (69.8 million after tax)	Construction of three spring catchments, installation of mainline to reservoir, 40m³ tank at Koplap
BANDECA	13 million	Construction of two spring catchments and associated pipework, renovation of reservoir tank at JamJam
Bali population	3.75 million	Excavation of 7.5-km trench from catchments to JamJam
Bali Rural Council	3.5 million	Fuel for digger for construction of access roads

In November 2004 the BANDECA President General wrote to the presidents of the divisional councils throughout Cameroon to advise them that 'the Bali water-by-gravity project has been completed and that potable water is now flowing in Bali!'[19] He further explained that, while they were waiting for the official inauguration of the new water supply, a handing-over ceremony had been organized at the Palace by the Fon of Bali, during which the contractor had given the keys of the project to the President General. The President General also used the occasion to announce that the BANDECA National Executive Committee (NEC) had decided that water would now be free, since the BANDECA annual development levy (1,000 CFA francs for men, 500 CFA francs for women) would cover the costs of maintenance. He also announced that he had applied to government to fund the construction of a bigger collection tank at Jamjam (which had already been approved) and the extension of the water supply to some of Bali's outlying villages. Thus, he said, 'the priority project of the last [BANDECA] General Assembly has been fully realized.'

But by the time the next BANDECA annual general meeting (AGM) was held, three months after the handover at the Palace, the water project was enveloped in a fog of dissatisfaction and rumour. The official inauguration of the project never took place and the water system was beset by problems. At first there was no water at all because the pipework at the lowest point broke under the pressure of the water – the static head in the system exceeded the strength of the plastic pipe. Once this was rectified by inserting stronger pipe into the relevant sections, however, the water supply was still very erratic and only available in parts of Bali and then only on some days. People at home and in the diaspora were angry. The mayor of the opposition-led BRC publicly criticized the management of the water project during the visit of the Governor of North West Province to Bali. Bali elites connected to the CPDM were concerned that the mayor's anti-government speech would scupper their chances to lobby for further resources. However, the mayor was not alone in his criticism: the half-empty grandstand in the centre of Bali testified to the number of elites in the domestic diaspora whose absence spoke of their dissatisfaction with recent developments at home. While such sentiments posed no threat to the viability of *nda kums* across Cameroon, the willingness of the *nda kums* to cooperate with BANDECA was potentially seriously compromised. Few were prepared to contribute further to the home association until the BANDECA Executive Committee had made good the fiasco of the water project.

Two competing explanations for the failure of the water system emerged. One, propagated by the BANDECA leadership, congratulated the Bali people on progress so far and looked forward to overcoming the *technical* challenges; the other, circulated via *radio trottoir*[20] and therefore referred to below as the 'popular' discourse (Nyamnjoh, 2005), scrutinized the chain of people and events that led to the failure of the water through the double lenses of local politics and personal relationships.

'In record time you have completed what few villages have ever done'[21]

The BANDECA leadership's explanation for the problems with the water project came to light at the 2005 BANDECA AGM. Held in Bali, the AGM was well-attended by local residents, representatives of the divisional councils in the domestic diaspora, and a representative from BCA-USA who was in Bali on a private visit. Also present were the BANDECA NEC, provincial heads of government services, the District Officer and the Fon of Bali. On the day of the meeting the expectant atmosphere was palpable as copies of two documents were passed around outside the Bali community hall. One was anonymous and comprised a series of stark questions and accusations about the 'failure' of the water. The other was a letter written eight months previously by the water engineer from Limbe who had originally designed the water-by-gravity project, and which had been sent to the BANDECA President General and copied to the DO, the mayor, the gendarmerie brigade commander in Bali Subdivision, the contractor, the Chair of the Bali Water Committee and the Fon of Bali. Therein, the water engineer explained that a site visit in July 2004 had prompted him to record his misgivings about the work being done lest he be held responsible for what he felt would be the project's inevitable failure. He noted a litany of problems: the project design and plans had not been followed; the trenches for the pipeline had not been dug deep enough or not at all in places, with some sections of pipeline laid on the ground surface; the pipes used in places were insufficient to withstand water pressure; different (unstudied) spring sources had been constructed without knowing their yield in the dry season; the hydraulic grade line of the pipeline had been altered, causing water to flow back into the catchments; and the pipes supplied lacked a clear indication of their diameter and pressure, causing potential mix-ups. Unfortunately the engineer had died by the time the AGM was held, leaving behind him a series of unanswered questions.

The AGM was thus shaping up to be a potentially explosive affair as people arrived expecting the BANDECA NEC to account for what was widely referred to as the 'failure of the water'. The question of the quality of the pipework was uppermost in delegates' minds. One set of speculations revolved around which person(s) along the project chain had 'chopped monies' by buying cheaper or smaller pipes than required; another set centred on who was to be held responsible for the poor work that had led to the breaking of the pipes. The technicians, the contractor, the subcontractor, the BANDECA leadership and the Fon of Bali, among others, were variously implicated in some way. Who had pocketed money? Why did BANDECA accept an incomplete project from the government contractor? Why was a handing-over ceremony conducted in the Palace 'in secret', rather than in a public celebration?

Answers to these questions were not forthcoming at the AGM. In his annual address, the President General recounted BANDECA's achievements and major activities. He explained that water-by-gravity had indeed arrived, if in somewhat slightly lower volumes than envisaged, and he congratulated the Bali people on their contributions to the project, listing the amounts raised at each divisional council fundraising event. He added that the project would need to be 'reinforced' through harnessing further spring sources in order to increase the volume of water but he did not elaborate on the reasons for the current poor state of the water supply. Later, the Chair of the Water Committee simply stated in his report on the water-by-gravity project that the supply was inadequate for Bali; that the Water Committee recommended the payment of water dues; and that government should be lobbied for money to construct more tanks. When the floor was finally opened to debate, the very first questioner asked the President General to respond to the water engineer's letter that had been circulating outside the meeting. In answering, the President General explained that the government contract had been executed well by the contractor, but that there had been an unspecified problem with the pipework that had been rectified. Seemingly unsatisfied, the questioner (a leader in the domestic diaspora) again pressed the President General to explain the causes of the specific technical faults noted by the water engineer, to large applause in the hall. At this point the Fon of Bali intervened and endorsed the President General's position. The President General then went on to explain that the problem of low yield in the system was due to water usage, rather than to any specific technical fault. He claimed that the population of Bali had grown since the feasibility studies had been undertaken. He did not divulge the estimated population to be served by water according to the original plans (which the contractor claimed was 6,000) but rather quoted the mayor's estimate that Bali's population now stood at 115,000.[22] The problem of population growth had been compounded, he claimed, by the fact that Bali people had become wasteful in their water usage since BANDECA had announced that water was free. Not only did modern homes (that is, those with private connections) use greater volumes of water, but people had been using the water in their gardens. There was a need, he claimed, to 'civilize our people – just because something is free it doesn't mean it should be abused'. He pointed out that in the past Bali used one tank of water (at Jamjam) every three days, whereas now three and a half tanks are used each day. The solutions, he proposed, were first to secure further government funding to expand the water supply system, and second to reverse the decision that water would be free. At this point and amid much disquiet in the hall, the conference chair suggested that an independent technical committee be set up to look into the matter. This suggestion was accepted by the AGM and discussion about the water project was effectively removed from the floor.

'Water has no political colour'?

In the days and weeks after the AGM it became clear that the widespread disquiet in Bali and in the diaspora had not been quelled. Presidents of many of the divisional councils reported that their members were angry that their contributions appeared to have amounted to nothing or, worse, had lined the pockets of those involved with the project. The resounding message was that BANDECA would not receive any further contributions from the domestic diaspora until water flowed in Bali. It was up to the BANDECA leadership to sort out the situation that had unfolded. Indeed, the disquiet in Bali and in the diaspora was mobilized in such a way as to demand better accountability from the leadership. So, while it is possible to interpret the discussions at the BANDECA AGM as an attempt by the Bali elite to close down opportunities to discuss the water project openly, it is also true that the delegates won significant concessions. In particular, the AGM did not accept the President General's stated wish to stand down at the meeting. Rather, it was felt that, as one of Bali's most 'viable elites', he bore a responsibility to see the troubled water project through to completion. He was thus required to remain in post for a further two years. As one delegate pointed out, 'we judge people by what they finish, not what they attempt'.

Nevertheless, people were dissatisfied with the BANDECA leadership's official explanation for the failure of the water project. Instead a second, 'popular' version of events explained the water project failure with reference to the intersection of politics and personal relationships in Bali. The failure of BANDECA's official explanation to engage with this debate served only to fuel it further, much to the frustration of several BANDECA leaders and government officials. In their opinion, and since the facts were incontrovertible, people were wilfully misinterpreting what had happened in order to make political capital from the whole episode. The refrain 'water has no political colour' was often invoked by such officials, but was not widely believed by the population.

In Bali as across much of North West Province of Cameroon, 'politics' has become defined by the struggle between the ruling CPDM party and the opposition Social Democratic Front (SDF) party. Key social and political institutions are judged by how they map onto this political landscape. In Bali, many key elites in government employment (particularly in Yaoundé) are connected to the CPDM as individuals, including the Fon of Bali who sits on the CPDM central committee, and the BANDECA President General who is a Minister Plenipotentiary. On the other hand, BRC is dominated by SDF councillors and is led by an SDF mayor, who also holds the post of BANDECA Secretary. The political divisions between these individuals were cross-cut by personal relationships and interests that served further to bind the Fon and the President General together in opposition to the mayor. Thus the key governing institutions in Bali – the Palace, the council and the home association – existed in tension with one another, while the incumbents in the Palace and home association were often eyed with suspicion by a population in Bali Town mostly sympathetic to the SDF.

In this context, the water supply had become a political football between the SDF-led rural council and the (predominantly) CPDM-led home association. Both BRC and BANDECA wanted to prevent the other from taking control of the water and making political capital from it. Before the water-by-gravity project, BRC had put forward a proposal that it should take over the water from BANDECA, citing as justification the government's new decentralization programme and BANDECA's apparent failure to manage the water effectively. BRC also claimed that it would reduce the price of water in Bali to 100 CFA francs per cubic metre. BANDECA responded by saying that water supply would be free once they had converted it to a gravity system. In the event, the government handed the water back to BANDECA because, it claimed, the association had been managing the water prior to the gravity project, and the decentralization programme had yet to come into force.

The mayor and the BANDECA leadership had ample opportunity to turn the water project to their political advantage. The period of fundraising for the water, for example, coincided with the run-up to a national presidential election in Cameroon, and the President General of BANDECA was also the CPDM campaign manager in Bali. It was thus convenient for the President General to make public pronouncements that the home association under his leadership could 'provide our people with pure and permanent spring water, with endless scope for extension'.[23] When the water failed to meet expectations, however, the mayor seized the opportunity to question publicly BANDECA's and the government's handling of the contract, and to make anti-government statements more generally.

Yet the water project was more than simply a political football between the council and the home association. It dovetailed with other agendas such as the need for elites to demonstrate their personal benevolence and commitment to the 'Bali people'. So, many of BANDECA's public pronouncements about the water project actually played down the government's support for the project in favour of talking up a Bali patriotism that celebrated community participation and ownership, and elite sacrifice for the 'Bali people'. Speaking at the BANDECA AGM, for example, the Fon of Bali made the following statement:

> Water-by-gravity belongs to the Bali Nyong'a community. When the need was discerned, assistance was given by the government but it was inadequate, so BANDECA filled the gap, increasing the project from

three to five catchments ... It is not government's water. This water cannot be taken by Bali Rural Council. It can only be run by the Bali community and it is our responsibility.

The interests of the BANDECA leadership were thus served by being seen to provide a significant development project for the village. Perhaps this was why the President General's promises about the provision of 'free' water to 'our people' conveniently sidestepped the fact that, according to the provincial government, the BANDECA water-by-gravity system was just the first phase in both a quantitative expansion and a qualitative improvement in Bali's water supply. Even at the AGM it was claimed that water would flow once the problems of supply and storage had been fixed: government funding to replace the storage tank at Jamjam had already been secured, and a feasibility study for the development of three further catchments had already been submitted to the Ministry of Mines, Water and Power. However, according to the Provincial Delegate for Mines, Water and Power in Bamenda, an estimated further 100 million CFA francs would be required to undertake the work, which even when completed would likely only serve up to 15,000 people.[24] The more modest scope of the water project was not made public knowledge during the fieldwork period.

What was most striking about the water project, however, was the fact that the home association was widely held to be responsible for the overall poor execution of what was fundamentally a government contract to construct a water supply. As is so often the case, it is the silences that are most revealing. Following the AGM, there was muted criticism of government in relation to the water project both in Bali and in the domestic and international diasporas. This is by no means insignificant in a context where criticism of government is usually not difficult to uncover. Rather, the failure of the water project was attributed within Bali itself to the home association and the Palace. So not only is there a risk for home associations when they take responsibility and credit for large development projects, but they may also provide cover for government incompetence. Following the logic of the 'politics of belonging' it is possible to interpret the Bali water project as a classic example of the way in which home associations are incorporated into the strategies of national political elites. Such a reading would interpret the government's 'donation' of the water project as an attempt to buy the loyalty of its clients in BANDECA while BANDECA, in turn, is buying the loyalty of its clients in the village. In this respect it matters less that the project is done well or not than that the grant is seen to be made. Then, when the project was poorly executed, Bali CPDM elites ensured that the home association deflected criticism from government.

Yet this argument is difficult to sustain given the interweaving of politics, personal ambition and traditional hierarchy in Bali. It is true, for example, that the BANDECA leadership publicly propagated a set of technical reasons for the failure of the water project rather than suggest that government was at fault in its project management. But it is also true that the same leadership did not seek to maximize the political capital from the government grant in the first place; in fact, they downplayed the government funding. Such a strategy might be part of an overall attempt by elites to be seen themselves successfully delivering water to the Bali population: people would have been less inclined to contribute in cash or kind to what they perceived to be a 'government project'. Similarly, the AGM could be read as an exercise in stifling public criticism of the government: it was chaired by two elites connected to the CPDM, and the meeting itself was monitored by 'security' personnel wearing CPDM badges on their lapels. It was one of the conference chairs who removed the water issue from the floor by suggesting that an independent technical committee be set up to look into it. However, while the AGM saw plenty of lively debate, the lack of open and sustained criticism of key individuals connected to the CPDM can also be attributed to the presence of the Fon of Bali throughout the meeting. A direct attack on the President General, for example, given his relationship to the Fon of Bali, would have been read as an attack on the Fon himself, which would be completely inappropriate in a public venue such as the AGM. For example, the mayor's criticisms of government and the BANDECA leadership brought censure by CPDM elites for his failure to observe Bali 'culture'. An interpretation of the water project that privileges a political elite reading therefore misses the opportunity to consider how politics, traditional hierarchy and the home association have become interwoven in the provision of development in Bali. It also overlooks the ways in which communities understand very well how to make use of their own political elites in order to extract resources from them and from the state.

Transnational (dis)connections

The loss of confidence in BANDECA was also felt by some in the international diaspora. There was much email debate about what had gone wrong with the water project, often based on even more partial and incomplete information than was available in Cameroon. And in the international diaspora too there was little enthusiasm to support the home association further until water flowed in Bali. But what could the international diaspora do to hold BANDECA accountable? As it turned out, very little, other than to retreat from engagement with the home association. Given the primary reliance of the water-by-gravity project on domestic funds, this did not pose a great threat. Certainly the international censure seemed not to move the leadership, who did not feel themselves to be accountable to those outside Cameroon. Indeed, the President General already considered the international diaspora too distant: he wanted to see more of them come home to Bali.

In the UK, the difficulties encountered by the water-by-gravity project simply compounded the misgivings that BCDA-UK already had about the home association in Bali. In fact, they had not cooperated with BANDECA directly since the mid-1990s, when their donation of about £600 for the town's water supply failed to be acknowledged in a published list of donors. This incident led to a debate within the group on their relationship with BANDECA, during which they opted to remain independent rather than become a 'branch' of the home association in Cameroon. They were so incensed about the donation that they wrote to the Chair of the Bali Water Committee, sending a photocopy of the receipt for monies transferred and demanding to know why their contribution had been overlooked in favour of contributions by individuals and other diaspora groups such as BCA-USA. As with the Bali elites in Cameroon, the UK group's contributions are closely tied to the desire for recognition at home and are part of a wider sense of competition. As a Bali man in London put it, 'if people in Cameroon hear what one [diaspora] group has done, they will contact their people in the UK and ask them what they are doing ... why aren't you doing anything?'[25] But the group felt they had never received a proper account of what their money had been spent on. Verbal reports, on which they relied, were no substitute for receipts and statements for monies received and spent. To add to their misgivings, there was also widespread distrust of the BANDECA leadership's connections to the CPDM. The UK diaspora was worried about potentially contributing to projects that might be used by CPDM elites for personal political capital. Their insistence on accountability, however, did not seem to have gone down well at home:

> We [in the UK] are very conscious of good government. Back home they see us as strict like the British people, they say 'you are following the culture of the British who are very strict' ... [whereas they think the American diaspora are] generous, open and giving. And then they say that here, we want to know everything before we give a penny ... it's not that we hold tight to everything; we want to see how these things are spent.[26]

The nature of communication between the UK and Cameroon did not help those in Bali or in the UK to come to a mutual understanding of their roles and responsibilities. In the UK, information about the water project was gained on an ad hoc basis and relied on personal contacts. Bits of information were either picked up by members on visits home (often not to Bali itself but to Buea or Limbe); recounted to the group by visitors to the UK from Cameroon; or gleaned from phone conversations and email discussion forums with others in the diaspora. So, in our research we found that members of BCDA-UK were not only unaware that government had met approximately 75 per cent of the project costs; they were also unaware of the major fundraising tour undertaken by the President General and BANDECA's mobilization of the other 25 per cent.

The twin problems for the international diaspora of the lack of accountability and the lack of information are well demonstrated by the attempt by members of the US-based Bali email discussion forum to collate, and seek answers to, a whole series of questions about the failure of the project, who was to be held responsible, and what could be done. The questions were not sent directly to BANDECA but to a preferred contact in Bali. His frank responses to their questions did little to allay the fears of those in the US about what had happened. As in the domestic diaspora and in the UK, many contributors to the discussion forum blamed the contractor, and therefore the BANDECA leadership and the Fon for signing the contract off when the work had been poorly done. People called for clarification of the roles of BRC, BANDECA and the Palace, and there were many who felt that the BRC should take control of the water. Again, however, criticism of the national government was unusually muted in a forum where it was often forthcoming.

Conclusions

Bali's water saga reveals the strengths and weaknesses of home associations as development providers. Following the partial failure of the first stage of the water-by-gravity project, the President General was expected to extract further funding from government. By late 2006, a second contract of 30 million CFA francs had been secured, which was awarded by the Ministry of Mines, Water and Power to a new contractor. The second stage of the project involved the construction of a surface dam below the first catchment, a treatment and purification plant, and extra pipework. The project was inaugurated by the Minister of Energy and Water Resources in February 2007, during which he announced a final stage of the Bali water-by-gravity project with a contract for 82 million CFA francs to construct a second dam and a second treatment unit. The President General of BANDECA finally stood down at the April 2007 AGM and was able to claim in his outgoing speech that 'the problem of output, which had been the principal shortcoming of the first project, has finally been resolved'.[27]

In the interim the Bali Water Committee continued to pump some water to Bali using the electric pump system at Gola, racking up 500,000 CFA francs in monthly electricity bills. The Bali Water Committee increased the water rate by 100 CFA francs per cubic metre, but the continued hostility towards charging for water among the Bali population meant that huge debts with the electricity supplier mounted. In this way the population of Bali compelled those in the domestic diaspora to clear BANDECA's debts with the electricity supplier and to replace the electric pump with more efficient pumps. In his stepping-down speech at the 2007 AGM, the President General summed up the collective efforts made to supply water to Bali as follows:

> I pay tribute to the entire population of Bali, who bore with fortitude the difficult days of insufficient water. I congratulate the Water Committee of BANDECA, who successfully managed the limited supply. I salute the elite of Bali, who never relented in their efforts to push before the authorities of the nation the needs of this Sub-Division. And in your name, I thank the Government of President Paul Biya, for pumping the colossal sum of 187,000,000 francs into our water supply alone. Few communities in Cameroon have been so blessed.

Three conclusions can be drawn from the Bali water-by-gravity project. First, it reveals that, despite the possibilities for development that international diasporas pose, domestic diasporas may in practice have more to offer in terms of capital, people and ideas. Bali's international diaspora has long been involved in paying for water in the village, but the water-by-gravity project relied more heavily on funds raised within Cameroon. Second, the water project provided an opportunity for Bali's elite to demonstrate their benevolence and their commitment to Bali. But it also revealed the capacity for those at home and in the domestic diaspora to hold elites to account and to extract resources from them and from the state. The BANDECA President General's attempt to stand down in 2005 after the first phase of the water project was overruled at the AGM. Rather, the home association wanted the President General, as a 'viable' elite, to make sure the water supply was working before he resigned his position. Two more government contracts were successfully secured under his tenure. In this way 'the village', which has always been reluctant to pay water bills and the electricity bills they are related to, put pressure on elites to dig into their own pockets and to extract resources from government. In contrast the international diaspora has less capacity for exerting leverage over the leaders of BANDECA. For them the need for communication and project monitoring and evaluation is a pre-requisite for greater involvement in this scale of project. Third, home associations have a more effective role in lobbying for and mobilizing resources than in managing large infrastructure projects, so that ultimately it is clear that though the home association might like to claim the water as one of its projects, it was only possible to deliver it through central government financing. There are limits to the scale of project that home associations, even very well organized ones like BANDECA, can realistically achieve. Instead the water project was a rather muddled collaboration, which succeeded because it is still possible for personal and political enemies to work together in the interests of their home.

Notes

1. 11 February 1948, F.B. Carr Touring Notes, File NW/Fa/1937/1, CNA, (Bamenda).
2. 4 March 1948, Secretary's Office Enugu Province (A.M. Gerrard) to Resident Buea, File NW/Rd.1952/1, CNA (Bamenda).
3. 28 September 1952, SDO Bamenda, File NW/Rd.1952/1, CNA (Bamenda).
4. 1 October 1955, Chief Engineer Victoria to Executive Engineer Bamenda, File NW/Rd.1952/1, CNA (Bamenda).
5. 28 November 1956, File NW/Rd.1952/1, CNA (Bamenda).
6. 8 November 1957, File NW/Rd.1952/1, CNA (Bamenda).
7. Interview, Bali, March 2005.
8. Statement by the President General of BANDECA, BANDECA fundraising for the Bali water-by-gravity project, Buea, 20 June 2004.
9. Letter from President General BANDECA to the Ministry of Mines, Power and Water, 21 September 2004.
10. Statement by the President General of BANDECA, BANDECA fundraising for the Bali water-by-gravity project, Buea, 20 June 2004.
11. Interview, contractor, Bamenda, April 2005; interview, Provincial Delegate for Mines, Water and Power, Bamenda, February 2005.
12. Statement by the President General of BANDECA, BANDECA fundraising for the Bali water-by-gravity project, Buea, 20 June 2004.
13. 'Bali Nyong'a water-by-gravity project' release of Bali Nyong'a Development and Cultural Association, Yaoundé Divisional Branch, to all *nda kums* in Yaoundé, 28 June 2004.
14. E.g. a Limbe businessman donated 2 million CFA francs; the mayor of Tiko donated 500,000 CFA francs.

15. Bali *nda kum*, Bamenda, April 2005.
16. Interview, DO Bali Subdivision, Bali, December 2004.
17. 'Welcome remarks addressed to the National Executive Committee of BANDECA by the Bali Divisional President of BANDECA, B.A. Gwannua Ndangam, on the occasion of community fund raising for the Bali water project on Monday 2 August 2004 at the Bali Community Hall'.
18. Based on figures presented by the contractor to the 'Reception Ceremony and the Handing Over of the Bali Water Supply by Gravity co-sponsored by the Ministry of Mines and BANDECA', 20 November 2004. .
19. Letter from the President General of BANDECA to the President of Bamenda Divisional Council, 22 November 2004.
20. Stephen Ellis translates *radio trattoir* as 'pavement radio', meaning '…the popular and unofficial discussion of current affairs in Africa, particularly in towns' (1989, 321).
21. President General of BANDECA, policy speech to BANDECA AGM, Bali, 12 February 2005.
22. More reliable figures from the District Medical Officer suggest that Bali's population is actually in the region of 60,000. The inflation of population figures is most likely related to the BRC's attempt to have Bali promoted to Division status.
23. Statement by the President General of BANDECA, BANDECA fundraising for the Bali water-by-gravity project, Buea, 20 June 2004.
24. Interview, Bamenda, April 2005.
25. Interview, BCDA-UK member, London, November 2006.
26. Interview, BCDA-UK member, London, November 2006.
27. BANDECA President General, Bali, 7 April 2007.

PART FOUR
Home associations, migration and development

10 CONCLUSIONS

. . . .

This book began by identifying three overarching questions. What is the structure and character of African home associations? What development work do African home associations do? And how do we understand the political work of home associations? The detailed answers to those questions have emerged through parts Two and Three of the book, but here we revisit them while adding a fourth and a fifth question: Can African diaspora groups be engaged by international development policy-makers? And, should African diaspora groups be engaged by international development policy-makers?

The structure of home associations

African home associations have persisted since the early twentieth century. They ebb and flow but never quite go away, existing in a dialectical relationship with many of the abstractions we have used to describe their structure and geography. All the categories we have used to try to describe the character of these associations (such as ethnicity, place, nation and subnation) are themselves partly transformed by home associations. So to say 'home associations are ethnic associations' is to start with an overdrawn distinction between the two terms – home associations have been integral to the process of crystallizing ethnic identities, while ethnic identities provide the rationale for home associations to exist. This is why so often the fit between home associations and ethnic groups turns out to be so poor. Equally, to say that 'home associations are place-based associations' runs the risk of treating place as an unchanging descriptor, cast in stone and secure, whereas the situation that emerges from the case studies is one in which both the meanings and the institutions of home are being made and remade in the diaspora. Home associations are integral to the ongoing production of places, even while place is the rationale for home associations to exist.

To search for a model of the geography (or spatial structure) of home associations is to chase a rainbow. The structures vary over time and space. To look for explanations for why one association has a home branch and another does not, why one association has elections and another does not, why one has a strong branch in the UK and another does not, why one has no international branches at all and another does, requires careful unpicking of their long historical trajectories. However, there are some overarching factors that seem to us to be important in determining what particular form any one association takes.

First, historic (often pre-colonial) political structures have a significant influence. The difference between hierarchical and egalitarian societies seems to be carried forward into the structure of associations. The centrifugal forces in the Manyu and Newala examples make it hard for association leaders to mobilize the masses. Second, the availability of capital in the homeplace and in the diaspora has a major impact on the character of the association and this in turn is a consequence of the particularities of migration histories from any one place. Migration is a differential process, so the capacities of diaspora communities vary in relation to who migrated, where they migrated to, when they migrated, and what they did after they had migrated. The character of a home association also reflects the size and economic strength of the diaspora. Where the number of people who are economically successful is small (such as those from Newala) the association is also relatively small. This is crucial from a policy perspective, because it draws attention to the spatially uneven nature of home association work. Equally important is the availability of capital within the homeplace. The more opportunities there are at home the greater the incentive to maintain contact.

Third, the precise political–economic contexts at any moment in Africa is also an important factor governing the character of home associations. The contraction of associations in the 1960s and 1970s in Tanzania and their expansion in the 1980s and 1990s is an obvious example of the effect of both political and economic changes. However, despite fundamentally similar economic circumstances, the character of the associations that grew up in the 1990s in Tanzania is qualitatively different from the expansion of associations at the same time in Cameroon. The post-independence outlawing of tribal associations and the nation-building exercise in Tanzania has placed any associational activity apparently based on ethnic mobilization under public scrutiny. DDTs and other home associations thus reflect geographical and administrative boundaries, even if their members also share an ethnic or sub-ethnic identity. In contrast the revival of Cameroonian associations in the 1990s reflected both the civil unrest of the early part of that decade and the establishment's response to that unrest. Associations were both an expression of local autonomy from the centralized state and also the state's (apparently) successful attempt to reassert its control. As a result while the home associations may have had democratic structures and mass membership they were also always politically fraught, trying to paper over different party loyalties and different attitudes to the central government within the association.

In Britain, we can draw the tentative conclusion that UK government policy has relatively little effect on the structure of international African home associations. Within the UK, shifts in government policy (particularly at local government level) will have only a small impact on associations because existing engagement is so limited. The current shift away from funding community organizations that are perceived to foster 'bonding capital' within minority communities and towards those identified as producing 'bridging capital' between minority and majority communities will logically produce a less conducive environment for home associations (Department of Communities and Local Government, 2008). Notwithstanding our scepticism about the assumption that home associations do only foster 'bonding capital', the fact that there is such limited contact between our case study African home associations and the British state (whether national or local) suggests that any shift in policy is not going to be that significant. Still, other British government departments (for example the Department for International Development) are taking an increased interest in home associations, which might lead to more opportunities for some of these associations to expand.

It is therefore very difficult to generalize about the structure of internationalized African home associations, but two key findings emerge from this research. The first is that it is erroneous to imagine them as a transnational network of branches radiating out from a central home-place. None of the four case study associations included in this research matched this imagined geography. Some associations, such as MECA, do not even have a branch in the homeplace. One homeplace can generate numerous overlapping home associations (as happens in Rungwe and Manyu). Members of the diaspora can choose which home association to join, or they may simultaneously be members of several. Furthermore, the communication and resource flows between members or 'branches' of associations in different places are often intermittent and opportunistic. It is ultimately more useful to think of home associations as practices rather than structures. MECA particularly at times seems more a state of mind than an association.

The second key finding about structure is that although home associations have attracted attention because of their apparently recent transnationalization, in each of the four case studies the African dimension of the home association is still more important than the British dimension in terms of flows of money, ideas and people between home and diaspora. This is why much of the material in Part Three of the book discusses home associations' work in Africa. In the Tanzanian case we found no examples of DDTs or other home associations in the UK that mapped on to domestic migrants' associations in Tanzania. Tanzanian associations in the UK are characterized primarily by shared national identities, rather than affinities to rural homeplaces. The different approaches to nation-building in Cameroon and Tanzania shape their diasporas in Britain. However, our observation that the international diaspora is relatively insignificant for African development is based on the British diasporas only. Further comparative work is needed in order to establish how and why different diasporas might be more important in different homeplaces.

The question of development

Home associations' contribution to development goes further than the mobilization of resources. In terms of the size of capital flows, home associations fall behind governments and international donors as investors in public goods in Africa. They have a limited capacity for fundraising, service delivery and project management. But they are not trivial institutions, and in fact their significance is far greater than their material outputs might suggest. Their significance stems from the challenge they present to existing definitions of development through their investments in projects that would not normally be included under mainstream development as defined in Western development discourse. Some of the projects that the four home associations have undertaken are relatively familiar, such as the construction of schools, health facilities, water supplies, toilets, town halls, libraries, internet cafes and orphanages. As well as raising money themselves, home associations also lobby centralized bureaucracies in an attempt to secure government or donor support for large infrastructural development projects. The Bali water-by-gravity project is a case in point here and also serves as a reminder that it is often impossible to separate home associations, governments and donors as the agents of a particular development project. Other types of project that home associations undertake are more distinctive, such as the construction of mortuaries, churches and flagpoles, the restoration of palaces and cultural buildings, the funding of health fairs led by medics from the diaspora, the paying of legal costs in land disputes, and the provision of consumer goods (such as computers and cars) to traditional rulers. But the uniqueness of home associations' developmental work also emerges from the ways in which they seek the development of 'their people' as much as their homeplace. The two are, in fact, inseparable. This is why the members of home associations considered the welfare activities for those away from home, which are their primary concern, to be developmental.

Home associations' welfare activities in the domestic and international diasporas include the provision of social and financial support and advice. In the domestic diaspora, some associations have even constructed their own community halls to provide a venue for meetings and other events. The solace and practical support that home associations are able to offer their members during important events such as births, baptisms, circumcision or initiation, marriage, illness and death are the most enduring of all their activities and their greatest strength.

The importance of welfare means that home associations have become one venue among many for constructing ideas about what defines the 'culture' and the 'cultural practices' of a given homeplace. Home associations engage in normative debates about cultural practices such as chieftaincy disputes, burial and death celebrations, often advocating the modernization of such activities. The modernizing agenda and didactic tone (of 'forward' elites educating 'backward' villagers) evident here is often mirrored in home associations' material development activities, such as the construction of mortuaries and the emphasis on education through school construction and scholarships. But the cultural work that diasporas do is not only about changing practices at home; it is also about maintaining and adapting elements of 'tradition' and 'culture' in the diaspora. Culture is rehearsed through the meetings and occasions organized by domestic and international home associations. Key life stages are celebrated in neotraditional ways that conserve language, music, values, food, songs, dance, clothing, masquerades, secret societies and cosmologies. Development, then, is not just about more schools and health facilities; it is about better burial practices, better 'traditional' festivities and better knowledge of 'culture' (such as the learning of vernaculars) by more people.

The capacity of home associations to improve the material quality of life in the homeplace is limited and awkward, but distinctive. Their development projects are sometimes overambitious, ill-conceived, perverse or reflect the personal political ambitions of the leadership. From the perspective of development professionals the capacity of individuals within home associations to plan and implement successful development projects is inevitably limited because they are amateurs with little or no training. It is unlikely that log-frames, monitoring procedures or independent evaluation reports are used. As volunteers, the leaders of home associations lack time and other resources. Home associations are also potentially exploitative: a variety of social pressures are put on both the leadership and the rank and file to 'participate' in projects, while elites often manage debates so that decisions are taken in camera in advance of public meetings. Leaders can be more answerable to their own political masters in the central state than to their members, and frequently impose their ideas on those in the village. They let governments off the hook by providing the goods and services that government ought to provide but has failed to. But on the other hand it is precisely their amateurism that gives home associations their distinctiveness as agents of development. Amateurism enables them to step outside the routine formulas for delivering development. Home associations do put money into local communities, and while this may bring some benefit in terms of poverty reduction through backwards linkages and local economic growth, the greater benefit comes in improving quality of life through investment in public goods and services, albeit on a relatively limited scale. Home associations do provide a mechanism for those in Africa to engage the international diaspora, though it is a mechanism that has to overcome significant problems around communication, trust and understanding. Where there is a membership, home associations can hold leaders to account, though perhaps not in ways predicted by Eurocentric theories of liberal democracy. Home associations provide space for deliberation without ever assuming the possibility of a bland consensus. Moreover, home association leaders are embedded in social relations at home, which means that their developmental work is less constrained by the temporal and fashion cycles associated with external development agents. Home associations do not always wait for the government to deliver development, they do it themselves and as a result can pursue their own development priorities. They can hold government to account by revealing its developmental failures, or by forcing government to support services (such as schools) that they have initiated.

Despite all their problems and limitations, African home associations still offer transformative possibilities. In terms of civil society institutions that can be used to deliver development, home associations are organically and historically rooted in a way that alternative structures such as NGOs and donors are not. We recognize that home associations are also problematic, but continually highlighting their failures runs the risk of implicitly endorsing the monopoly that alien (Western) institutions have over development.

The question of politics

It is naïve to imagine that home associations are not engaged in political work. In Cameroon, home associations often have an explicit political position articulated in terms of the ancillary role that they offer in supporting government's development efforts. However, there is also an implicit politics that is closely connected to national ideas weaving together notions of ethnicity, belonging and territory. This political work is usually discussed through the language of ethnically defined 'cultures'. Culture in Cameroonian associations ranks as equally important to development. Indeed it is sometimes inseparable from development in the eyes of association members. In Tanzania, however, public dis-cussion of ethnicity is highly circumscribed. Nevertheless, home associa-tions may still have the instrumental effect (Ferguson 1990) of enabling the emergence of ethnic patron–client networks because they draw their solidarity from ethnicity.

Embracing home associations as development providers means tolerating their political work. Home associations are political actors, even though most associations explicitly reject this claim, instead depoliticizing their impacts by invoking the language of 'development' and 'culture'. In both Cameroon and Tanzania, home associations are participants in ethno-territorial place-based politics (though this is a far more potent politics in Cameroon than in Tanzania at present), and in this sense they are a symptom of political belonging. They can be manipulated to work in the interests of the preservation of power for governing political parties in rural constituencies, particularly in the context of decentral-ization. This is an instrument effect of power, rather than a planned strategy on the part of the central state. So while they can provide another vehicle for delivering the rural vote, both on a 'contractual' basis (central state funding – actual, promised or aspirational – for projects exchanged for campaigning) and by providing a platform for ambitious rural politicians to advance their own careers, this does not always play out so neatly in practice. Home associations may deflect criticism from central government by taking the blame for dysfunctional aspects of the patrimonial state; but they can also highlight the failures of the state by delivering or initiating projects successfully, and may even mock the government in an attempt to goad it into action.

However, in highlighting the relationship between home associations and political belonging, analyses have yet to deal adequately with the positive aspects of place-based loyalties, which we have argued are the centripetal forces that hold home associations together and cannot be wished away. The obligations people feel to family and neighbours are often expressed as obligations to a homeplace. Our response has been to begin to construct a progressive politics of place that distinguishes between the reactionary elements of political belonging and the potentially progressive pole of moral conviviality. The latter expresses the way in which loyalty to 'home' can provide the language, ideas and values to enable cooperation. It is the solvent that dissolves the differences between people and enables them to establish the right way to live comfortably together within a place. Moral conviviality is much quieter than political belonging – it does not announce its presence in the same way; identifying moral conviviality requires reading history for mobility and mixture rather than fixity and homogeneity. In any place home associations are caught in the balance between political belonging and moral conviviality.

Ideas of modernization often assume that as a society becomes more modern, its attachment to place declines. Reciprocally, attachment to place is seen as irrational and a sign of backwardness. There is a view in African studies and development studies (as well as in some government policies on integration, such as in the UK) that transformative development at the grassroots is only possible if civil society can transcend the confines of locality and forge larger-scale alliances across space. From such a perspective home associations cannot be transformative, because though they sometimes operate on a transnational scale, they are held together by a shared attachment to a place. In consequence they often reinforce historical inequalities and oppressive structures. However, the evidence from the four home associations shows that attachment to place can actually drive a process of progressive change, for example by challenging oppressive practices surrounding widowhood and witchcraft accusation. Place and the moral conviviality associated with home are thus potentially progressive concepts even though they are often assumed to be politically reactionary.

Home associations are not necessarily ethnic associations. MECA provides the clearest refutation of this since it brings together several ethnic groups both in Cameroon and Britain. In Britain, MECA is just one of a plethora of Manyu and even Anglophone Cameroonian groups in which the Manyu diaspora is active. In Tanzania, NDF is dominated by Makonde, and the Rungwe associations are dominated by Nyakyusa, but neither association unites all members of either ethnic group. Among the Tanzanian associations in the international diaspora ethnicity is of minor (or no) importance in delineating membership. Location, extended kin and friendship groups are more important. The Bali home associations are perhaps the closest approximation to ethnic homogeneity because they bring together people claiming Bali Nyong'a ethnicity. Yet even here there is scope to challenge this claim: Bali Nyong'a identity is an amalgam that has been stuck together, within living memory, from multiple different ethnic identities and these internal differences retain meaning for some people. In the international diaspora, spouses and friends from other ethnic groups are accommodated within home association meetings and younger generations self-consciously associate on a non-ethnic basis. This was perhaps most clearly demonstrated at a cultural gala and fundraising event held in London by BCDA-UK in summer 2007. The event was showcasing Bali Nyong'a 'tradition' but non-Bali Nyong'a spouses wore traditional attire and joined in the dances; and the Cultural Secretary of BCDA-UK performed traditional dances with other home associations from Cameroon who had also been invited. As the Manyu husband of a Bali Nyong'a woman said, 'I am proud to wear [the traditional Bali attire] ... it doesn't matter that I'm not a Bali man'.

Can and should home associations be engaged by development policy-makers?

Development donors wishing to engage diaspora groups should leave the decision about whether or not to collaborate in the hands of the diaspora groups themselves. Home associations should be left to set their own agendas and should be free to choose whether or not to engage with mainstream development associations. What makes home associations interesting developmental actors is that they invest in things that would not normally be included in the usual list of development projects. They undertake their work in ways that would not be acceptable to many funders because they lack formal legal status as organizations, because their management of finances is not always transparent, because they do not follow the protocols of the development project cycle, and because they are closely associated with political agendas. Home associations are the 'mimic men' of international development. They are like develop-ment organizations but the likeness is never perfect. They adopt the language, form and practices of development organizations but there is

Table 10.1 Percentage of people receiving remittances from overseas in the home areas (survey data)

	Bali	Manyu	Rungwe	Newala
In the homeplace (%)	19	15	8	3
Domestic diaspora (%)	19	30	13	2
Number	556	552	578	587

Table 10.2 Overseas remittances in the home areas by size (%) (survey data)

	<£10	£10–£24.99	£25–£49.99	£50+	Number of people receiving remittances from overseas
Bali	5	21	28	47	156
Manyu	3	9	24	64	181
Rungwe	5	15	39	41	75
Newala	24	35	24	18	17

always a slippage that reveals the difference. But like the mimic men of the colonial past, home associations make the development industry uncomfortable precisely because they straddle two worlds and therefore they always have more knowledge about a place and how it works than those who come from outside. This is why there is such ambivalence about them as development actors. Home associations do development differently, and they might even do it better. Formal engagement by the machinery of development could damage the distinctiveness of home associations by forcing them into a straitjacket of rules, standard practices and indicators. But this anxiety is not one that should be a concern for those outside associations; it is for those who run these groups to decide if they want to take that risk. For those bodies that are outside diaspora groups who claim that they want to engage diasporas (DFID, 2003, 2007; Home Office, 2003) the strategy is clear. They should make a significant amount of taxpayers' money available to diaspora groups and see if diaspora organizations are interested in coming forward with proposals about how to use it.

A single policy towards home associations is likely to produce different outcomes in different places. In particular, given the variations in home associations' capacities to deliver development and existing disparities in international remittances (Tables 10.1 and 10.2), a policy of supporting home associations is likely to exaggerate an already uneven geography of diaspora development. This is true both between and within countries. So, for example, a policy that supports diaspora groups in Britain to do development work in Africa is more likely to benefit Cameroon than Tanzania, because Cameroonian home associations have clearer links to specific rural homeplaces. Tanzanian diaspora groups in the UK currently do very little development work in Tanzania, partly because their diverse memberships make it difficult to pinpoint a particular project. Within Africa a strategy of supporting home associations would support those communities with more educated, professional migrants, which tend to be wealthier communities in the first place. In itself this perpetuation of inequality is not an outright barrier to engagement (it is true after all of many interventions in the name of development that those best placed to benefit are not always the intended beneficiaries), but it seems to us to be missing from much of the debate about the relationship between migration and development. Those places with fewer migrants will be disadvantaged. Home associations are not a panacea to the problem of getting development aid to rural areas.

As we finished this book in early 2008, both Tanzania and Cameroon appeared briefly in international headlines. Tanzania endured the political cataclysm of losing its prime minister and entire cabinet in a corruption scandal. Cameroon saw the return of violent mass protests on to the streets of its cities for the first time in a decade. Both countries are in the process of change and their home associations will change with them; but there is plenty of evidence to suggest that in some form or another their home associations will endure.

BIBLIOGRAPHY

Abbott, C.W. (2006) 'Nigerians in North America: new frontiers, old associations?' in K. Konadu-Agyemang, B.K. Takyi and J.A. Arthur (eds) *The new African diaspora in North America: trends, community building, and adaptation* Lexington Books, Lanham MD, 141-165.

Abdul-Korah, G.B. (2007) '"Where is not home?" Dagaaba migrants in the Brong Ahafo region, 1980 to the present', *African Affairs*, 106, 422, 71-94.

Abrahamsen, R. (2003) 'African studies and the postcolonial challenge', *African Affairs*, 102, 407, 189-210.

Achebe, C. (1960) *No longer at ease*, Heinemann, Oxford.

Adeyanju, C.T. (2000) *Transnational social fields of the Yoruba in Toronto*, MA Thesis, University of Guelph.

Adi, H. (2002) 'The African diaspora, "development" and modern African political theory', *Review of African Political Economy*, 9, 237-251.

Agbese, P.O. (1998) 'Hometown associations and conflict management: the experience of the Agila Development Association', in R. Honey and S. Okafor (eds) *Hometown associations: indigenous knowledge and development in Nigeria*, Intermediate Technology Publications, London, 75-88.

Ajibewa, A. and S. Akinrinade (2003) *Globalisation, migration and the new African diasporas: towards a framework of understanding.* Paper presented to the International Workshop on Migration and Poverty in West Africa, Sussex Centre for Migration Research, University of Sussex, 13-14 March.

Akyeampong, E. (2000) 'Africans in the diaspora: the diaspora and Africa', *African Affairs*, 99, 183-216, 395.

Akyeampong, E. (2005) 'Diaspora and drug trafficking in West Africa: a case study of Ghana', *African Affairs*, 104, 416, 429-447.

Al-Ali N., R. Black and K. Koser (2001) 'Refugees and transnationalism: the experience of Bosnians and Eritreans in Europe', *Journal of Ethnic and Migration Studies*, 27, 4, 615-634.

d'Alisera, J. (2004) *An imagined geography: Sierra Leonean Muslims in America*, University of Pennsylvania Press, Philadelphia PA.

Alpers, E.A. (1972) 'Towards a history of the expansion of Islam in East Africa: the matrilineal peoples of the southern interior', in T.O. Ranger and I.N. Kimambo (eds) *The historical study of African religion*, Heinemann, London, 172-201.

Alpers, E.A. (2000) 'Recollecting Africa: diasporic memory in the Indian Ocean world', *African Studies Review*, 43, 1, 83-99.

Amazee, V.B. (1990) 'The "Igbo scare" in the British Cameroons, c. 1945–61', *Journal of African History*, 31, 281-293.

Amazee, V.B. (1994) 'The role of the French Cameroonians in the unification of Cameroon,

1916–1961', *Transafrican Journal of History*, 23, 195–234.

Ammassari, S. (2004) 'From nation-building to entrepreneurship: the impact of elite return migrants in Côte d'Ivoire and Ghana', *Population, Space and Place*, 10, 2, 133-154.

Ammassari, S. and R. Black (2001) *Harnessing the potential of migration and return to promote development: applying concepts to West Africa*, Sussex Migration Working Paper, Sussex Centre for Migration Research.

Amoako, J. (2006) 'Ethnic identity, conflict and diasporic constructions in the New World: the case of Asante in North America', in K. Konadu-Agyemang, B.K. Takyi and J.A. Arthur (eds) *The new African diaspora in North America: trends, community building, and adaptation*, Lexington Books, Oxford.

Anderson, B. (1991) *Imagined communities: reflections on the origins and spread of nationalism*, Verso, London.

Anthias, F. (1998) 'Evaluating "diaspora": beyond ethnicity?' *Sociology*, 32, 3, 557-580.

Appadurai, A. (1996) *Modernity at large: cultural dimensions of globalization*, University of Minnesota Press, Minneapolis.

Ardener, S. and S. Burman (eds) (1996) *Money-go-rounds: the importance of rotating savings and credit for women*, Berg, Oxford.

Arthur, J.A. (2006) 'The new African diaspora in North America: policy implications', in K. Konadu-Agyemang, B. K. Takyi, and J. A. Arthur, (eds) *The new African diaspora in North America: trends, community building, and adaptation*, Lexington Books, Lanham MD, 287-302.

Askew, K. (2002) *Performing the nation: Swahili music and cultural politics in Tanzania*, University of Chicago Press, London.

Attah-Poku, P. (1996) 'Asanteman immigrant ethnic association: an effective tool for immigrant survival and adjustment problem solution in New York City', *Journal of Black Studies*, 27, 1, 56-76.

Awasom, N.F. (1998) 'Colonial background to the development of autonomist tendencies in Anglophone Cameroon, 1946–1961', *Journal of Third World Studies*, 15, 168-183.

Awasom, N.F. (2000) 'The reunification question in Cameroon history: was the bride an enthusiastic or a reluctant one?', *Africa Today*, 47, 2, 91-119.

Babou, C.A. (2002) 'Brotherhood solidarity, education and migration: the role of the *dahiras* among the Murid Muslim community of New York', *African Affairs*, 101, 403, 151-170.

BANDECA (2007) 'Our purpose', *http://bandeca.org/id1.html*, last accessed on 20 June 2008.

Barkan, J., M. McNulty, and M. Ayeni (1991) 'Hometown voluntary associations, local development and the emergence of civil society in Western Nigeria', *Journal of Modern African Studies*, 29, 3, 457-480.

Baroin, C. (1996) 'Religious conflict in 1990–1993 among the Rwa: secession in a Lutheran diocese in northern Tanzania', *African Affairs*, 95, 381, 529-554.

Bates, R. (1974) 'Ethnic competition and modernization in contemporary Africa', *Comparative Political Studies*, 6, 457-484. Reproduced in J. Hall (1994) *The state: critical concepts*, Routledge, London, 174-196.

Bayart, J.-F. (1993) *The state in Africa: the politics of the belly*, Longman, London.

Bebbington, A. (2000) 'Re-encountering development: livelihood transitions and place transformations in the Andes', *Annals of the Association of American Geographers*, 90, 3, 495-520.

Beck, L.J. (2001) 'Reining in the marabouts? Democratization and local governance in Senegal', *African Affairs*, 100, 401, 601-621.

Becker, F. (2006) 'Rural Islamism during the "war on terror": a Tanzanian case study', *African Affairs*, 105, 421, 583-603.

Bejeng, P. (1985) *The passing of a great leader: Galega II of Bali-Nyonga*, Nooramac, Douala.

van den Bersselaar, D. (2005) 'Imagining home: migration and the Igbo village in colonial Nigeria', *Journal of African History*, 46, 1, 51-73.

Bhabha, H. (1994) *The location of culture*, Routledge, London.

Black, R., M. Collyer, R. Skeldon and C. Waddington (2006) 'Routes to illegal residence: A case study of immigration detainees in the United Kingdom', *Geoforum*, 37, 4, 552-564.

Bolt, P. (1996) 'Looking to the diaspora: the overseas Chinese and China's economic development, 1978–1994', *Diaspora,* 5, 3, 25-36.

Boone, C. (2003) *Political topographies of the African state: territorial authority and institutional choice,* Cambridge University Press, Cambridge.

Boyce-Davies, C.E. (ed.) (2007) *Encyclopaedia of the African diaspora: origins, experiences, and culture,* ABC-CLIO, Santa Barbara CA.

Brabazon, J. (2003) *Liberia: Liberians united for reconciliation and democracy (LURD),* Africa Programme Armed Non-State Actors Project Briefing Paper no. 1, Chatham House, London.

Brah, A. (1996) *Cartographies of diaspora: contesting identities,* Routledge, London.

Braziel, J.E. and A. Mannur. (2003) 'Nation, migration, globalization: points of contention in diaspora studies', in J.E. Braziel and A. Mannur (eds) *Theorizing diaspora,* Blackwell, Oxford, 1-22.

Brennan, J. (2002) *Nation, race, and urbanization in Dar es Salaam, Tanzania, 1916-1976.* Unpublished PhD thesis, Northwestern University.

Brubaker, R. (2002) 'Ethnicity without groups', *Archives Européennes de Sociologie,* XLIII, 2, 163-189.

Brubaker, R. (2005) 'The "diaspora" diaspora', *Ethnic and Racial Studies,* 28, 1, 1-19.

Brubaker, R. and F. Cooper (2000) 'Beyond "identity"', *Theory and Society,* 29, 1-47.

Buggenhagen, B.A. (2001) 'Prophets and profits: gendered and generational visions of wealth and value in Senegalese Murid households', *Journal of Religion in Africa,* 31, 4, 373-401.

Burton, A. (2002) 'Adjutants, agents, intermediaries: the native administration in Dar es Salaam Township, 1919–1961', in A. Burton (ed.) *The urban experience in Eastern Africa c.1750–2000,* British Institute in East Africa, Nairobi.

Burton, A. (2005) *African underclass: urbanisation, crime and colonial order in Dar es Salaam 1919–1961,* James Currey, Oxford.

Byfield, J. (2000) 'Introduction: rethinking the African diaspora', *African Studies Review,* 43, 1, 1-9.

Caglar, A. (2006) 'Hometown associations, the rescaling of state spatiality and migrant grassroots transnationalism', *Global Networks,* 6, 1, 1-22.

Campbell, G. (2006) 'Le commerce d'esclaves et la question d'une diaspora dans le monde de l'océan indien', *Cahiers des anneaux de la mémoire,* no. 9.

Carter, S. (2005) 'The geopolitics of diaspora', *Area,* 37, 1, 54-63.

Chadwick, E. (1950) 'What is community development?' *Eastern Outlook,* 1-2.

Charsley, S. (1969) *The princes of Nyakyusa,* East African Publishing House, Nairobi.

Chiabi, E.M. (1997) *The making of modern Cameroon: a history of substate nationalism and disparate union, 1914–1961,* University Press of America, Lanham, MD.

Chikanda, A. and B. Dodson (2007) *The Zimbabwean diaspora: the struggle for rights and recognition.* Paper presented at the Canadian Association for African Studies annual conference, New College, University of Toronto, 18 May 2007.

Chikezie, C.E. (2005) 'Accountability, Africa and her diaspora', available online at www.openDemocracy.net, last accessed 26 September 2005.

Chilver, E. (1964) 'A Bamiléké community in Bali-Nyonga: a note on the Bawok', *African Studies,* 23, 3-4, 121-127.

Chilver, E. (1967) 'Paramountcy and protection in the Cameroons: the Bali and the Germans, 1889–1913', in P. Gifford and W.R. Louis (eds) *Britain and Germany in Africa: Imperial Rivalry and Colonial Rule,* Yale University Press, New Haven, 479-511.

Chilver, E. (1970) *Historical notes on the Bali chiefdoms of the Cameroons Grassfields,* 'Two reports to the Bali-Chamba Historical and Cultural Society, Report 1 Origins, migration and composition. Report 2 The Bali-Chamba of Bamenda: settlement and composition'.

Chilver, E. and P. Kaberry (1961) 'An outline of the traditional political system of Bali-Nyonga', *Africa,* 31, 4, 355-371.

Chilver, E. and U. Röschenthaler (2002) *Cameroon's tycoon: Max Esser's expedition and its consequences,* Berghahn, Oxford.

Clapham, C. (1998) 'Introduction: analysing African insurgencies', in C. Clapham (ed.) *African guerrillas*, James Currey, Oxford, 1-18.

Clayton, A.J. (1993) *Christianity and Islam in south-east Tanzania: a study of religious appropriation among Makonde*. Unpublished PhD thesis, University of Manchester.

Clifford, J. (1994) 'Diasporas', *Cultural Anthropology*, 9, 3, 302-338.

Cohen, A. (1969) *Custom and politics in urban Africa: a study of Hausa migrants in Yoruba towns*, Routledge and Kegan Paul, London.

Cohen, R. (1997) *Global diasporas: an introduction*, University College London Press, London.

Collier, P. (2000) *Economic causes of civil war and their implications for policy*, World Bank, Washington DC.

Collier, P. and A. Hoeffler (2001) *Greed and grievance in civil war*, working paper no. WPS2355. World Bank, Washington DC.

Copans, J. (2000) 'Mourides des champs, mourides des villes, mourides du téléphone portable et de l'internet', *Afrique contemporaine*, no. 194, 24-33.

Cresswell, T. (2004) *Place: a short introduction*, Blackwell, Oxford.

Cruise O'Brien, D., M.C. Diop and M. Diouf (2002) *La construction de l'État au Sénégal*, Karthala, Paris.

Crush, J. (ed.) (1995) *Power of development*, Routledge, London.

Curtis, K. (1992) 'Cooperation and cooptation: the struggle for market control in the Bukoba District of colonial Tanganyika', *International Journal of African Historical Studies*, 25, 3, 505-538.

Daley, P. (1998) 'Black-Africans in Great Britain: spatial concentration and segregation', *Urban Studies*, 35, 10, 1703-1724.

Davies, R. (2007) 'Reconceptualising the migration–development nexus: diasporas, globalisation and the politics of exclusion', *Third World Quarterly*, 28, 1, 59-76.

Delancey, M.W. and H.M. Mokeba (1988) *Historical dictionary of the Republic of Cameroon*, Scarecrow Press, Lanham MD and London.

Department of Communities and Local Government (2008) *The Government's response to the Commission on Integration and Cohesion*, Communities and Local Government Publications, London, February.

DFID [Department for International Development] (2003) *Getting it right together: black and minority ethnic groups and DFID's development agenda – scoping study*. Department for International Development, London.

DFID [Department for International Development] (2007) *Moving out of poverty – making migration work better for poor people*. Department for International Development, London.

van Dijk, R.A. (1997) 'From camp to encompassment: discourses of transsubjectivity in the Ghanaian Pentecostal diaspora', *Journal of Religion in Africa*, 27, 2, 135-159.

Diop, M.C. (1981) 'Fonctions et activités des *dahira* mourides urbains (Sénégal)', *Cahier d'Études Africaines*, 81-83, XXI –1-3, 79-91.

Diouf, M. (2000) 'The Senegalese Murid trade diaspora and the making of a vernacular cosmopolitanism', *CODESRIA Bulletin*, 1, 19-30.

Ebune, J.B. (1992) *The Growth of Political Parties in Southern Cameroons 1916–1960*, CEPER, Yaoundé.

Ebune, J.B. (2004) 'Contributions of self-help associations to the growth and development of British Southern Cameroons, 1922-1962: a historical perspective', *Epasa Moto*, 2, 1, 59-80.

Economist, The (2004) 'Out of Africa', *Economist*, 9 October, 25-26.

Edmondson, L. (2001) 'National erotica: the politics of "traditional" dance in Tanzania', *Drama Review*, 45, 1, 153-170.

Edmondson, L. (2007) *Performance and politics in Tanzania: the nation on stage*, Indiana University Press, Bloomington.

Ellis, S. (1989) 'Tuning in to pavement radio', *African Affairs*, 88, 321-330, 352.

Ellison, J. (1999) *Transforming obligations, performing identity: making the Nyakyusa in a colonial context*. Unpublished PhD thesis, University of Florida.

Englund, H. (2002) 'The village in the city, the city in the village: migrants in Lilongwe', *Journal of Southern African Studies*, 28, 1, 137-154.

Englund, H. (2004) 'Cosmopolitanism and the devil in Malawi', *Ethnos*, 69, 3, 293-316.

Escobar, A. (1995) *Encountering development: the making and unmaking of the third world*, Princeton University Press, Princeton NJ.

Escobar, A. (2001) 'Culture sits in places: reflections on globalism and subaltern strategies of localization', *Political Geography*, 20, 2, 139-174.

Eyoh, D. (1998) 'Through the prism of a local tragedy: political liberalisation, regionalism and elite struggles for power in Cameroon', *Africa*, 68, 3, 338-359.

Eyoh, D. (1999) 'Community, citizenship and the politics of ethnicity in post-colonial Africa', in P. Zeleza and E. Kalipeni (eds) *Sacred places and public quarrels: African cultural and economic landscapes*, Africa World Press, Trenton NJ, 271-300.

Faist, T (2008) 'Migrants as transnational development agents: an inquiry into the newest round of the migration-development nexus', *Population, Space and Place*, 14, 21-42.

Falk Moore, S. (1996) 'Post-socialist micro-politics: Kilimanjaro, 1993', *Africa*, 66, 4, 587-606.

Fanso, V.G. (1986) 'Traditional and colonial African boundaries: concepts and functions in inter-group relations', *Présence Africaine*, 58-75, 137-140.

Fanso, V.G. (1989) *Cameroon history for secondary schools and colleges: the colonial and post-colonial periods* (Vol. 2), Macmillan, Basingstoke.

Fanso, V.G. (1999) 'Anglophone and Francophone nationalisms in Cameroon', *Round Table*, 88, 281-296.

Farah, A.O., M. Muchie, and J. Gundel (eds) (2007) *Somalia: diaspora and state reconstitution in the Horn of Africa*, Adonis and Abbey, London.

Fardon, R. (1996) 'The person, ethnicity and the problem of "identity" in West Africa', in I. Fowler and D. Zeitlyn (eds) *African crossroads: intersections between History and Ethnography in Cameroon*, Berghahn Books, Oxford, 17-44.

Fardon, R. (2006a) *Widening local worlds in West Africa*. Paper presented to Anthropology, University of Lisbon Institute of Social Science, 2 June 2006, http://www.ics.ul.pt/agenda/seminarioantropologia/pdf/richard_fardon.pdf, accessed 16 February 2008.

Fardon, R. (2006b) *Lela in Bali: history through ceremony in Cameroon*, Berghahn, Oxford.

Farrant, M., A. MacDonald, and D. Sriskandarajah (2006) *Migration and development: opportunities and challenges for policymakers*, Migration Research Series, no. 22, International Organization for Migration, Geneva.

Ferguson, J. (1990) *The anti-politics machine: 'development', depoliticization, and bureaucratic power in Lesotho*, Cambridge University Press, Cambridge.

Ferguson, J. (1999) *Expectations of modernity: myths and meanings of urban life on the Zambian Copperbelt*, University of California Press, Berkeley.

Ferguson, J. (2006) *Global shadows: Africa in the neoliberal world order*, Duke University Press, Durham NC.

Fisiy, C. and M. Goheen (1998) 'Power and the quest for recognition: neo-traditional titles among the new elite in Nso, Cameroon', *Africa*, 68, 3, 383-402.

Fohtung, M.G. (1992) [1962] 'Self-portrait of a Cameroonian, taken down by Peter Kalle Njie and edited by E.M. Chilver', *Paideuma*, 38, 219-248.

Fokwang, J. (2003) *Chiefs and democratic transition in Africa: an ethnographic study in the chiefdoms of Tshivhase and Bali*. Unpublished MA thesis, University of Pretoria.

Fonchingong, C.C. (2004) 'The travails of democratization in Cameroon in the context of political liberalisation since the 1990s', *African and Asian Studies*, 3, 1, 33-59.

Foucher, V. (2002) 'Les "évolués", la migration, l'école: pour une nouvelle interprétation de la naissance du nationalisme casamançais', in M.C. Diop (ed.) *Le Sénégal contemporain*, Karthala, Paris, 375-424.

Frost, D. (2002) 'Diasporan West African communities: the Kru in Freetown and Liverpool', *Review of African Political Economy*, 29, 92, 285-300.

Gabriel, J.M. (1999) 'Cameroon's Neopatrimonial Dilemma', *Journal of Contemporary African Studies*, 17, 2, 173-196.

GCIM [Global Commission on International Migration] (2005) *Migration in an interconnected world: new directions for action*, Global Commission on International Migration, Switzerland.

van der Geest, S. (2006) 'Between death and funeral: mortuaries and the exploitation of liminality in Kwahu, Ghana', *Africa*, 76, 4, 485-501.

Geiger, S. (1997) *TANU Women: gender and culture in the making of Tanganyikan nationalism, 1955–1965,* Heinemann, Portsmouth, NH.

Germenji, E. and I. Gedeshi (2008) *Highly skilled migration from Albania: an assessment of current trends and the ways ahead,* Working Paper T-25, Development Research Centre on Migration, Globalisation and Poverty, University of Sussex.

Geschiere, P. and J. Gugler (1998) 'The urban–rural connection: changing issues of belonging and identification', *Africa*, 68, 3, 309-319.

Geschiere, P. and F. Nyamnjoh (1998) 'Witchcraft as an issue in the "politics of belonging": democratization and urban migrants' involvement with the home village', *African Studies Review,* 41, 3, 69-91.

Geschiere, P. and F. Nyamnjoh (2000) 'Capitalism and autochthony: the seesaw of mobility and belonging', *Public Culture,* 12, 2, 423-452.

Geschiere, P. and F. Nyamnjoh (2001) 'Autochthony as an alternative to citizenship: new modes in the politics of belonging in postcolonial Africa', in E. Kurimoto (ed.) *Rewriting Africa: toward renaissance or collapse?* National Museum of Ethnology, Osaka, 209-237.

Ghosh, B. (2006) *Migrants' remittances and development: myths, rhetoric and realities,* International Organization for Migration, Geneva.

Gibbon, P. (1998) *'Limping towards a ditch without a crutch: the brave new world of Tanzanian cotton marketing cooperatives',* Centre for Development Research Working Paper Subseries, no. iii.98.18, http://www.diis.dk/graphics/CDR_Publications/cdr_publications/working_ papers/ wp-98-18.htm, accessed 4 January 2008.

Gibbon, P. (2001) 'Civil society in Tanzania: a 40-year perspective', *Development and Change,* 32, 5, 819-844.

Gibson-Graham, J.K. (2004) 'Area studies after poststructuralism', *Environment and Planning A,* 36, 405-419.

Gifford, P. (2001) *African Christianity: its public role,* 2nd edition, Hurst, London.

Gilroy, P. (1993) *The Black Atlantic: modernity and double consciousness,* Verso, London.

Gilroy, P. (1994) 'Diaspora', *Paragraph,* 17, 1, 207-212.

Glickman, H. (2005) 'The Nigerian "419" advance fee scams: prank or peril?' *Canadian Journal of African Studies,* 39, 3, 460-489.

Goldring, L. (1998) 'The power of status in transnational social settings', in M.P. Smith and L.E. Guarnizo (eds) *Transnationalism from below,* Transaction Publishers, London, 165-195.

Gomez, M.A. (2005) *Reversing sail: a history of the African diaspora,* Cambridge University Press, Cambridge.

de la Gorgendière, L. (2007) *Ghanaian associations in Canada: motivation and cooperation for development at home and abroad.* Paper presented at Second AEGIS European Conference on African Studies, African Studies Centre, Leiden, 11–14 July.

Grillo, R. and B. Riccio (2004) 'Translocal development: Italy–Senegal', *Population, Space and Place,* 10, 2, 99-111.

Gueye, C. (2002) *Touba: la capitale des mourides,* Karthala, Paris.

Gugler, J. (2002) 'The son of the hawk does not remain abroad: the urban–rural connection in Africa', *African Studies Review,* 45, 1, 21-41.

Gunderson, F. and B. Gregory Barz (eds) (2000) *Mashindano! Competitive music performance in East Africa,* Mkuki na Nyota Publishers, Dar es Salaam.

Gwanmesia, T.G. (2003) *Community participation in development in Bali subdivision: the case of health care and potable water supply.* Unpublished Postgraduate Teachers' Diploma dissertation in Geography, University of Yaoundé I.

ter Haar, G. (1998) *Halfway to paradise: African Christians in Europe,* Cardiff Academic Press, Cardiff.

ter Haar, G. (2004) 'Chosen people: the concept of diaspora in the modern world', in S. J. Sutcliffe (ed.) *Religion: empirical studies,* Ashgate, Aldershot, 91-106.

de Haas, H. (2005) 'International migration, remittances and development: myths and facts',

Third World Quarterly, 26, 8, 1269-1284.

de Haas, H. (2007a) *Migration, remittances and social development*, United Nations Research Department for Social Development, Geneva.

de Haas, H. (2007b) *The myth of invasion: irregular migration from West Africa to the Maghreb and the European Union*, International Migration Institute, Research Report, Oxford University, http://www.imi.ox.ac.uk.

de Haas, H. and O. Bakewell (2007) 'African migrations: continuities, discontinuities and recent transformations', in P. Chabal, U. Engel and L. de Haan (eds) *African Alternatives*, Brill, Leiden, 95-118.

Hagberg, S. (2004) 'Ethnic identification in voluntary associations: the politics of development and culture in Burkina Faso', in H. Englund and F.B. Nyamnjoh (eds) *Rights and the politics of recognition in Africa*, Zed, London,195-218.

Hakielimu (2007) *Is secondary education progressing? Key findings from government reviews of SEDP implementation*, Hakielimu, Dar es Salaam.

Hall, S. (1990) 'Cultural identity and diaspora', in J. Rutherford (ed.) *Identity: community, culture, difference*, Lawrence and Wishart, London, 222–237.

Hall, S. (1996) 'New ethnicities', in D. Morley and K.-H. Chen (eds) *Critical dialogues in cultural studies*, Routledge, London, 441-449.

Harris, H. (2006) *Yoruba in diaspora: an African church in London*, Palgrave Macmillan, Basingstoke.

Hart, G. (2001) 'Development critiques in the 1990s: cul de sacs and promising paths', *Progress in Human Geography*, 25, 649-658.

Henry, L. (2004) 'Morality, citizenship and participatory development in an indigenous development association: the case of GPSDO and the Sebat bet Gurage of Ethiopia', in S. Hickey and G. Mohan (eds) *Participation: from Tyranny to transformation?* Zed, London, 140-155.

Henry, L. and G. Mohan. (2003) 'Making homes: the Ghanaian diaspora, institutions and development', *Journal of International Development*, 15, 611-622.

Henry, L., G. Mohan and H. Yanacopulos (2004) 'Networks as transnational agents of development', *Third World Quarterly*, 25, 5, 839-855.

Hepner, T.R. (2003) 'Religion, nationalism and transnational civil society in the Eritrean diaspora', *Identities*, 10, 269-293.

Herbert, J., J. May, J. Wills, K. Datta, Y. Evans and C. McIlwaine (2008) 'Multicultural living? Experiences of everyday racism amongst Ghanaian migrants in London', *European Urban and Regional Studies*, 15, 2, 103-117.

Hickey, S. (2002) 'Transnational NGDOs and participatory forms of rights-based development: converging with the local politics of citizenship in Cameroon', *Journal of International Development*, 14, 841-857.

Hickey, S. (2004) *'Hometown associations' as social movements for citizenship: a case study from Northwest Cameroon*. Paper presented at the 47th annual meeting of the African Studies Association, New Orleans, LA, 11–14 November.

Hickey, S. (2007a) 'Caught at the crossroads: citizenship, marginality and the Mbororo Fulani in northwest Cameroon', in D. Hammett, P. Nugent and S. Dorman (eds) *Making nations, creating strangers: states and citizenship in Africa*, Brill, Leiden, 83-104.

Hickey, S. (2007b) *Citizenship, 'hometown associations' and progressive politics in Northwest Cameroon: the case of MBOSCUDA*. Paper presented at workshop on 'Reconceptualizing diaspora and African hometown associations', University of Leicester, 8–9 May.

Home Office (2003) *Voluntary and community sector infrastructure: a consultation document*, Home Office, London.

Honey, R. and S. Okafor (eds) (1998a) *Hometown associations: indigenous knowledge and development in Nigeria*, Intermediate Technology Publications, London.

Honey, R. and S. Okafor (1998b) 'Introduction', in R. Honey and S. Okafor (eds) *Hometown associations: indigenous knowledge and development in Nigeria*, Intermediate Technology Publications, London, 1-2.

Hunt, W. (1925) *An assessment report on the Bali clan in the Bamenda Division of Cameroons Province*, Cameroon National Archives, Buea.

Hyden, G. (1980) *Beyond ujamaa in Tanzania: underdevelopment and an uncaptured peasantry*, Heinemann, London.

Iheme, E. (2005) 'Response to strengthening civil society in the south: challenges and constraints – a case study of Tanzania', *International Journal of Not-for-Profit Law*, 8, 1, 54-62. http://www.icnl.org/knowledge/ijnl/vol8iss1/special_3r.htm, accessed 20 February 2008.

Iliffe, J. (1969) 'The age of improvement and differentiation 1907–1945', in I.N. Kimambo and A.J. Temu (eds) *A history of Tanzania*, East African Publishing House, Dar es Salaam, 123-160.

Iliffe, J. (1979) *A modern history of Tanganyika*, Cambridge University Press, Cambridge.

Ionescu, D. (2006) *Engaging diasporas as development partners for home and destination countries: challenges for policymakers*, Migration Research Series, no. 26, International Organization for Migration, Geneva.

Ishemo, S. (2002) 'From Africa to Cuba: an historical analysis of the Sociedad Secreta Abakuá (Naniguismo)', *Review of African Political Economy*, 29, 92, 253-272.

Ishumi, A.G.M. (1995) 'Provision of secondary education in Tanzania: historical background and current trends', in J. Semboja and O. Therkildsen (eds) *Service provision under stress in East Africa: the state, NGOs and people's organizations in Kenya, Tanzania and Uganda*, Centre for Development Research, Copenhagen, 153-165.

Jeffreys, M. (1957) 'The Bali of Bamenda', *African Studies*, 16, 108-13.

Jeffreys, M. (1962) 'Some notes on the customs of the Grassfields Bali of Northwestern Cameroon', *Afrika und Ubersee*, 46, 3, 161-168.

Jennings, M. (2002) 'Almost an Oxfam in itself': Oxfam, *Ujamaa* and development in Tanzania', *African Affairs*, 101, 509-530.

Jerman, H. (1997) *Between five lines: the development of ethnicity in Tanzania with special reference to the Western Bagamoyo District*, Saarijarvi: Transactions of the Finnish Anthropological Society, no. 38 and the Nordic Africa Institute, Uppsala.

Jindra, M. (2005) 'Christianity and the proliferation of ancestors: changes in hierarchy and mortuary ritual in the Cameroon Grassfields', *Africa*, 75, 3, 356-377.

Jones, P.S. (2000) 'Why is it alright to do development "over there" but not "here"? Changing vocabularies and common strategies of inclusion across the "First" and "Third" Worlds', *Area*, 32, 3, 237-41.

de Jong, F. (1997) 'The production of translocality: initiation in the sacred grove in South Senegal', *Focaal*, no. 30/31, 61-83.

de Jong, F. (1999) 'Trajectories of a mask performance: the case of the Senegalese *kumpo*', *Cahier d'Études Africaines*, 153 (XXXIX-1), 49-71.

Jua, N. (1997) 'Contested meanings: rulers, subjects and national integration in post-colonial Cameroon', in P. Nkwi and F.B. Nyamnjoh (eds) *Regional balance and national integration in Cameroon: lessons learned and the uncertain future*, ASC/ICASSRT, Yaoundé, 62-66.

Jua, N. (2005) 'The mortuary sphere, privilege and the politics of belonging in contemporary Cameroon', *Africa*, 75, 3, 325-54.

Kabki, M. (2007) *Transnationalism, local development and social security: the functioning of support networks in rural Ghana*. African Studies Centre, Leiden.

Keck, M.E. and K. Sikkink (1998) *Activists beyond borders: advocacy networks in international politics*, Cornell University Press, London.

Kelsall, T. (2000) 'Governance, local politics and districtization in Tanzania: the 1998 Arumeru tax revolt', *African Affairs*, 99, 397, 533-51.

Kelsall, T. (2002) 'Shop windows and smoke-filled rooms: governance and the re-politicization of Tanzania', *Journal of Modern African Studies*, 40, 579-619.

Kerlin, M.D. (2000) 'New agents of socio-economic development: Guinea-Bissauan hometown associations in Portugal', *South European Society and Politics*, 5, 3, 33-55.

Killingray, D. (1994) 'Africans in the United Kingdom: an introduction', in D. Killingray (ed.) *Africans in Britain*, Frank Cass, Essex, 2-27.

Kilson, M.L. and R.I. Rotberg (1976) (eds) *The African diaspora: interpretive essays*, Harvard University Press, London.

Kingdon, Z. (2002) *A host of devils: the history and context of the making of Makonde spirit culture*, Routledge, London.

Kiondo, A.S.Z. (1993) 'Structural adjustment and non-governmental organisations in Tanzania: a case study', in P. Gibbon (ed.) *Social change and economic reform in Africa*, Uppsala, Nordic Africa Institute.

Kiondo, A.S.Z. (1995) 'When the state withdraws: local development, politics and liberalisation in Tanzania', in P. Gibbon (ed.) *Liberalised development in Tanzania: studies on accumulation processes and local institutions*, Nordic Africa Institute, Uppsala, 109-176.

Kleis, G.W. (1980) 'Confrontation and incorporation: Igbo ethnicity in Cameroon', *African Studies Review*, 23, 3, 89-100.

Kleist, N. (2008) 'Mobilising "the Diaspora": Somali transnational political engagement', *Journal of Ethnic and Migration Studies*, 34, 2, 307-23.

Kofele-Kale N. (ed.) (1980) *An African experiment in nation building: the bilingual Cameroon Republic since reunification*, Westview Press, Boulder CO.

Konings, P. (2001) 'Mobility and exclusion: conflicts between autochthons and allochthons during political liberalization in Cameroon', in M. de Bruijn, R. van Dijk and D. Foeken (eds) *Mobile Africa: Changing patterns of movement in Africa and beyond*, Brill, Leiden, 169-194.

Konings, P. and F.B. Nyamnjoh (2003) *Negotiating an Anglophone identity: a study of the politics of recognition and representation in Cameroon*, Brill, Leiden.

Koponen, K. (1995) *Development for exploitation: German colonial policies in mainland Tanzania, 1884–1914*, Lit Verlag, London.

Koser, K. (ed.) (2003a) *New African diasporas*, Routledge, London.

Koser, K. (2003b) 'Mobilizing new African diasporas: an Eritrean case study', in K. Koser (ed.) *New African diasporas*, Routledge, London, 111-123.

Kothari, U. (2008) 'Global peddlers and local networks: migrant cosmopolitanisms', *Environment and Planning D: Society and Space*, 3, 26, 500-16.

Kuba, R. and C. Lentz (2006) *Land and the politics of belonging in West Africa*, Brill, Leiden

Kwakye-Nuako, K. (2006) 'Still praisin' God in a new land: African immigrant Christianity in North America', in K. Konadu-Agyemang, B.K. Takyi and J.A. Arthur (eds) (2006) *The new African diaspora in North America: trends, community building, and adaptation*, Lexington Books, Lanham MD, 121-140.

Lambert, M.C. (1999) 'Have Jola women found a way to resist patriarchy with commodities? (Senegal, West Africa)', *Political and Legal Anthropology Review*, 22, 1, 85-93.

Lampert, B. (2007) *Diaspora and development? Nigerian organisations in London and their transnational linkages with 'home'*. Paper presented at COMPAS seminar, Oxford, 10 May.

Lange, S., H. Wallevik and A. Kiondo (2000) *Civil society in Tanzania*, Bergen: Chr. Michelsen Institute (CMI Report R 2000:6).

Laville, S. (2007) 'Big Daddy's boy: Idi Amin's son jailed in Britain over Somali gang murder', *Guardian*, 4 August.

Lentz, C. (1994) 'Home, death and leadership: discourses of an educated elite from north-western Ghana', *Social Anthropology*, 2, 2, 149-169.

Lentz, C. (2006a) *Ethnicity and the making of history in northern Ghana*, Edinburgh University Press, London.

Lentz, C. (2006b) 'Decentralisation, the state and conflicts over local boundaries in northern Ghana', *Development and Change*, 37, 4, 901-919.

Leslie, J.A.K. (1963) *A survey of Dar es Salaam*, East African Institute of Social Research and Oxford University Press, London.

LeVine, V.T. (1964) *The Cameroons: from mandate to independence*, University of California Press, Berkeley CA.

LeVine, V.T. (1971) *The Cameroon Federal Republic*, Cornell University Press, Ithaca NY.

Levitt, P. (2001) 'Transnational migration: taking stock and future directions', *Global Networks*, 1, 3, 195-216.

Liebenow, G. (1971) *Colonial rule and political development in Tanzania: the case of the Makonde,* East African Publishing House, Tanzania.

Lissu, T.A. (2000) '*Repackaging authoritarianism: freedom of association and expression and the right to organize under the proposed NGO policy for Tanzania*', http://www.leat.or.tz/publications/authoritarianism/, accessed 1 February 2008.

Little, K. (1965) *West African urbanization: a study of voluntary associations in social change*, Cambridge University Press, London.

Little, K. (1972) 'Voluntary associations and social mobility among West African women', *Canadian Journal of African Studies*, 6, 2, 278-88.

Lonsdale, J. (1992) 'The moral economy of the Mau Mau: wealth, poverty and civic virtue in Kikuyu political thought', in B. Berman and J. Lonsdale (eds) *Unhappy valley: conflict in Kenya and Africa,* Vol. 2: *Violence and ethnicity*, James Currey, London, 315-504.

Lugalla, J. (1993) 'Structural adjustment policies and education in Tanzania' in P. Gibbon (ed.) *Social change and economic reform in Africa,* Nordic Africa Institute, Uppsala.

McCurdy, S. (1996) 'The 1932 "war" between rival Ujiji (Tanganyikan) associations: understanding women's motivations for inciting political unrest', *Canadian Journal of African Studies/Revue Canadienne des Etudes Africaines*, 30, 10-31.

McFarlane, C. (2006) 'Transnational development networks: bringing development and postcolonial approaches into dialogue', *Geographical Journal*, 172, 1, 35-49.

MacGaffey, J. and R. Bazenguissa-Ganga (2000) *Congo–Paris: transnational traders on the margins of the law*, James Currey, Oxford.

McGregor, J. (2007) 'Joining the BBC (British Bottom Cleaners): Zimbabweans and the UK care industry', *Journal of Ethnic and Migration Studies*, 33, 5, 801-824.

McIlwaine, C. (2007) 'From local to global to transnational civil society: re-framing development perspectives on the non-state sector', *Geography Compass*, 1.

Mahler, S. (1998) 'Theoretical and empirical contributions toward a research agenda for transnationalism', in M.P. Smith and L.E. Guarnizo (eds) *Transnationalism from below*, Transaction Publishers, London, 64-100.

Manchuelle, F. (1997) *Willing migrants: Soninke labour diasporas, 1848–1960*, James Currey, Oxford.

Manger, L. and M.A.M. Assal (2006) 'Diasporas within and without Africa – dynamism, heterogeneity, variation', in L. Manger and M.A.M. Assal (eds) *Diasporas within and without Africa: dynamism, heterogeneity, variation*, Nordic Africa Institute, Uppsala, 7-31.

Manning, P. (2003) 'Africa and the African diaspora: new directions of study', *Journal of African History*, 44, 487-506.

Manuh, T. (2003) "'Efie" or the meanings of "home" among female and male Ghanaian migrants in Toronto, Canada and returned migrants to Ghana', in K. Koser (ed.) *New African diasporas*, Routledge, London, 140-159.

Marsland, B. (2006) Hawataki maendeleo*: authority, resistance and identity in Kyela District.* Paper presented to workshop on 'Community driven development and local actors', University of Bradford, 14th June 2006.

Marx, K. (1973 [1857]) *Grundrisse*, London, Penguin.

Massey, D. (1993) 'Power-geometry and a progressive sense of place', in J. Bird, B. Curtis, T. Putnam, G. Robertson and L. Tickner (eds) *Mapping the futures: local cultures, global change*, Routledge, London, 59-69.

Massey, D. (1994) 'A global sense of place', in D. Massey (ed.) *Space, place and gender*, University of Minnesota Press, Minneapolis, 146-156.

Massey, D. (2006) 'Space, time and political responsibility in the midst of global inequality', *Erdkunde*, 60, 2, 89-95.

Maxwell, D. (2007) *African gifts of the spirit: Pentecostalism and the rise of a Zimbabwean transnational religious movement*, James Currey, Oxford.

Mazzucato, V. (2005) *Ghanaian migrants' double engagement: a transnational view of development and integration policies*, Global Migration Perspectives no 48, Global Commission on International Migration, Geneva.

Mazzucato, V. (2008) 'The double engagement: transnationalism and integration. Ghanaian migrants' lives between Ghana and The Netherlands', *Journal of Ethnic and Migration Studies*, 34, 3, 199-216.

Mazzucato, V., R. van Dijk, C. Horst, and P. de Vries (2004) 'Transcending the nation: explorations of transnationalism as a concept and phenomenon', in D. Kalb, W. Pansters and H. Siebers (eds) *Globalization and development: themes and concepts in current research,* Kluwer Academic Press, Dordrecht, 131-162.

Mazzucato, V., M. Kabki and L. Smith (2006) 'Transnational migration and the economy of funerals: changing practices in Ghana', *Development and Change,* 37, 5, 1047-1072.

Mbuagbaw, T.E., R. Brain and R. Palmer (1987) *A History of the Cameroons,* Longman, Harlow.

MECA-Yaoundé (1996) *Manyu Elements Cultural Association MECA-Yaoundé: Constitution,* mimeo.

Mercer, C. (1999) 'Reconceptualising state–society relations in Tanzania: are NGOs "making a difference"?' *Area,* 31, 3, 247-258.

Mercer, C. (2002) 'NGOs, civil society and democratization: a critical review of the literature', *Progress in Development Studies,* 2, 5-22.

Mercer, C., G. Mohan and M. Power (2003) 'New perspectives on the politics of development in Africa', *Geoforum,* 34, 417-418.

Merz, B.J., L.C. Chen and P.F. Geithner (eds) (2007) *Diasporas and development,* Harvard University Press, Cambridge MA.

Mesaki, S. and J. Mwankusye (1998) 'The saga of the Lindi–Kibiti road: political ramifications', in P. Seppälä and B. Koda (eds) *The making of a periphery: economic development and cultural encounters in southern Tanzania,* Mkuki na Nyota, Dar es Salaam, 58-74.

Michels, S. (2004) *Imagined power contested: Germans and Africans in the Upper Cross River Area of Cameroon 1887–1915,* Lit Verlag, Münster.

Mihanjo, E.P. and N.N. Luanda (1998) 'The south-east economic backwater and the urban floating wamachinga', in P. Seppälä and B. Koda (eds) *The making of a periphery: economic development and cultural encounters in southern Tanzania,* Mkuki na Nyota, Dar es Salaam, 222-232.

Mohan, G. (2002) 'Diaspora and development', in J. Robinson (ed.) *Development and displacement,* Oxford University Press, Oxford, 77-140.

Mohan, G. (2006) 'Embedded cosmopolitanism and the politics of obligation: the Ghanaian diaspora and development', *Environment and Planning A,* 38, 867-883.

Mohan, G. (2008) 'Making neoliberal states of development: the Ghanaian diaspora and the politics of homelands', *Environment and Planning D: Society and Space,* 26, 3, 464-479.

Mohan, G. and A.B. Zack-Williams (2002) 'Globalisation from below: conceptualising the role of the African diasporas in Africa's development', *Review of African Political Economy,* 29, 92, 211-236.

Moya, J.C. (2005) 'Immigrants and associations: a global and historical perspective', *Journal of Ethnic and Migration Studies,* 31, 5, 833-864.

Murray, P. (2007) *Profile of UK diaspora civil society groups involved in international development. Interests, attitudes and involvement: a mapping exercise,* Connections for Development, London.

Mwamfupe, D. (1998) *Changing village land, labour and livelihoods: Rungwe and Kyela Districts, Tanzania,* African Studies Centre Working Paper 29, Leiden.

Nangumbi, A.A. (1998) 'Mystical forces and social relations in Makonde oral culture' in P. Seppälä and B. Koda (eds) *The making of a periphery: economic development and cultural encounters in southern Tanzania,* Mkuki na Nyota, Dar es Salaam, 265-284.

Nathan, L. (2005) *The frightful inadequacy of most of the statistics': a critique of Collier and Hoeffler on causes of civil war,* Crisis States Research Centre Discussion Paper no.11, London School of Economics and Political Science, London.

Ndangam, G. (1988) 'The biography of V.S. Galega II (1906–1985)', in V. Titanji, et al. (eds) *An introduction to the study of Bali-Nyonga: a tribute to His Royal Highness Galega II, traditional ruler of Bali-Nyonga from 1940–1985,* Stardust Printers, Yaoundé, 43-66.

NDF [Newala Development Foundation] (n.d.) *Newala Development Foundation,* mimeo.

Ndione, B. (forthcoming) 'Territoires urbains et réseaux sociaux: les processus de migration internationale dans les quartiers de la ville sénégalaise de Kaolack', *African Diaspora.*

Ndjio, B. (2006) 'Intimate strangers: neighbourhood, autochthony and the politics of belonging', in P. Konings and D. Foeken (eds) *Crisis and creativity: exploring the wealth of the African neighbourhood,* Brill, Leiden, 66-86.

Ndofor-Tah, C. (2000) *Diaspora and development: contributions by African organisations in the UK to Africa's development*, African Foundation for Development, London.

Newland, K. with E. Patrick (2004) *Beyond remittances: the role of diaspora in poverty reduction in their countries of origin,* report for the Department for International Development, Migration Policy Institute, Washington DC.

Ngoh, V.J. (2001) *Southern Cameroons, 1922–1961: A Constitutional History,* : Ashgate, Aldershot.

Niger-Thomas, M. (2000) *'Buying futures': The upsurge of female entrepreneurship crossing the formal/informal divide in South West Cameroon*, Leiden University Press, Leiden.

Njeuma, M.Z. (1995) 'Reunification and political opportunism in the making of Cameroon's independence', *Paideuma*, 41, 27–37.

Nkwi, P.N. (1997) 'Rethinking the role of elites in rural development: a case study from Cameroon', *Journal of Contemporary African Studies*, 15,1, 67-86.

Nkwi, P.N. and A. Socpa (1997) 'Ethnicity and party politics in Cameroon: the politics of divide and rule', in P. Nkwi and F.B. Nyamnjoh (eds) *Regional balance and national integration in Cameroon: lessons learned and the uncertain future,* ASC/ ICASSRT, Yaoundé, 138-149.

Nkwi, W. (2006) 'Elites, ethno-regional competition in Cameroon, and the Southwest Elites Association (SWELA) 1991-1997', *African Study Monographs*, 27, 3, 123-143.

Nyamndi, N. (1988) *The Bali Chamba: a political history*, Editions Cape, Paris.

Nyamnjoh, F.B. (1999) 'Cameroon: a country united by ethnic ambition and difference', *African Affairs*, 98, 390, 101-118.

Nyamnjoh, F.B. (2005) 'Images of Nyongo amongst Bamenda Grassfielders in Whiteman Kontri', *Citizenship Studies*, 9, 3, 241-269.

Nyamnjoh, F.B., D. Durham and J. Fokwang (2002) 'The domestication of hair and modernized consciousness in Cameroon: a critique in the context of globalization', *Identity, Culture and Politics,* 3, 2, 98-124.

Nyamnjoh, F.B. and M. Rowlands (1998) 'Elite associations and the politics of belonging in Cameroon', *Africa*, 68, 3, 320-337.

Nyberg-Sorensen, N., N. van Hear and P. Engberg-Pedersen (2002) *The migration-development nexus: evidence and policy options.* Migration Series, no. 8, International Organization for Migration, Geneva.

O'Connor, A. (1983) *The African city*, Hutchinson, London.

Oben, T.M. and R.M. Akoko (2004) '"Motions of support" and ethno-regional politics in Cameroon', *Journal of Third World Studies*, XXI, 1, 241-258.

OECD (2006) *International Migration Outlook: SOPEMI 2006 edition*, OECD Publications, Paris.

Offidele, E.P.O. (1947) 'Growth and influence of tribal unions', *West Africa Review*, 18, 937-941.

Olukoju, A. (2007) *Desertion, dereliction, and destitution: the welfare of stranded seamen in colonial West Africa, ca. 1921–34.* Paper presented at *Belonging in Europe* conference, Equiano Centre, University College London, 6–8 November.

Olukoshi, A.O. (1997) 'Associational life', in L. Diamond, A. Kirk-Greene and O. Oyediran (eds) *Transition without end: Nigerian politics and civil society under Babangida*, Vantage Publishers, Ibadan, 450-476.

Orozco, M. (2002) 'Globalization and migration: the impact of family remittances in Latin America', *Latin American Politics and Society*, 44, 2, 41-66.

Orozco, M. (2006) 'Diasporas, philanthropy and hometown associations: the Central American experience', *Inter-American Dialogue*, 22 March 2006.

Orozco, M. with M. Lapointe (2004) 'Mexican hometown associations and development opportunities', *Journal of International Affairs*, 57, 2, 31-51.

Orozco, M. and R. Rouse (2007) *Migrant hometown associations and opportunities for development: a global perspective*, Migration Policy Institute, http://www.migrationinformation.org/USfocus/display.cfm?ID=579, accessed 22 February 2008.

Orozco, M and K. Welle (2005) 'Hometown associations and development: ownership, correspondence, sustainability and replicability', in B.J. Merz (ed.) *New patterns for Mexico: observations on remittances, philanthropic giving, and equitable development*, Harvard University Press, Cambridge MA.

Osaghae, E.E. (1994) *Trends in migrant political organizations in Nigeria: the Igbo in Kano,* French Institute for Research in Africa, University of Ibadan, Ibadan.

Owusu, T.Y. (2000) 'The role of Ghanaian immigrant associations in Toronto, Canada', *International Migration Review* 34, 4, 1155-1181.

Owusu, T.Y. (2006) 'Transnationalism among African immigrants in North America: the case of Ghanaians in Canada', in K. Konadu-Agyemang, B.K. Takyi and J.A. Arthur (eds) *The new African diaspora in North America: trends, community building, and adaptation,* Lexington Books, Lanham MD, 273-286.

Page, B. (2000) '"A priceless commodity": The production of water in Anglophone Cameroon 1916–1999'. Unpublished PhD thesis, University of Oxford.

Page, B. (2007) 'Slow going: the mortuary, modernity and the hometown association in Bali-Nyong'a, Cameroon', *Africa,* 77, 3, 419-441.

Palmer, C. (1998) 'Defining and studying the modern African diaspora', *Perspectives,* http://www.historians.org/perspectives/issues/1998/9809/9809VIE2.CFM, accessed 2 October 2007.

Pantoja, A.D. (2005) 'Transnational ties and immigrant political incorporation: the case of Dominicans in Washington Heights, New York', *International Migration,* 43, 123-146.

Patterson, T.R. and R.D.G. Kelley (2000) 'Unfinished migrations: reflections on the African diaspora and the making of the modern world', *African Studies Review,* 43, 1, 11-45.

Pérouse de Montclos, M.-A. (2003) 'A refugee diaspora: when the Somali go west', in K. Koser (ed.) *New African diasporas,* Routledge, London, 37-55.

Pieterse, J. (2003) 'Social capital and migration: beyond ethnic economies', *Ethnicities,* 3, 1, 29-58.

Pinkerton, C., G. McLaughlin, and J. Salt (2004) *Sizing the illegally resident population in the UK. Home Office Online Research Report 58/04,* http://www.homeoffice.gov.uk/rds/pdfs04/rdsolr 5804. pdf, accessed 20 February 2008.

Piot, C. (1999) *Remotely global: village modernity in West Africa,* University of Chicago Press, Chicago.

Portes, A. (1997) *Globalization from below: the rise of transnational communities,* Transnational Communities Programme Working paper series, WPTC-98-01.

Portes, A., C. Escobar and A. Walton Radford (2007) 'Immigrant transnational organisations and development: a comparative study', *International Migration Review,* 41, 1, 242-281.

Portes, A. and P. Landolt (2000) 'Social capital: promise and pitfalls of its role in development', *Journal of Latin American Studies,* 32, 2, 529-547.

Potts, D. (2000) 'Urban unemployment and migrants in Africa: evidence from Harare 1985–1994', *Development and Change,* 31, 4, 879-910.

Potts, D. (2005) 'Urban growth and urban economies in Eastern and Southern Africa: trends and prospects', in D.F. Bryceson and D. Potts (eds) *African urban economies: viability, vitality or vitiation?* Palgrave Macmillan, Basingstoke, 67-104.

Pratten, D. and S.A. Baldo. (1995) '"Return to roots": processes of legitimacy and accountability in Sudanese migrant associations', in M. Edwards and D. Hulme (eds) *Non-governmental organizations: performance and accountability: beyond the magic bullet,* Earthscan, London, 119-130.

Ranger, T. (1975) *Dance and society in Eastern Africa, 1890–1970: the Beni Ngoma,* Heinemann, Portsmouth, NH.

Ranger, T. (1979) 'European attitudes and African realities: the rise and fall of the Matola chiefs of south-east Tanzania', *Journal of African History,* 20, 1, 63-82.

Ranger, T. (2007) 'Scotland Yard in the bush: medicine murders, child witches and the construction of the occult: a literature review', *Africa,* 77, 2, 272-283.

Ratha, D. and Z. Xu (2008) *Migration and remittances factbook,* World Bank, Washington DC.

de Regt, M. (2006) 'Ethiopian women increasingly trafficked to Yemen', *Forced Migration Review,* 25, 37-38.

de Regt, M. (2007) *Ethiopian women in the Middle East: the case of migrant domestic workers in Yemen.* Seminar paper presented at the African Studies Centre, Leiden, 15 February.

REPOA (2007) *Tanzanian non-governmental organizations – their perceptions of their relationships with the Government of Tanzania and donors, and their role in poverty reduction and development,* Special Paper 07.21, Research on Poverty Alleviation, Mkuki na Nyota, Dar es Salaam.

Reynolds, R. (2002) 'An African brain drain: Igbo decisions to immigrate to the US', *Review of African Political Economy*, 92, 273-284.

Riccio, B. (2001) 'From "ethnic group" to "transnational community"? Senegalese migrants' ambivalent experiences and multiple trajectories', *Journal of Ethnic and Migration Studies*, 27, 4, 583-599.

Riccio, B. (2003) 'More than a trade diaspora: Senegalese transnational experiences in Emilia-Romagna, Italy', in K. Koser (ed.) *New African diasporas*, Routledge, London, 95-110.

Rigby, A. (2006) 'Civil society, reconciliation and conflict transformation in post-war Africa', in O. Furley and R. May (eds) *Ending Africa's wars: progressing to peace*, Ashgate, Aldershot, 47-62.

Robinson, J. (2006) *Ordinary cities: between modernity and development*, Routledge, London.

Robinson, J. (2007) *Cities in a world of cities*. Paper presented at the Annual Meeting of the Association of American Geographers, San Francisco, 17-21 April.

Röschenthaler, U. (2004) 'Transacting obasinjom: the dissemination of a cult agency in the Cross River area', *Africa*, 74, 2, 241-276.

Ruel, M.J. (1964) 'The modern adaptation of associations among the Banyang of the West Cameroon', *Southwestern Journal of Anthropology*, 20, 1, 1-14.

Ruel, M.J. (1969) *Leopards and leaders: constitutional politics among a Cross River people*, Tavistock, London.

Rungwe District Council (2005) *Rungwe District Council Profile*, Tukuyu, Tanzania.

Safran, W. (1991) 'Diasporas in modern societies: myths of homeland and return', *Diaspora*, 1, 1, 83-99.

Sahlins, M. (1994) 'Goodbye to Tristes Tropes: ethnography in the context of modern world history', in R. Borowsky (ed.) *Assessing Cultural Anthropology*, McGraw Hill, New York, 377-395.

Sahlins, M. (1999) 'What is anthropological enlightenment? Some lessons of the twentieth century', *Annual Review of Anthropology*, 28, i–xxiii.

Sander, C. and S.M. Maimbo (2003) *Migrant labor remittances in Africa: reducing obstacles to developmental contributions*, Africa Region Working Paper no. 64, World Bank, Washington DC.

Sanders, T. (2003) 'Imagining the Dark Continent: the Met, the media and the Thames torso', *Cambridge Anthropology*, 23, 2, 53-66.

Schmitz, J. (1994) 'Cités noires: les républiques villageoises du Fuuta Tooro (Vallée du fleuve Sénégal)', *Cahiers d'Études Africaines*, XXXIV, 1-3(133-135), 419-460.

Seppälä, P. (1996) 'The politics of economic diversification; reconceptualising the informal sector in south east Tanzania', *Development and Change*, 27, 3, 557-578.

Seppälä, P. (1998a) 'Introduction', in P. Seppälä and B. Koda (eds) *The making of a periphery: economic development and cultural encounters in southern Tanzania*, Mkuki na Nyota, Dar es Salaam, 7-36.

Seppälä, P. (1998b) 'The recovery of cashew production in Southern Tanzania', in P. Seppälä and B. Koda (eds) *The making of a periphery: economic development and cultural encounters in southern Tanzania*, Mkuki na Nyota, Dar es Salaam, 118-137.

Seppälä, P. and B. Koda (eds) (1998) *The making of a periphery: economic development and cultural encounters in southern Tanzania*, Mkuki na Nyota, Dar es Salaam.

Shepperson, G. (1976) 'Introduction', in M.L. Kilson and R.I. Rotberg (eds) *The African diaspora: interpretive essays*, Harvard University Press, London, 1-10.

Sherrington, R. (2007) *Developing disparities in Tanzania*. Unpublished PhD thesis, University of Manchester.

Sherwood, M. (1995) *Manchester and the 1945 Pan-African Congress*, Savannah Press, London.

Sherwood, M. (2007) *The first Pan-African conference, London, 1900*. Paper presented at the Belonging in Europe Conference, Equiano Centre, University College London, 6–8 November.

Shivji, I.G. (1986) *Law, State and the Working Class in Tanzania*, James Currey, London.

Sieveking, N., M. Fauser and F. Ngo Youmba (2007) *The negotiation of development by African migrant organisations: examples from Germany and Spain*. Paper presented at AEGIS European Conference on African Studies, African Studies Centre, Leiden, 11–14 July.

de Silva Jayasuriya, S. (2007) (ed.) *Sounds of identity: the music of Afro-Asians*, Semar Publishers, The Hague.

de Silva Jayasuriya, S. and R. Pankhurst (eds) (2003) *The African diaspora in the Indian Ocean*, Africa World Press, Trenton NJ.

Simone, A.-M. (2001) 'Between ghetto and globe: remaking urban life in Africa', in A. Tostensen, I. Tvedten and M. Vaa (eds) *Associational life in African cities: popular responses to the urban crisis*, Nordic Africa Institute, Uppsala, 46-63.

Smith, L. (2007) *Tied to Migrants: transnational influences on the economy of Accra, Ghana*, African Studies Centre, Leiden.

Smith, R. (1998) 'Transnational localities: community, technology and the politics of membership within the context of Mexico and US migration', in M.P. Smith and L.E. Guarnizo (eds) *Transnationalism from below*, Transaction Publishers, New Brunswick NJ, 196-238.

Sommers, M. (2001) *Fear in Bongoland: Burundi refugee youth in Urban Tanzania*, Berhahn, Oxford.

Styan, D. (2003) 'La nouvelle vague? Recent Francophone African settlement in London', in K. Koser (ed.) *New African diasporas*, Routledge, London, 17-36.

Tadreg (2007) *Tanzanian cashew situation analysis 2007*, Tanzania Development Research Group, Dar es Salaam.

Takougang, J. (2003) 'The 2002 legislative election in Cameroon: a retrospective on Cameroon's stalled democracy movement', *Journal of Modern African Studies*, 41, 3, 421-435.

Titanji, V., M. Gwanfogbe, E. Nwana, G. Ndangam and A. Lima (eds) (1988) *An introduction to the study of Bali-Nyonga. A tribute to His Royal Highness Galega II, Traditional Ruler of Bali-Nyonga from 1940–1985*, Stardust Printers, Yaoundé.

Tölölyan, K. (1996) 'Rethinking diaspora(s): stateless power in the transnational moment', *Diaspora*, 5, 1, 3-36.

Tostensen, A., I. Tvedten and M. Vaa (2001) 'The urban crisis, urban governance and associational life', in A. Tostensen, I. Tvedten and M. Vaa (eds) *Associational life in African cities: popular responses to the urban crisis*, Nordic Africa Institute, Uppsala, 7-26.

Trager, L. (1998) 'Hometown linkages and local development in south-western Nigeria: whose agenda? What impact?' *Africa*, 68, 3, 360-382.

Trager, L. (2001) *Yoruba hometowns: community, identity, and development in Nigeria*, Lynne Rienner, Boulder CO.

Tripp, A.-M. (1994). 'Rethinking civil society : gender implications in contemporary Tanzania', in J. Harbeson, D. Rothchild and N. Chazan (eds) *Civil Society and the State in Africa*, Lynne Reinner, Boulder CO, 149-168.

Tripp, A.-M. (1997) *Changing the rules: the politics of liberalization and the urban informal economy in Tanzania*, University of California Press, California.

Uduku, O. (2002) 'The socio-economic basis of a diaspora community: *Igbo bu ike'*, *Review of African Political Economy*, 92, 301-311.

Ugba, A. (2006) 'African Pentecostals in 21st century Ireland', *Studies: an Irish Quarterly Review*, 95, 378, 163-174.

URT [United Republic of Tanzania] (2000) *Secondary Education Master Plan 2001–2005*, Ministry of Education and Culture, Dar es Salaam.

URT [United Republic of Tanzania] (2003) *2002 Population and housing census*, http://www.tanzania.go.tz/census/, accessed 14 January 2008.

URT [United Republic of Tanzania] (2004) *Secondary education development plan, 2004–2009*, Ministry of Education and Culture, Dar es Salaam.

URT [United Republic of Tanzania] (2005) *Tanzania Human Development and Poverty Report 2005*, Mkuki na Nyota, Dar es Salaam.

Vertovec, S. (2004) 'Migrant transnationalism and modes of transformation', *International Migration Review*, 38, 3, 970-1001.

Vertovec, S. (2006) *Diasporas good? Diasporas bad?*, Centre on Migration, Policy and Society Working Paper no. 41, University of Oxford.

Vertovec, S. and R. Cohen (eds) (1999) *Migration, diasporas and transnationalism*, Edward Elgar, Cheltenham.

Vincent, J. (1970) 'The Dar es Salaam townsman: social and political aspects of city life', *Tanzania Notes and Records*, 71, 149-156.

de Vries, P. (2007) 'Don't compromise your desire for development! A Lacanian/ Deleuzian rethinking of the anti-politics machine', *Third World Quarterly*, 28, 1, 25-43.

Welch, C. (1966) *Dream of Unity*, Cornell University Press, Ithaca NY.

Wembah-Rashid, J.A.R. (1998) 'Is culture in south-eastern Tanzania development-unfriendly?' in P. Seppälä and B. Koda (eds) *The making of a periphery: economic development and cultural encounters in southern Tanzania*, Mkuki na Nyota, Dar es Salaam, 39-57.

Werbner, P. (1998) 'Diasporic political imaginaries: a sphere of freedom or a sphere of illusions?' *Communal/Plural*, 6, 1, 11-31.

Werbner, P. (2000) 'Introduction: the materiality of diaspora – between aesthetic and "real" politics', *Diaspora*, 9, 1, 5-20.

Werbner, P. (2002) 'The place which is diaspora: citizenship, religion and gender in the making of chaordic transnationalism', *Journal of Ethnic and Migration Studies*, 28, 1, 119-133.

Willis, J. (2001) '"Beer used to belong to older men": drink and authority among the Nyakyusa of Tanzania', *Africa*, 71, 373-390.

Wilson, M. (1951) *Good company: a study of Nyakyusa age-villages*, Beacon Press, Boston.

Wilson, M. (1957) 'Joking relationships in central Africa', *Man*, 57, July, 111-112.

Wilson, M. (1959) *Communal rituals of the Nyakyusa,* Oxford University Press, London.

Woods, D. (1994) 'Elites, ethnicity and "home town" associations in the Côte d'Ivoire: an historical analysis of state-society links', *Africa*, 64, 4, 465-483.

World Bank (2001) *Migrants' capital for small-scale infrastructure and small enterprise development in Mexico*, World Bank, Washington DC.

World Bank (2006) *Global development finance 2006: the development potential of surging capital flows*, World Bank, Washington DC.

Wright, M. (1971) *German missions in Tanganyika 1891–1941: Lutherans and Moravians in the Southern Highlands*, Oxford University Press, Oxford.

Wright, M. (1972) 'Nyakyusa cults and politics in the later nineteenth century', in T.O. Ranger and I.N. Kimambo (eds) *The historical study of African religions*, Heinemann, London, 153-170.

Yenshu, E.V. (2003) 'Levels of historical awareness. The development of identity and ethnicity in Cameroon', *Cahiers d'Etudes Africaines*, XLIII, 3, 171, 591-628.

Yenshu, E.V. (2005) *On the viability of local autonomy associations: associating identity and development in the home-based associations*, unpublished report.

Yenshu, E.V. and G.N. Ngwa (2001) 'Changing inter-community relations and the politics of identity in the Northern Mezam Area', *Cahiers d'Etudes Africaines*, XLI, 1, 163-190.

Young, R. (2003) *Postcolonialism: a very short introduction*, Oxford University Press, Oxford.

Zack-Williams, A.B. (1995) 'Development and diaspora: separate concerns?' *Review of African Political Economy*, 65, 349-367.

Zeleza, P.T. (2005) 'Rewriting the African diaspora: beyond the Black Atlantic'. *African Affairs*, 104, 414, 35-68.

Zelinsky, W. (2001) *The enigma of ethnicity: another American dilemma*, University of Iowa Press, Iowa City.

INDEX

● ●

treatment, 73; progressive politics of, 24-5, 29, 153, 232; reactionary stereotype, 52
Pogoro Association, Tanganyika, 113
political diaspora associations, 61
political parties, trans-ethnic, 26
'political tribalism', 25
political-economic context, home association character, 226
'politics of belonging', 17; reactionary elements, 232
Portugal, Pelundo diaspora, 65, 69
'post-development', 18
Potts, D., 145
Presbyterian Church, 36
Priestner, William, 206
primary schooling, prioritization, 198
private insurance, resistance to, 143
privatization, Tanzania social services, 125

racism, struggles against, 61
Railway Asiatic Union, Tanganyika, 109
Ranger, Terrence, 110
ranked membership societies, 79
re-ethnicization process, Cameroon, 98
refugee commuinities, 57
Registrar of Societies, Tanzania, 121-2, 124
reification, identity, 20
remittances, 7, 49, 50; collective, 20; financial constraint, 148; Ghanaian from Holland, 234; individual, 18; internal, 120; international disparities, 234; private, 8; to Bali Water Committee, 207
Reynolds, R., 66
Riccio, B., 61
Roman Catholics, schools, 197
Ruel, M.J., 71
Rungwe District, Tanzania, 43; associations, 123, 233; diaspora new school support, 196; District Council, 186; domestic diaspora, 33, 126, Lutheran missions, 191, 197; migrants education support, 185; Moravian missionary school, 188; Nyakyusa, 201; pre-colonial, 45 Small Tea Growers Association, 192; 'traditional rulers 'imposition, 47; transport infrastructure, 44-6
Rungwe District Education Trust (RUDET), 45, 123, 126, 185-6, 188, 190, 192-3, 196, 199; cess income stream, 189; decline of, 201
Rungwe District Technical Schools Fund (RDTSF), 191
Rungwe East Development Foundation (RUEDEFO), 45, 106, 186, 192
Rungwe West Development Foundation (RUWEDEFO), 46, 106
rural development: NGO colonization of, 22; state capacity, 34
Rural Integrated Project Support Programme, 195
Ruvuma Development Association, 122
Rwanda, ethnic conflict, 28

Safwa ethnic group: diaspora, 191; language, 121
sapeurs, Congolese traders, 61
Schmitz, J., 70-1
scholarships, 145, 180, 184
school fees, 183
secret societies, 78, 87, 150
Selya Development Foundation (SEDEFO), 46, 107, 186, 192
Senegal: burial repatriation, 60; Casamance region, 70; Associations of Italy, 61
Seppälä, P., 105
SHIMABU (Busekelo Development Association), 21, 46, 107, 192; Dar es Salaam director, 22
Singapore, cashew processing, 41
Slough, UK, 33
SNV (Netherlands development organization), 182-3
Social Democratic Front (SDF), Cameroon, 36, 214-15
Société National des Eaux du Cameroun (SNEC), 206-8
Societies Ordinance, Tankanyika 1954, 117-18
Somali Youth League, 62
Somalia/Somaliland, rebuilding efforts, 57
Soninke, ethnic group: miners *chambres,* 63; trading networks, 61
Southern Upcountries African Association, 117
Spain, diaspora groups funding, 53
St Anne's Lutheran Church, Swahili congregation, 139
state, the African, 17; development goods capacity, 99; 1980s provision collapse, 19, 125; social services capacity/incapacity, 123
subjectivity(ies) 'diaspora, 20-1
Sudanese Association, Tanganyika, 113
Swahili society, 41; language, 121

Tanganyika African National Union (TANU), 108, 110, 118, 120-1
Tanganyika European Civil Servants Association, 108
Tanganyika Territory African Civil Services Association, 109
Tanganyika, labour migration from, 115
Tanganyikan Welfare and Commercial Organization, 113
Tankanyika Association, 112
Tanzania, 14, 26; British colonial era, 107; burial societies, 137, 140; chieftans abolition, 47; diaspora wedding committees, 142; domestic diaspora development role, 202; economic restraints, 34; education provision, 30, 200; ethnicity attitudes/ policies, 27-8, 126, 177, 231; home associations, 18, 226; independence, 120; international diaspora, 179; local state, 195; nation-building project, 19, 35, 103, 121, 176; nationalist rise, 110; 1990s political liberalization, 198; postcolonial state, 42; school